S0-DJF-970

INTERNATIONAL TRADE SOURCES

RESEARCH AND INFORMATION GUIDES IN BUSINESS, INDUSTRY, AND ECONOMIC INSTITUTIONS
VOLUME 12
GARLAND REFERENCE LIBRARY OF SOCIAL SCIENCE
VOLUME 1068

Research and Information Guides in Business, Industry, and Economic Institutions

Wahib Nasrallah, *Series Editor*

Franchising in Business
A Guide to Information Sources
by Lucy Heckman

Staff Training
An Annotated Review of the Literature
by William Crimando and T.F. Riggar

Global Countertrade
An Annotated Bibliography
by Leon Zurawicki and Louis Suichmezian

The New York Stock Exchange
A Guide to Information Sources
by Lucy Heckman

The American Stock Exchange
A Guide to Information Resources
by Carol Z. Womack and Alice C. Littlejohn

U.S. Securities and Exchange Commission
A Research and Information Guide
by John W. Graham

The International Financial Statistics Locator
A Research and Information Guide
by Domenica M. Barbuto

International Trade Sources
A Research Guide
by Mae N. Schreiber

International Trade Sources
A Research Guide

Mae N. Schreiber

Garland Publishing, Inc.
New York and London
1997

Library of Congress Cataloging-in-Publication Data

Schreiber, Mae N.
International trade sources : a research guide / by Mae N. Schreiber.
p. cm. — (Research and information guides in business, industry, and economic institutions ; 12) (Garland reference library of social science ; v. 1068)
Includes indexes.
ISBN 0-8153-2109-0 (alk. paper)
1. International trade—Bibliography. 2. International business enterprises—Bibliography. 3. Business information services—Handbooks, manuals, etc. I. Title. II. Series. III. Series: Garland reference library of social science ; v. 1068.
Z7164.C8S33 1997
[HF1379]
016.382—dc20 96-30183
CIP

Printed on acid-free, 250-year-life paper
Manufactured in the United States of America

Series Foreword

The new information society has exceeded everyone's expectations in providing new and exciting media for the collection and dissemination of data. Such proliferation has been matched by a similar increase in the number of providers of business literature. Furthermore, many emerging technologies, financial fields, and management processes have amassed an amazing body of knowledge in a short period of time. Indicators are that packaging of information will continue its trend of diversification, confounding even the experienced researcher. How then will information seekers identify and assess the adequacy and relevancy of various packages to their research needs?

It is my hope that Garland's Research and Information Guides in Business, Industry, and Economic Institutions series will bridge the gap between classical forms of literature and new alternative formats. Each guide will be devoted to an industry, a profession, a managerial process, or a field of study. Organization of the guides will emphasize subject access to formats such as bibliographic and numeric databases on-line, distributed databases, CD-ROM products, loose-leaf services, government publications and books, and periodical articles. Although most of the guides will serve as locators and bridges to bodies of knowledge, some may be reference books with self-contained information.

Since compiling such guides requires substantial knowledge in the organization of information or the field of study, authors are selected on the basis of their expertise as information professionals or subject specialists. Inquiries about the series and its content should be addressed to the series editor.

Wahib Nasrallah
Langsam Library
University of Cincinnati

CONTENTS

PREFACE

International trade is a catalyst in transforming countries, policies, and trends. There is a need for information on international trade sources including exporting, importing, and marketing. Exports are engines of growth in the United States economy as they contributed to more than 40% in the rise of the gross national product (GNP) between 1986 and 1990. They are also expected to contribute to the World gross domestic product (GDP) which is expected to increase about 3.5% annually between 1995-2000.

The Uruguay Round of trade agreements, NAFTA (North American Free Trade Agreement) and other liberal trade agreements throughout Latin America and Asia will create new opportunities for U.S. exports.

There are many viewpoints about the relationship of trade, investment, government policies, to the role of multinational corporations and their effect on the world economy and industry.

This research guide is intended for international marketing students, librarians, researchers, and business people as an aid to locating reliable sources on industry, markets, countries, products, and regulations for doing business internationally. It is written from an American perspective.

It will include primary, secondary, and reference sources, periodicals, indexes, government documents, and computerized sources that have been available through February 1996. The basis for selection is that these can be found in a business, university, public, or depository library. With a few exceptions, the titles are predominately in the English language.

Included are over 800 sources; 95% of these entries will be descriptive. The annotations characterize the source and include the author, title, place of publication, publisher, publication date, pages, ISBN, ISSN,

LCCN, and SUDOCS number for government documents, and order numbers for publications from the National Technical Information Service (NTIS) if available.The SUDOCS number helps to identify and locate the government document in depository libraries. The NTIS (NTIS is a distributor for many non-depository government publications) publications are available for purchase, and order numbers are useful for identifying and purchasing them. Although the NTIS documents are government publications, they are not always found in depository libraries as these are not free. But most NTIS documents are reasonably priced.

The exceptions for ISBN and ISSN numbers are for the series such as *Price Waterhouse Information Guide Series, Country Report Series,* and *County Business Patterns*, and economic censuses, etc.

There are no journal articles or dissertations.

There are many people to thank for help and suggestions: my husband, Karl Schreiber, for his computer skills and support, Wahib Nasrallah and Phyllis Korper for their editing, Dr. John Thanopoulos, Renee Wilson, Joseph LaRose, Ruth Clinefelter, the Reference and Interlibrary Loan Staff at Bierce Library, and the marketing students who asked questions that led to this book.

ABBREVIATIONS

ASEAN	Association of South East Asian Nations
BEM	Big Emerging Markets
CBI	Caribbean Basin Initiative
DAE	Dynamic Asian Economies
Dept.	Department
EC	European Community
EU	European Union
FDI	Foreign Direct Investment
GATT	General Agreements on Tariffs and Trade
GDP	Gross Domestic Product
GNP	Gross National Product
GPO	Government Printing Office
HS	Harmonized System
IMF	International Monetary Fund
ISBN	International Standard Book Number
ISIC	International Standard Industrial Classification Code
ISSN	International Standard Serial Number
LAC	Latin American Countries
NAFTA	North American Free Trade Agreement
NTDB	National Trade Data Bank
NTIS	National Technical Information Services
OECD	Organisation for Economic Cooperation and Development
SIC	Standard Industrial Classification Code
SITC	Standard International Trade Classification
UBO	Ultimate Beneficial Owner
U.S.	United States
U.S. GPO	United States Government Printing Office

International Trade Sources

INTRODUCTION

Because there is no single source or method, there are thirteen possible ways to begin your research; the sample search shows a "user friendly" approach to this guide.

This book begins with an industry analysis and outlook to view the industry as a whole or a segment of the industry. Chapter II then looks at the challenges facing companies and industries. These hurdles need to be addressed.

In order to market a product in a foreign country, the user needs country information. Chapter III lists sources for countries. Chapter IV suggests guides for export or import or business.

It is not necessary to start at Chapter I. For example, a student researcher may find the guide *International Business Information: How to Find It, How to Use It* (Chapter IV) a more helpful starting point as it gives excellent explanations with search strategies and lists bibliographies for locating business information and looking in appropriate places.

For another an export or marketing guide may be more suitable for an overview. Exporting, importing, and marketing guides answer questions and procedures that need consideration before entering the international arena. Strategies, opportunities and practical considerations are other areas covered.

The indexes and abstracts are useful for recent information on a country, product, or trend. For some the country information sources such as: *Country Report Series, Europa World Yearbook* and the *Price Waterhouse Information Guide Series* may be the place to start. These publications profile a country from an economic, market, and tax perspective. However, they do not have the latest information on political changes such as the resignation of a prime minister, latest technology breakthrough, or currency crisis. Periodicals and newspapers are the complement to country sources for current information.

Some sources do not fall into precise categories. Country specific statistics such as *Japan: an International Comparison* are under country information (Chapter III, Asia, Japan). In contrast, statistics for a broader area are under Statistics (Chapter VII), such as *Statistical Yearbook for Asia and the Pacific* which has statistics for many countries, including Japan.

Specific marketing guides will be under country such as: *Doing Business in Mexico* will be under Mexico while a broader area guide such as *Cracking Latin America: A Country by Country Guide to Doing Business in the World's Newest Emerging Markets* is in Chapter IV Guides, Marketing.

For convenience, country specific sources will be under the country such as guides, background information, yearbooks, studies, and statistics, except for directories and periodicals.

Sources that don't fit country or regional areas are under "international" such as *Multinational Business* in the Periodicals chapter. Whenever there are breakdowns by region and there are sources that don't fit in these categories, they will be listed under "international."

Countries are geographically arranged by regions as much as possible but there are exceptions. The OECD countries are under Europe, although Japan and the U.S. (OECD members) don't really fit geographically in this category.

In some sources Russia may be under the Soviet Union, the U.S.S.R, or Eastern Europe. In this guide, it is geographically classified under Europe, then Commonwealth of Independent States (as much as possible). Eastern Europe is under Europe. For some of the statistical sources, Eastern and Western Europe are divided

Australia and New Zealand are classified geographically under Oceania, and the Middle East is geographically classified with Africa. China (People's Republic), Hong Kong, and Taiwan are listed as separate entries. Taiwan sometimes calls itself the Republic of China but it is listed under Taiwan.

There is uneven coverage due to source availability. For example, statistics for the U.S. are much easier to find than product specific export or marketing statistics for Liberia. Also there is also more information on Asian and European countries than lesser developed countries.

The following is a summary of the thirteen chapters:

I. The Industry Analysis and Outlook examine and assess key industries. The outlook looks at the industry as a whole while the analysis examines a segment of the industry.

II. Challenges. These are economic and industrial challenges. Different industries have different challenges. Some challenges include competition, trade barriers and policies.

III. Country Information. The general country information chapter of this guide provides political, economic, and historical data for various countries. The region and country specific section looks at a specific country. Additional information covers cultural, environmental, and labor and employment.

IV. Guides and Bibliographies. Business guides explain ways to find information on companies, markets, economies, and business questions. Others list extensive sources to consult. Exporting, importing, and marketing guides are basic "how to guides" for learning the essentials for successfully exporting, importing, or marketing.

V. Indexes and Abstracts. Indexes and Abstracts point to current sources of information on country, company, product, business environment, industry trend, government, or technological breakthrough.

VI. Periodicals and Newspapers are a good way for managers to keep current with events that affect business. Regionally oriented periodicals such as *Far Eastern Economic Review* deal with issues and trends of the area.

VII. Statistics. The statistics chapter includes: social, economic, financial, and demographic.

VIII. Electronic Sources. These include computerized sources, Internet, and Worldwide Web Sites.

IX. Directories. The directories chapter is used to find basic company or government agency information such as name, address, telephone, and fax number or financial information.

X. Dictionaries explain or define trade or business terms.

XI. Regulations, Laws, and Agreements. These are regulations, laws, and agreements that are important for doing business overseas.

XII. Classification Codes. This chapter has an explanation of these codes and manuals to identify these numbers.

XIII. Handbook and Yearbooks. These business handbooks, encyclopedias, and yearbooks contain useful information.

SAMPLE SEARCH

The following is a quick sample search for using this guide.

Topic: Select a product, country, and business. Exporting polyurethane to China is used for this sample search. Polyurethane is a type of plastic which has various names, such as urethane.

I. Select a guide

A. *A Basic Guide to Exporting*

1. Discusses ways to export successfully

2. Looks at decisions to be made before a company considers exporting

3. Suggests ways to conduct market research

4. Provides methods for selling overseas

B. *Business Opportunities in the Far East*

1. Examines problems and opportunities in the Far East

2. Analyzes the business, financial, and tax aspects of trading in China

II. Select an index

A. *Predicasts F & S Index International* and *PROMPT*

1. Provides marketing information on urethane resins for Asia with data on China, Japan, Malaysia, and Taiwan

2. Gives applications, consumption and projects to the year 2000 for urethane

3. States that the biggest single market outside Japan is China with a total consumption of 100,000 tons a year

B. *ABI/Inform*

This index gives the names of companies that will build polyurethane plants in China such as: Nippon Polyurethane Inc., Dupont, and ICI

III. Select a source for an industry overview on plastics

A. *U.S. Industrial Outlook* provides industry trends and forecasts, including industry, product and trade data, international competitiveness (U.S. is a major net exporter of plastics to the world).

B. Value Line Investment Survey. This source gives an industry survey from an investment point of view and lists companies and ranks them in terms of the industry.

IV. Select the *Harmonized Tariff Schedule of the United States* to identify the Harmonized Number for polyurethane (Chapter XII). The number is 3909.

V. Select the *National Trade Data Bank* to find the export figures of polyurethane (Chapter VIII)

A. Select the program U.S. merchandise trade by commodity and enter the number 3909.

B. The export data for polyurethane are given with total U.S. exports to the world, then a breakdown by country. The major countries the U.S. exports polyurethane to are: Japan,

Hong Kong, Korea, Singapore, the Netherlands, and Belgium.

C. The export data in the NTDB are very product specific.

VI. Select the *National Trade Data Bank* to find marketing information on China. Under the program market research reports, there are market research reports from various government agencies that change from month to month.

VII. Select a title in Chapter III for country information such as:

A. *Europa World Yearbook*
Gives a country profile with data on population, income, employment, government, money supply and external trade for China.

B. *Reference Book for World Traders*
Gives exporting basics, commodity restrictions , travel tips, and "doing business" information for China.

C. *Price Waterhouse Information Guide Series*
Gives investment climate, aims of the Chinese government policy, tax, and corporate information

VIII. Select a source for tax information such as: *Exporters Encyclopaedia*. Gives turnover tax rate as applied to commodities.

IX. Select a source to find trade barriers (Chapter II) such as: *National Trade Estimates...Report on Foreign Trade Barriers*. Gives trade barriers for China.

X. Select a source for current political, economic, and business developments such as *Asian Wall Street Journal* (Chapter VI). It has similar information as the *Wall Street Journal* but with emphasis on Asia with coverage of business, stock market, and companies.

CHAPTER 1

INDUSTRY ANALYSIS AND OUTLOOK

This chapter has industry analysis and outlook, both general and specific. Sources such as: *U.S. Industrial Outlook, Industry and Development: A Global Report, Standard and Poor's Industry Surveys*, and *Panorama of EU Industry* cover a broad range of industries. In addition to outlook, *Valueline* provides company analysis and rating in relation to the industry as a whole. In general, the government sources give industry analysis but will not evaluate companies.

Others such as those in *The National Trade Data Bank* are industry specific covering the computer, cosmetics, or machinery industry. See also *Inside U.S. Business* for an industry synopsis.

GENERAL

1. Darnay, Arsen, ed. *Manufacturing Worldwide: Industries Analyses, Statistics, Products, and Leading Companies and Countries*. Detroit, MI:Gale Research, Inc., 1995. 792 p. ISBN 0810396815.

This is a worldwide industry analysis of economic activity in 459 manufacturing industries including statistics with industry profiles, products, establishments, employment, selected ratios, leading companies, and countries. See next entry.

2. Darnay, Arsen, ed. *Manufacturing USA: Industry Analyses, Statistics, and Leading Companies*. 1994. Detroit, MI: Gale Research, Inc. ISSN 1044-7024. LCCN 478963.

This source analyzes over 450 U.S. manufacturing industries with data on employment, compensation, production, and expenditures. The ranking of leading companies are by sales within SIC and there are data on materials consumed with breakdown by material, quantity, delivered cost, and input-output tables broken down by sector industry. Volume I covers SIC 2011 to 3299 and Volume II covers SIC 3312 to 3399.

3. Darnay, Arsen, ed. *Service Industries USA: Industry Analyses, Statistics, and Leading Companies*. Detroit, MI: Gale Research, Inc. ISSN 1058-1626. LCCN 92645930.

This is an overview for 150 service industries with analyses and statistics of establishments, employment, revenues, ownership and occupation. It includes a profile of the industry: general statistics, indices of change, selected ratios, leading companies, occupations employed by the industry, and industry by state.

4. Hilstrom, Kevin, ed. *Encyclopedia of American Industries*. Detroit, MI: Gale Research, Inc. 1994. 2 vols. ISBN 0787601020.

Volume 1 covers 460 manufacturing industries with an overview of the industry and its health, organization and structure of the industry, background and development of the industry, current conditions, industry leaders, workforce, and U.S. position in the global marketplace in the industry, and industry information sources. Volume 2 covers service and nonmanufacturing industries.

5. Information Access Co. *Predicasts Forecasts*. Foster City, CA: Information Access Co. ISSN 0278-0135. LCCN 81-643080. Quarterly.

This is a compilation of forecasts for products, markets, and industry for the United States and North America using a modified 7 digit Standard Industrial Classification Code. It includes: consumption, shipments, capacity, productions, imports, and exports listing original source and annual growth. This is a quarterly with an annual cumulation.

6. Information Access Co. *Predicasts's Basebook*. Foster City, CA: Information Access Co. Annual.

This is an annual arranged by modified Standard Industrial Classification (SIC) Code that indicates the trends of products and industries. The series cover the time period 1970 to present (there is also an earlier edition) and includes: shipments, imports, exports, wholesale price, expenditures for new plant, equipment, and material, purchased fuels and electricity, payroll, employment, production workers, hours worked, and value added. Also there is an alphabetical index to SIC code, and growth rates for selected products.

7. Information Access Co. *PROMPT, Predicasts Overview of Markets and Technology*. Foster City, CA: Information Access Co. ISSN 0161-8032. LCCN 78-646645. Monthly. Available online. SEE ALSO *DIALOG* 16 and 216.

This abstract gives a marketing overview of specific industries such as food & beverages, textiles & fibers, containers & packaging, plastic materials, drugs & pharmaceuticals, coatings & pigments, plastic products, communications and appliances, and recreation.

8. Information Access Co. *Worldcasts. Product.* Foster City, CA: Information Access Co. ISSN 0163-6723. Quarterly.

This compiles forecasts on products, markets, industry, economic aggregates for the world as reported by experts in the trade and business press. Some industries included are: agriculture, forestry, fishing, mining & extractive industries, food, tobacco products, textile mill products, apparel, printing and publishing, chemicals, polymers, and primary metals.

9. Information Access Co. *Worldcasts. Regional.* Foster City, CA: Information Access Co. ISSN 0163-6731. Quarterly.

This has forecasts on products, markets, industry and economic aggregates as reported by experts in the field. Regions included are: West Europe, East Europe, Africa, Middle East, Americas (except U.S.), Asia and Oceania, and the World. This has production data, imports, exports, consumption, sales, and shipments by SIC code.

10. Media General Financial Services. *Industriscope*. Richmond, VA:Media General Financial Services. Monthly.

This monthly covers 8000 U.S. companies and arranges them by industry group including price, price change, ratio analysis, earnings, and dividends.

11. Moody's Investors Service. *Moody's Industry Review*. New York, NY: Moody's Investors Service. ISSN 1047-3114. LCCN 92-648945.

This loose-leaf examines the U.S. industry from advertising to wholesale distributors with financial data, latest annual rankings, revenues, net income, operating profit margin, return on capital, current assets, and price-earnings ratio, and 12-month price score, and a graph of market trends for NYSE composite index for each industry.

12. Office for Official Publications of the European Community. *Panorama of EU Industry*. Luxembourg: Office for Official Publications of the European Community. LCCN sn94017981. Annual.

This is an extensive survey of the European Community's manufacturing and service industries providing an overview, description of the industry, current situation, production, consumption, investment, employment, industry structure, recent trends, demand and supply, competition, and outlook. Some industries surveyed are: chemicals, food and drink, electrical engineering, textiles, leather, clothing and footwear, and rubber and plastics. Many tables with comparisons are included.

13. Organisation for Economic Co-operation and Development. (OECD) *Indicators of Industrial Activity*. Paris: Organisation for Economic Cooperation and Development. ISSN 0250-4278. LCCN 79-64888. Quarterly with an annual *Industrial Structures Statistics*. (Also available on diskette)

This source looks at short term trends in different industrial sectors broken down by International Standard Industrial Classification (ISIC) codes with data on adjusted seasonal variations, deliveries, producer prices and employment. The outlook is for OECD countries with graphs and statistics on total industry, mining and quarrying, manufacturing, food, beverages, and tobacco, textiles, wearing apparel, wood and wood products, paper and chemicals.

14. OECD. *Industrial Structure Statistics=Statistiques des Structures Industrielles*. Paris: Organisation for Economic Co-operation and Development. Annual. 1982-.

Long term trends in different industrial sectors are broken down by two and three digit ISIC codes in this publication with numbers on production, value added, employment, investment, wages and salaries of employees, number of establishments, and hours worked.These trends are for OECD countries. Chapter I has data originating from industrial surveys and foreign trade data. Chapter II has statistics derived from national accounts estimates. Data are more detailed than *Indicators of Industrial Activity* but not as current. Recent issues profile countries from Algeria to Zimbabwe with manufacturing value added, industrial production index, gross output, employment and manufacturing profitability.

SEE ALSO Rasie, Larry. *Directory of Business Information*.

A brief industry overview is given with description of the industry, status of the industry outlook, end users of the product, international status, sources of information, leading companies, and periodicals specific to the industry.

15. Sawinski, Diane M. and Wendy H. Masons, eds. *Encyclopedia of Global Industries*. Detroit, MI: Gale Research, Inc. ISSN 1084-8614. LCCN sn95-3479.

This source covers 115 of the world's industries including: biotechnology, cable and pay television services, computer software, engineering services, information retrieval services, motor vehicle and car bodies, pharmaceutical preparations, real estate, and telecommunications. This coverage looks at: industry background, development, organization, structure, current condition, research and technology, and work force.

16. Sawinski, Diane M., ed. *U.S. Industry Profiles: The Leading 100*. Detroit, MI: Gale Research, Inc. 1995. 673 p. ISBN 0787605336.

This has a U.S. industry snapshot, outlook, organization and structure, and America's position in the world. It also includes periodicals and newsletters of the industry covered.

17. Standard and Poor's Corporation. *Standard and Poor's Industry Surveys*. New York: Standard and Poor's Corporation. LCCN sn87-17035.

The surveys review various U.S. industries such as: aerospace, autos and autoparts, banking, and chemicals. There are analyses of the industry and a comparison and rating of companies with data on operating revenues, operating income, compound growth rate, index basis, net income, return on revenue, current ratio, price earnings ratio and dividend payment ratio.

18. United Nations. Industrial Development Organization. *Industry and Development: A Global Report*. United Nations. Industrial Development Organization. New York: United Nations. ISSN 0250-7935. LCCN 86-640935. Annual. 1985-.

This report has a comprehensive outlook with a survey of selected manufacturing industries and industrial growth performance for North

America, Japan, Western and Eastern Europe, Latin America and the Caribbean, Africa, and Asia. Coverage of the industry includes data on world production, world trade in the industry, largest companies in the industry, capacity, cost of production. Some industries covered are: textiles, footwear, furniture, petroleum, rubber products, plastics, metal products, electrical machinery, and transport equipment.

19. United Nations. Industrial Development Organization. *International Yearbook of Industrial Statistics*. Vienna: United Nations. 1995. ISBN 185898257X. LCCN 95-64826. Annual.

Information in this yearbook covers: industrial activity for 120 countries with data on industry and products.

20. U.S. Dept. of Commerce. Bureau of Industrial Economics. *U.S. Global Trade Outlook*. U.S. Dept. of Commerce. International Trade Administration. Washington, DC: U. S. Government Printing Office. 1995. LCCN sn95-27449. SUDOCS C 61.34/2: (also available on CD-ROM) Annual. 1994-.

This source provides insight into key industry sectors in the U.S. economy from a trade perspective. These sectors include cross sections of U.S. industries involved in the global economy such as: medical equipment and supplies, computer equipment, computer software, paper products, information services, and automotive parts. Selected countries are covered with the best export opportunities for those countries. Appendixes provide economic and trade data from 1983-1993 for 21 countries and region. Names and telephone numbers for industry specialists are included at the end of analysis.

21. U.S. Dept. of Commerce. International Trade Administration. *U.S. Industrial Outlook*. U. S. Dept. of Commerce. International Trade Administration. Washington, DC: U. S. Government Printing Office, 1994. LCCN 84-645436. SUDOCS C 61.34:994.

There are outlook, trends, and forecasts for about 350 U.S. industries in this source with names of a government contact person for each industry and telephone number. Tables on U.S. trade, shares of imports and exports of manufactured goods by country groupings, U.S. merchandise, total trade shares, product by country, relative price index of U.S. exports in its major foreign markets are included.

22. Value Line Investment Survey. *Value Line Investment Survey.* New York: Value Line, Inc. ISSN 0042-2401. LCCN sf 86-92098.

This source surveys U.S. industries through an investor's perspective beginning with an industry review, then an analysis of individual companies within the industry in terms of timeliness, safety, beta, quarterly revenues, dividends and earnings.

SPECIFIC

23. Aerospace Industries Association of America. *Aerospace Facts and Figures.* Washington, DC: Aerospace Industries Association of America. LCCN 46025007. Annual. 1945-.

This source includes information on the aerospace industry, civilian and military production, R&D, trade, employment, finances and trends.

SEE ALSO *Directory of Business Periodicals Special Issues.*

It has special issues that have the latest industry overview such as: "Facts and Figures for the Chemical Industry," "Annual Ceramic Business Outlook," and "Industry Forecast" for the plastics industry.

24. Electronic Industries Association. *Electronic Market Data Book.* Washington, DC: Electronic Industry Association. Marketing Services Dept. ISBN 07908--0056X. LCCN 72-627504. Annual. 1972-.

This statistical yearbook provides an overview of the electronics industry including trends, international trade, and stock index. The contents cover industry overview, consumer electronics, telecommunications, defense-related communications, computers, industrial and electronic components, and international electronics.

25. Marketing Services. Inc. *Automotive News: Market Data Book.* Detroit: Marketing Services, Inc. ISSN 0363-71960. LCCN sn84010453. Annual.1976-.

The information includes worldwide vehicle production and sales, registration, and prices for U.S.-built and imported cars.

26. Motor Vehicle Manufacturers Association of the United States. *World Motor Vehicle Data.* Detroit: Motor Vehicle Manufacturers Association of the United States. ISSN 0085-8307. LCCN 73-640507. Annual.

World production of motor vehicles by country and type, world production of motor vehicles for selected countries, top 40 manufacturers ranked by domestic production, world imports and exports, top 50 passenger cars sold by models, Africa imports, Asia imports, European imports and Western Hemisphere imports are areas covered in this source.

SEE ALSO *National Trade Data Bank.*

Under the program "Market Research Reports" (Disc 1) there are industry analyses for specific products and countries. These reports do not cover a broad industry but are specific such as: the microprocessor, bicycle, or electric utility industry, auto parts, construction, and plastics industry. These reports change from month to month. The analyses are those of specialists in the field and not of the International Trade Commission.

27. Organisation for Economic Co-operation and Development. *World Energy Outlook.* Paris: Organisation for Economic Co-operation and Development. Washington, DC: distributed by OECD Publications and Information Center.Annual.1977-.

Global Trends to 2010 on world energy and oil demand with

assumptions on energy price, macroeconomics, and power generation are some topics in this source. Outlook for energy is broken down by fuel type: oil, gas, coal, electricity, and nuclear power.

28. U.S. Dept. of Commerce. International Trade Commission. *Industry and Trade Summary*. Washington, DC: U.S. International Trade Commission.

These are summaries on products imported and exported into the U.S. Each report focuses on a different commodity or industry area with information or product uses, U.S. industry profile, foreign industry profile, U.S. and foreign producers and customs treatment. Analysis also contains factors affecting trends in consumption, production, and trade of the commodity. Some commodities covered are: lamps and lighting fittings, footwear, major primary olefins, heavy structural steel shapes, aircraft spacecraft and related equipment, polyethylene resins, and wood pulp.

U.S. Department of Commerce. (U.S. Dept.) *Industry Sector Analysis*. Washington, DC: U.S. Dept. of Commerce. International Trade Administration. Distributed by National Technical Information Service.

These are very brief documents packed with information and data for a particular industry and country. Some sectors included are:

29. *Industry Sector Analysis-Cosmetics Market Overview (Poland) 1994*. PB94-197399/GAR.

30. *Industry Sector Analysis-Footwear Industry Profile (Hungary) 1994*. PB94-202868/GAR.

31. *Industry Sector Analysis-Office Consumable, (Canada) 1993*. PB93-233658/GAR.

32. *Industry Sector Analysis-Pharmaceutical Industry (New Czech Republic) 1994*. PB94-202884/GAR.

33. *Industry Sector Analysis-Thermal Power Generating Equipment (Colombia)1993*. PB93-235224/GAR.

34. *Industry Sector Analysis-Water Supply Equipment (Venezuela), 1993*. PB93-238657/GAR.

U.S. Environmental Protection Agency. EPA Office of Compliance. *EPA Office of Compliance Sector Notebook Project: Profile of ...* Washington, DC: U.S. Government Printing Office, 1995.

These are industry profiles from an environmental perspective including: industry description, characterization of the industry, industry size and geographic distribution, top ten companies, economic trends, industrial processes, comprehensive environmental measures for similar sector industries. See the following:

35. U.S. Environmental Protection Agency (U.S. EPA). EPA Office of Compliance. *EPA Office of Compliance Sector Notebook Project: Profile of Dry Cleaning Industry*. Washington, DC: U.S. Government Printing Office, 1995. 86 p. ISBN 0160482682. SUDOCS EP 1.2:P94/30/clean

36. U.S. EPA. EPA Office of Compliance. *EPA Office of Compliance Sector Notebook Project: Profile of Electronics and Computer Industry*. Washington, DC: U.S. Government Printing Office, 1995. 142 p. ISBN 0160482690. SUDOCS EP 1.2:P94/28/electro

37. U.S. EPA. EPA Office of Compliance. *EPA Office of Compliance Sector Notebook Project: Profile of Inorganic Chemical Industry*. Washington, DC: U.S. Government Printing Office, 1995. 123 p. ISBN 01604822712. SUDOCS EP 1.2:P94/20/inorg

38. U.S. EPA. EPA Office of Compliance. *EPA Office of Compliance Sector Notebook Project: Profile of Iron and Steel Industry*. Washington, DC: U.S. Government Printing Office, 1995. 113 p. ISBN 0160482720. SUDOCS EP 1.2:P94/22/iron

This profiles the iron and steel industry from an environmental perspective with geographic distribution of establishments, steel works, blast furnaces, rolling and finishing mills, top U.S. iron and steel producers, economic trends, domestic market, international trade, and long term prospects.

39. U.S. EPA. EPA Office of Compliance. *EPA Office of Compliance Sector Notebook Project: Profile of Lumber and Wood Industry*. Washington, DC: U.S. Government Printing Office, 1995. 120 p. ISBN 0160482739. SUDOCS EP 1.2:P94/23/lumber

40. U.S. Environmental Protection Agency. EPA Office of Compliance. *EPA Office of Compliance Sector Notebook Project: Profile of Metal Mining Industry*. Washington, DC: U.S. Government Printing Office, 1995. 130 p. ISBN 0160482275. SUDOCS EP 1.2:P94/16/metal

This document profiles the metal mining industry. It includes: major base metal producing areas, precious metal producing areas, number of facilities per state, major uses for selected metal minerals, economic trends, and leading companies.

41. U.S. Environmental Protection Agency. EPA Office of Compliance. *EPA Office of Compliance Sector Notebook Project: Profile of Motor Vehicle Assembly Industry*. Washington, DC: U.S. Government Printing Office, 1995. 138 p. ISBN 0160482763. SUDOCS EP 1.2:P94/19/motor

It includes the size of the motor vehicle and motor vehicle equipment manufacturing establishments, geographic distribution of the industry, top ten motor vehicle manufacturers ranked by world production, and automotive material usage 1984-1994, and use of alternative fuel forecast.

42. U.S. Environmental Protection Agency. (U.S. EPA) EPA Office of Compliance. *EPA Office of Compliance Sector Notebook Project: Profile of the Nonferrous Metals Industry*. Washington, DC: U.S. Government Printing Office, 1995. 124 p. 6p. ISBN 0160482771. SUDOCS EP 1.2:P94/21/nonfer

43. U.S. EPA. EPA Office of Compliance. *EPA Office of Compliance Sector Notebook Project: Profile of the Non-Metal Mining Industry*. Washington, DC: U.S. Government Printing Office, 1995. 86 p. ISBN 016048278x. SUDOCS EP 1.2:P94/21/mining

44. U.S. EPA. EPA Office of Compliance. *EPA Office of Compliance Sector Notebook Project: Profile of the Organic Chemicals Industry*. Washington, DC: U.S. Government Printing Office, 1995. 126 p. ISBN 0160482798. SUDOCS EP 1.2:P94/21/organic

45. U.S. EPA. EPA Office of Compliance. *EPA Office of Compliance Sector Notebook Project: Profile of the Petroleum Refining Industry*. Washington, DC: U.S. Government Printing Office, 1995. 131 p. ISBN 0160482801. SUDOCS EP 1.2:P94/21/petrol

46. U.S. Environmental Protection Agency. EPA Office of Compliance. *EPA Office of Compliance Sector Notebook Project: Profile of the Printing and Publishing Industry*. Washington, DC:

47. U.S. Environmental Protection Agency. EPA Office of Compliance. *EPA Office of Compliance Sector Notebook Project: Profile of the Pulp and Paper Industry*. Washington, DC: U.S. Government Printing Office, 1995. 128 p. ISBN 016042828 SUDOCS EP 1.2:P94/21/pulp

48. U.S. Environmental Protection Agency. EPA Office of Compliance. *EPA Office of Compliance Sector Notebook Project: Profile of the Rubber and Plastics Industry*. Washington, DC: U.S. Government Printing Office, 1995. 130 p. ISBN 0160482801. SUDOCS EP 1.2:P94/21/rubber

49. U.S. Environmental Protection Agency. EPA Office of Compliance. *EPA Office of Compliance Sector Notebook Project: Profile of the Stone, Clay, Glass, and Concrete Products Industry*. Washington, DC: U.S. Government Printing Office, 1995. 101 p. ISBN 0160482801. SUDOCS EP 1.2:P94/18/concrete

50. U.S. Environmental Protection Agency. EPA Office of Compliance. *EPA Office of Compliance Sector Notebook Project: Profile of the Wood Furniture and Fixtures Industry*. Washington, DC: U.S. Government Printing Office, 1995. 116 p. ISBN 0160482704. SUDOCS EP 1.2:P94/21/wood

51. Ward's Reports, Inc. *Ward's Automotive Yearbook*. Detroit: Ward's Reports, Inc. ISSN 0083-7229. LCCN 40-33639. Annual. 1938-

This source contains an overview of the global auto industry with worldwide production, new vehicle programs, top world producers, industry trends, key new vehicle programs, and automotive statistics for different countries.

CHAPTER II

CHALLENGES

The challenges are economic and industrial. The chapter is divided into: competition and trade, competitive assessment by industry, trade barriers, and trade policies. It includes: ways to compete economically or industrially such as: (1) producing a unique product or service (2) overcoming industry problems (3) being more productive or efficient (4) navigating trade barriers and (5) having an effective trade policy.

COMPETITION AND TRADE

52. Arnold, Bruce Gregory. *How the GATT Affects U.S. Antidumping and Countervailing-Duty Policy.* Washington, DC: U.S. Congressional Budget Office, U.S. Government Printing Office, 1994. 85 p. SUDOCS Y 10.2:T 27.

This study reports that the U.S. laws treat the pricing of imports in the U.S. market differently than the pricing of domestically produced goods. Over time, the antidumping and countervailing duty laws have become a source of protection for U.S. firms from foreign competition. The report covers predatory pricing, price discrimination, selling below cost, government subsidies, and controversies over U.S. antidumping and countervailing duty laws.

53. Carnevale, Anthony Patrick. *America and the New Economy.* Washington, DC: U.S. Dept. of Labor, Employment and Training Administration. 1991. 126p. SUDOCS L 37.2: AM 3/2.

This publication describes the new economy based on a new set of competitive standards that are transforming organizations, economic cycles, jobs and skill requirements. It includes: a new economic life cycle and a tranformation of America for the new economy. It covers: the automotive, food, chemical and pharmaceutical industries, and new market standards. It has tables on the productivity of other nations as a percentage of American productivity, 1950-1989; value of output per person in the U.S. and other nations, 1950-1989.

54. Dollar, David and Edward N. Wolff. *Competitiveness, Convergence and International Specialization*. Cambridge, Mass.: MIT Press, 1993. 228 p. ISBN 0262041359. LCCN 9202798.

This source attempts to answer questions on the competitiveness of the U.S. industries, the role of international trade, and the role of government. It looks at trends in shares of total manufacturing output produced by OECD member nations for 1961-1987, employment shares on the industry level, and the percentage shares of world export for 1963-1985 (U.S., Japan, and Germany by commodity group). One striking feature of international trade among industrialized economies is the degree of specialization. Also industries in which the U.S. continues to be strong exporters are generally industries that the government directly or indirectly supports.

55. Fraser, Robert, ed. *The World Trade System*. Harlow, Essex, U.K.: Longman Group. Distributed by Gale Research , Inc. 1991. 435 p. ISBN 0582086965. LCCN 92124705.

Part I gives a brief history of the world trading system since 1945 including the establishment of worldwide economic organizations, the pattern of trade in the early post war years, the oil crisis in the 70's, the economic integration in Western Europe, the international debt crisis, the developments in the Soviet Union and Eastern Europe, GATT, and Uruguay Round. Part II has global organizations. Part III gives country information, and Part IV covers international commodities including a brief summary about the importance of the commodity, data on major producers of the commodity, major exporters of the commodity and major countries that import the commodity.

56. *Michael E. Porter on Competition and Strategy*. Cambridge, Mass: Harvard Business School Press, 1991. 89 p. ISBN 0875842720.

Formulating a strategy begins by analyzing the competition. Corporate strategy must include diversification to succeed, but the success ratio is low. Information technology gives companies a competitive edge. A nation's competitiveness depends on its industries being innovative and upgraded. Government's role is as a catalyst and challenger -- to push companies to higher levels of competitive performance, provide tax incentives for long term capital gains, and to encourage long term investment, and to pressure Japan to buy more manufactured goods. These are some concepts in this book.

57. Miller, E. Williard and Ruby M. Miller. *America's International Trade: A Reference Handbook.* Santa Barbara, CA.: ABC-CLIO, 1995. 325 p. ISBN 0874367700. LCCN 95014135.

This handbook traces the evolution of the U.S. trade policy from a protectionist stand to a free trade policy. It includes a chronology of U.S. trade legislation, government organizations dealing with trade, international organizations, and a directory of World Trade Centers. It looks at three regional economies that have evolved: the European Union dominates Europe and Africa; Japan dominates Asia; and the U.S. is dominant in North and South America. It does not include country information.

58. Ohmae, Kenichi. *The Borderless World.* New York: HarperCollins, 1994. 223 p. ISBN 00063776657. LCCN gb94-44491.

The theme is that world consumers are the determining factor in the buying of products. They set the performance standards and there are no borders for products. Managers of multinational corporations need to reexamine their views on strategy and competition from the customer perspective. The role of government is changing in this interlinked global economy.

59. Sachwald, Frederique, ed. *European Integration and Competitiveness: Acquisition and Alliances in Industry*. Aldershot, Hants, England: Edward Elgar Publishing, 1994. 338 p. ISBN 1852789564. LCCN 9334133.

The aim of this book is to show how European firms have resorted to external growth operations to implement their strategies and strengthen their competitiveness. It includes: the logic behind the Single Market, defines competitiveness, analyzes the competitive game in each sector and assesses the position of Europe and European firms. The industries covered are: automobile, automobile components, chemicals, pharmaceuticals, electronic components, and consumer electronics.

60. Thurow, Lester. *Head to Head: The Coming Economic Battle Among Japan, Europe, and America*. New York: Warner Books, Inc., 1992. 336 p. ISBN 0446394971. LCCN 92-37621.

Thurow looks at the changing world order with its new rules and at the coming economic battle among Japan, Europe, and the U.S. He evaluates the three countries and puts forth an American game plan that begins by studying the competition, finding those countries in the world with the best economic performance, measuring the U.S. economic performance with theirs, understanding why they are better, matching then surpassing their performance. After improving America's productivity, he discusses investment, savings, and education in order to remain competitive.

61. U.S. Congress. House Committee on Foreign Affairs. Subcommittee on Asian and Pacific Affairs. *U.S.-Asia Economic Relations: Hearings Before the Subcommittee on Asian and Pacific Affairs, Joint with Subcommittee on International Economic Policy and Trade of the Committee on Foreign Affairs, House of Representatives. One Hundred Second Congress, Second Session, April 2 and 29, 1992.* Washington, DC: U.S. Government Printing Office. 1993. 242 p. ISBN 0160399084. LCCN 93-135432. SUDOCS Y 4.F 76/1:As 4/26.

This study looks for reasons the United States is losing the competitive struggle with Asia, and Japan, in particular. It measures the openness of the Japanese market to U.S. exports, and tracks investments, capital flows, trade and employment productivity. One fundamental difference is in corporate goals of U.S. and Japanese companies.

62. U.S. Congress. House. Committee on Government Operations, Commerce, Consumer, and Monetary Affairs Subcommittee. *The North American Free Trade Agreement (NAFTA) and Its Impact on the Textile/Apparel/Fiber and Auto and Auto Parts Industry: Hearings Before the Commerce, Consumer, and Monetary Affairs Subcommittee of the Committee on Government Operations, House of Representatives. One Hundred Third Congress, First Session.* 1993. Washington, DC: U.S. Government Printing Office, 1993. 233p. SUDOCS Y 4.G 76/7:AM 3/3.

The impact of NAFTA on the textile industry will be minor, but in the automotive industry it may lead to an increase of labor intensive jobs moving to Mexico. However, countering these negatives are: labor costs are a decreasing component of the automotive manufacturing costs, Mexico has higher infrastructure costs than the U.S. , Mexico's supplier is weak and much of the low skilled labor has already moved from the U.S. These are some issues covered by this hearing.

63. U.S. Congress. Joint Economic Committee. *Global Economic and Technological Change: Japan and the Asia-Pacific Region: Hearing Before the Subcommittee on Economic Goals and International Policy of the Joint Economic Committee. One Hundred Second Congress, Second Session.* Washington, DC: U.S. Government Printing Office, 1993. LCCN 0160385393. SUDOCS Y 4.EC 7:G 51/4/Pt. 3.

Japan has been called the core economy of the Asia-Pacific region. This hearing examines recent Japanese trade and investment increases in the East Asian and Pacific region. Japan's investment strategy is to circumvent protectionist trade barriers and to focus on manufacturing investments to provide a springboard into the global market. It compares Japan's trade and investment lead in the region vs. the lagging U.S. position and the growing Japanese assertiveness and activism in world trade.

64. U.S. Congress. Office of Technology Assessment. *Competing Economies: America, Europe and the Pacific Rim.* Washington, DC: U.S. GPO, 1993. 375 p. ISSN 0160359333. LCCN 91-602088. SUDOCS Y 3.T 22/2:2 EC7.

This report discusses improving the U.S. economic environment in manufacturing performance and ways Federal institutions can cooperate with industry to develop competitive strategies in the high-tech industries. The strategies include: trade, financial, and technology policies.

65. U.S. Dept. of Commerce. *Competing to Win in a Global Economy.* Washington, DC: U.S. Government Printing Office, 1994. 107 p. ISBN 0160452333. SUDOCS C 1.2: W 72.

The U.S. economy is back on track but if the objectives are raising living standards and creating better paying jobs, the critical elements to competitive trade are: civilian technology, education, training, retraining, community development, and health care. The long term challenges are: more savings and investment, productivity growth and labor compensation. Some problems are: family income growth is uneven and long terms trade imbalances remain. There are recommendations for improving competitiveness.

66. U.S. Dept. of Commerce. International Trade Commission. *Annual Report.* Washington, DC: U.S. Government Printing Office. SUDOCS ITC 1.1:.

This annual covers investigations of trade and tariff matters and includes congressional reports on: studies analyzing the competitiveness of U.S. industries, examinations under chapter 337 of the Tariff Act of 1930, and a summary of investigations for the year such as: the Dynamic Effects of Trade Liberalization, Steel, Semiannual Report, the Economic Effects of Significant U.S. Import Restraints, Live Cattle and Beef: U.S. and Canadian Industry Profiles, Trade and Factors of Competition.

67. Yoffie, David B. ed. *Beyond Free Trade.* Boston, MA.: Harvard Business School Press, 1993 . 466 p. ISBN 0875843441. LCCN 92-29834.

This three year study attempts to explain the changing patterns of world trade and global competition. Some findings are: comparative advantages and national competitive advantages continue to be important in global trade, American firms and the U.S. continue to dominate most of the industries studied, and the U.S. has lost significant market share although it is the world's largest exporter.

COMPETITIVE ASSESSMENT BY INDUSTRY

68. National Commission to Ensure a Strong Competitive Airline Industry. *Change, Challenge and Competition.* Washington, DC: U.S. Government Printing Office, 1993. 30 p.

This investigation looks at the airline industry, identifies impediments to a strong and competitive airline industry, makes recommendations for dealing with the obstacles and reports on the need for efficiency.

The U.S. Dept. of Commerce studies the present and future competitiveness of various industries from solid wood products to semiconductors. The assessments vary but include the following: executive summary, definition of the industry, U.S. industry performance, U.S. position in world markets, trends in world trade, competitive factors, and U.S. Government policies.

U.S. Dept. of Commerce. *A Competitive Assessment of the* ... Washington, DC: . Government Printing Office (U.S. GPO). The ones distributed by the U.S. Government Printing Office have SUDOCS number. The ones distributed by the National Technical Information Service have an Order number such as a PB and six digits.

Some titles are:

69. *A Competitive Assessment of the U.S. Fiber Optics Industry.* 1994. Springfield, VA: National Technical Information Services. PB94-134806CDG.

70. *A Competitive Assessment of the U.S. Industrial Air Pollution Control Equipment Industry.* 1991 SUDOCS C 61.2:IN 2/2.

71. *A Competitive Assessment of the U.S. Power Tool Industry*. 1992. SUDOCS C 61.2:P 87.

72. *A Competitive Assessment of the U.S. Sports Equipment Industry.* 1989. SUDOCS C 61.2:Sp 6.

73. *The Competitive Status of the U.S. Electronics Sector from Materials to Systems.* 1990. SUDOCS C 61.2:EL 2/3.

TRADE BARRIERS

74. U.S. Office of the U.S. Trade Representative. *National Trade Estimates... Report on Foreign Trade Barriers* Washington, DC: U.S. GPO. SUDOCS PREX 9. 10: Annual. 1986-.

This annual compiles important foreign trade barriers for each country from Australia to the former Yugoslavia. The report classifies the barriers into eight categories such as: import policies; standards, testing, labeling and certification; government procurement (i.e. "buy national"); lack of intellectual property protection; and export subsidies.

TRADE POLICIES

75. Batra, Raveendra N. *The Myth of Free Trade: A Plan for America's Economic Revival.* New York: Scribner, 1993.

Batra holds the view that free trade is the reason the U.S. economy is in trouble. He examines the effects of U.S. free trade policy on 11 of its major trading partners, the relationship between international trade and pollution, and concludes that free trade benefits everyone except the U.S.

76. Brittan, Leon. *European Competition Policy: Keeping the Playing Field Level.* London: Brassey's. Distributed by Macmillan Publishing Co. 1992. 112 p. ISBN 1857530772.

The source explains the European Competition Policy including: its foundations and guiding principles, application, scope, procedures for enforcement, and its application to merger policy and procedure.

77. Comanor, W. S. et al. *Competition Policy in Europe and North America: Economic Issues and Institutions.* New York: Harwood Academic, 1990. 260 p. ISBN 3718650592. LCCN 900044952.

This source compares and gives background on the attitudes and evaluation of competition policies in Europe, Canada, and the U.S. The role and enforcement of competition policy vary from country to country. It states that a well drafted competition policy promotes economic performance with a minimum of detrimental side effects.

78. Eden, Lorraine, ed. *Multinationals in North America.* Calgary: University of Calgary Press, 1994. 557 p. ISBN 1895176476. LCCN 94233184.

The focus of this source is on the actions of multinational enterprises (MNE) in North America (NA) and the government policies of the United States, Canada, and Mexico. It looks at recent changes in the North American economy and the relationship between MNE and the governments. It identifies emerging trends and implications of these trends for policy makers. It includes: multinationals and foreign direct investment in NA, location strategies of U.S. MNE after NAFTA, and characteristics of Japanese MNE in NA.

79. Organisation for Economic Cooperation and Development. *Main Developments in Trade.* Paris: Organisation for Economic Cooperation and Development. LCCN sn 94042184. Annual. 1993-. Also available on diskette.

This annual describes the recent evolution of trade flows and important trade measures and policies for the current year. Its aim is to assist the OECD trade Committee on trade issues. It includes a summary and assessment of foreign trade developments, various trade negotiations, GATT disputes, economic and trade trends that affect OECD countries.

80. U.S. Competitiveness Policy Council. *Annual Report to the President & Congress: Building a Competitive America.* Washington, DC: U.S. GPO. ISSN 1063-5548. LCCN 92640557 SUDOCS Y 3.C73/6:1/yr.

This report defines the competitiveness problem of the U.S., and recommends short and long term strategy. Some recommendations are: setting national goals, investing in the workforce, promoting industry, and investing in physical capital.

81. U.S. Congress. House. Committee on Foreign Affairs. *Country Reports on Economic Policy and Trade Practices: Report Submitted to the Committee on Foreign Affairs, Committee on Ways and Means of the U.S. House of Representatives, Committee on Foreign Relations Committee on Finance of the U.S. Senate by the Department of State in Accordance with Section 2202 of the Omnibus Trade and Competitiveness Act of 1988.* Washington, DC: U. S. GPO. SUDOCS Y 4.F 76/1:C 83/3/994. Annual. 1989-.

This document provides an analysis of economic and trade practices for countries that trade with the U.S. including: key economic indicators, overview of macroeconomic trends, exchange rate policies, structural policies that affect U.S. exports to that country, debt management policies, significant barriers to U.S. exports and investments, export subsidiary policies, protection of U.S. intellectual property rights, and worker rights.

82. U.S. Congress. Committee on Foreign Affairs. *East Asia Policy: Round Table Before the Committee on Foreign Affairs and its Subcommittee on Asia and the Pacific. House of Representatives. One Hundred Third Congress, Second Session.* Washington, DC: U.S. Government Printing Office, 1994. 75 p. ISBN 0160448115. SUDOCS Y 4.F 76/1:AS 4/30.

This hearing brings together government officials and the business community to discuss right and wrong policies for the area. Some recommendations are: the U.S. must state clearly its strategic objectives in Asia; Asians need to be convinced the U.S. will follow through on its commitment; policies for the region need to be integrated and address economic, financial, trade, and technology issues. This region is important for the prosperity of the U.S. as they account for about 46% of the incremental world imports over the course of this decade.

83. U.S. Congress. Office of Technology Assessment. *Global Communications: Opportunities for Trade and Aid.* Washington, DC: U.S. Government Printing Office, 1995. 183 p. SUDOCS Y 3.T 22/2: 2G 51/5:.

Communication and information technologies can mutually service foreign aid and trade goals. These technologies are of critical importance, and they are the fastest growing sectors in the world. This report assesses the tradeoffs between U.S. trade policy with respect to these industries and the U.S. foreign policy objective of promoting international stability and nation building.

84. U.S. Congress. Office of Technology Assessment. *Multinationals and the U.S. Technology Base.* Washington, DC: U.S. Government Printing Office, 1994. 211 p. ISBN 0160451876. SUDOCS Y 3.T 22/2:2M 91.

Multinational enterprises are critical to the health of the U.S. technology base and the implications for public policy are that they must be maintained. The nation's health is not solely related to R & D spending but to strategic investment behavior of multinationals. Some findings are: research and technology activities tend to be concentrated in the country of national origin; the U.S. typically exports five times more technology than it imports; trade follows investment and the Japanese investment in the U.S. exceeds U.S.investment in Japan by a factor of 3 to 1. Because of this imbalance in global trade and investment, U.S. policy should be: to expand multilateral trade agreements to encompass obstacles to foreign trade and restrict business practices and other barriers to comparable market access.

85. U.S. Dept. of Commerce. Trade Coordinating Committee. *The National Export Strategy: Third Annual Report to the United States Congress.* Washington, DC: U.S. Government Printing Office, 1995. 145 p. SUDOCS C 1.2:Ex 7/8.

According to this report, the U.S. national export strategy is working and achieving the goal of expanding exports to over $1.2 trillion by the year 2000. It looks at the U.S. trade performance, the by the year 2000. It looks at the U.S. trade performance, the macroeconomic picture (U.S. has regained its position from Germany as the largest exporter), lowering obstacles to exports, Trade Promotion Coordinating Committee Small Business Strategy, and tables for trade promotion expenditures by classification such as: negotiating open markets and lowering/removing trade barriers and trade promotion expenditure by agency.

86. U.S. Dept. of Commerce. Trade Promotion Coordinating Committee. *The National Export Strategy: Annual Report to the United States Congress*. Washington, DC: U.S. Dept. of Commerce, 1994. 158 p. SUDOCS C 61.8:115/9/spec.

This second annual report enumerates the 65 recommendations to improve the government's export promotion programs called for in the previous year and details the progress in the past year such as: supporting U.S. bidders in global competition, improving trade finance, removing obstacles to exporting, helping small-medium sized business, and focusing on new opportunities.

87. U.S. Dept. of Commerce. Trade Promotion Coordinating Committee. *Toward a National Export Strategy: U.S. Exports=U.S. Jobs: a Report to the United States Congress*. Washington, DC: U.S. Government Printing Office, 1993. 104 p. LCCN 93-231570. SUDOCS C 1.2:Ex 7/6.

The development of a national export strategy is expected to generate exports worth a trillion dollars and create 6 million new jobs by the year 2000. The strategy includes: (1)"one stop shops" in four major cities to replace the maze of offices exporters must contact (2) strategic country marketing plan for key U.S. export markets (3) high level advocacy for U.S. companies pursuing major foreign government procurement opportunities (4) annual "unified budget" for U.S. government export promotion activities coordinated by the National Economic Council, the Office of Management and Budget and the Trade Promotion Coordinating Committee.

SEE ALSO U.S. International Trade Commission. *The Year in Trade: Operations of the Trade Agreement Program.*

88. U.S. Office of the President. *Trade Policy Agenda and the ... Annual Report of the President of the United States on Trade Agreement Programs*. Washington, DC: U.S. Government Printing Office. LCCN sn93-44057. SUDOCS PREX 9.11: Annual. 1989-.

Successful trade policies are vital to the U.S. economy by stimulating output of goods and services, better paying jobs, and increasing competitiveness. This annual has an agenda for the year, a review of the previous year, summary of U.S. exports of goods and services, and data and negotiations such as the approval of Congress and president for the Uruguay Round of Multilateral Trade Negotiation.

89. Weintraub, Sidney, ed. *Integrating the Americas: Shaping Future Trade Policy*. New Brunswick, USA: Transaction Publishers, 1994. 197 p. ISBN 1560007699. LCCN 94-038585.

This book expresses different views about the economic integration and the future trade policy of the Americas. It includes: the historical pillars of U.S. trade policy, Latin American trade policy and its future, the uncertain prospects for free trade, NAFTA and its "unstable equilibrium," proposal for a U.S. - Brazilian free trade association, and a matrix of trade figures for East Asia, the EU and NAFTA, and MERCOSUR (Southern Cone Common Market in South America).

CHAPTER III

COUNTRY INFORMATION

The country information chapter is divided into: general, region and country, and additional information. The **general** includes any source or series that covers many countries and provides political, economic, and historical data for specific countries such as the *Europa World Yearbook*.

The series may be country specific. Each series has a slightly different perspective such as: *Country Report Series* looks at an individual country from an economic and political aspect, whereas the *Price-Waterhouse* series "*Doing Business in...*" emphasizes more tax information and the legal system, and *Disease and Environmental Alert Reports* focuses on the environmental and sanitary considerations as well as population, religion, and ethnic makeup of a particular country.

The **region** and **country** specific section covers a particular region or country, such as: *Asian Development Outlook* (regional area outlook), or *The EC 1992* (marketing implications for the area).

Studies on ways countries adjust to the changing trends in the global economy are also included as these countries will be the leaders. There are also studies on ways the developing countries can industrialize.

Any specialized guide, almanac, yearbook, or study for a region or country will be in this chapter. With this arrangement, information on a particular country will be in one area. For example, under Japan, there will be background, guides, and statistics such as: *Asia & Japan Business Information Sourcebook, Exporting to Japan, Japan, Marketing and Advertising Yearbook*. The exceptions are periodicals and directories.

Additional information includes: cultural, environmental and labor and employment data.

GENERAL

90. Croner, Ulrich Horst Edward. *Reference Book for World Traders*, 19--; *a loose leaf handbook covering information required for market research and for planning and executing exports and imports*. Queens Village, NY: Croner Publications. ISBN 0875140009. LCCN 61-10661.

Volume 1 covers exporting basics such as: filling out a shipper's export declaration, state listing of small business development centers, tariff structure of the countries, import license requirements, restrictions, postal information, international telegrams, telex rates, and shipping lines directory. Volume 2 has country information with international affiliation, currency, trade, ports, commodity restrictions, airlines, electric current, office hours, travel tips, and doing business in countries. It also includes: advertising agencies, banks, free trade zones, and trade directories.

91. The Dorling Kindersley Publishing, Inc. *The Dorling Kindersley World Reference Atlas*. New York, London: Dorling Kindersley, 1994. 732 p.

This atlas includes country information on: population, religion, political, economic and social issues, tourism, GNP per capita, GNP ranking, unemployment, health, wealth, and crime with charts and graphs.

92. Economist Intelligence Unit. *Country Report Series*. London: The Economist Intelligence Unit. Quarterly. (SEE ALSO LEXIS/NEXIS for online source)

The *Country Report* series has concise background and analysis of economic and political developments for 180 countries. Each report is country specific and includes the following data: economic indicators principal exports, outlook, forecast, direction of foreign trade, currency trends, and economic structure. It has an annual called *Country Profile*.

93. Euromonitor Plc. *World Economic Prospects: A Planners Guide to International Market Conditions*. London: Euromonitor Plc., 1993. 297 p. ISBN 0863385125. LCCN G.B. 93015501.

The interrelationship between economics, politics, and

demographics are synthesized both quantitatively and qualitatively for 78 countries to evaluate the market potential for each country including: country overview, political stability and risk, economic profile, labor force, and population.

94. Europa Publications Limited. *Europa World Yearbook* London; Europa Publications Limited. ISSN 0956-2273. LCCN 89-649752. Annual. 1945-

Part I has information on international organizations. Part II covers countries from Afghanistan to Zimbabwe providing recent history, location, climate, language, religion, government, and economic affairs. Statistics include finance, industry, money supply, and external trade, and employment.

95. Gale Research, Inc. *Craighead's International Business Travel, and Relocation Guide to 71 Countries 1994-95*. Detroit, MI: Gale Research, Inc. 1994-95. 1603 p. ISSN 1058-3904. LCCN 92-660542.

This handy relocation guide has 71 country profiles including: official name, head of state, overview, travel advisory, climate, people, government and politics, history, economy, recent developments, trends, language, business procedures, operating conditions, business customs, currency, communication, mail, and health and safety.

96. Gale Research Inc. *Worldmark Encyclopedia of the Nations, 8th ed. Detroit*, MI: Gale Research, Inc. 1995. 5 vol. ISSN 0810398788. LCCN 94-38556.

This five volume set is divided into: United Nations, Africa, Americas, Asia & Oceania, and Europe with country information covering location, population, languages, history, transportation, government, labor, industry, foreign trade, and foreign investment.

97. Hargreaves, David and Monica Eden-Green et al. *World Index of Resources and Population*. Brookfield, VT.: Dartmouth Pub. 1994. 417 p. ISBN 1855215039. LCCN 93-038638.

Sixty-one countries are examined in terms of political and

economic risk assessment, economic profile, minerals industry profile, and strategic factors. Also forecasting of population, minerals industries and energy industries are other topics discussed.

98. International Reports. *International Country Risk Guide*. New York: International Reports. LCCN 81-645809. ISSN 0278-6680. 1986-.

This looks at countries from an investor's viewpoint and assesses political and country risks.

99. Organisation for Economic Cooperation and Development. *OECD Economic Surveys*. Paris: Organisation for Economic Cooperation and Development.

The series include specific information on OECD countries including trends, prospects, outlook, macroeconomic policies, structural reform, and financial markets. There are tables on current and capital spending (per cent of GNP), currency composition of foreign debt, employment, population ratio and its component. The survey includes: Australia (ISBN 0196-08360), Austria, (ISBN 0474-5124), Belgium, Canada, Czechoslovakia, Finland, and Hungary, etc.

100. Price Waterhouse. *Price Waterhouse Information Guide Series*. New York: Price Waterhouse.

Each guide is entitled *Doing Business in...*(country) and covers an individual country from an auditor's perspective with data on investment climate, business environment, aims of government policy, economic development plan, political and legal system, and trade opportunities. Very good tax information covering: corporate income taxes, corporate residence, foreign worker's levy, and property tax. Price-Waterhouse also publishes the *Corporate Taxes: a World Wide Summary* that has tax rules from Antigua to Zimbabwe.

101. *Statesman's Year Book*. London: Macmillan. ISSN 0081-4601. LCCN 04-3776. Annual.

This one volume source covers international organization and countries of the world from A-Z profiling each country with: area, population, constitution and government, economy, energy, industry, labor, trade unions, and references. Information is similar to *Europa World Year Book* but more concise.

102. Third World Journalists. *Third World Guide*. Rio de Janeiro: Editora Terceiro Mundo. LCCN sn 87036114. Annual. 1984-

This source provides basic social, political, and economic information. It gives an overview of demographics, children, health, arms in numbers, transnationals, poverty, and international trade. It has forecasts and trends such as: most of the world population growth will be in Africa, Asia and Latin America and the population of the South will be younger and the North will be older. There are tables on: fertility in figures, food and import dependency, country debt and food production per capita. Profiles of third world countries from Afghanistan to Zimbabwe are included with indicators on children per woman, infant mortality (per 1000 births) and life expectancy.

103. U.S. Dept. of Commerce. International Trade Administration. *Investment Climate Statement*. Washington DC: U.S. International Trade Administration, distributed by National Technical Information Service.

This series has an investment climate statement for a particular country. It is periodically updated with information on: economic conditions, a country overview, government policy, receptivity to foreign investment, transfer policy, dispute settlement, and economic trends. Foreign investment data are provided.

104. U.S. Dept. Of Commerce. National Technical Information Service. *Country Commercial Guides*. Springfield, VA: National Technical Information Service.

Each country report presents a comprehensive view of the country's marketing environment including economic and political conditions, trade regulations, best market and investment prospects, and travel tips.

105. U.S. Dept. of Defense. Armed Forces Medical Intelligence Center. Epidemiology and Environmental Health Division. *Disease and Environmental Alert Reports (DEAR)*. Washington, DC: U.S. Government Printing Office, 1996. 1 v. ISBN 96072754. SUDOCS D 5.202:D65. Also distributed by NTIS. PC181020796.

This report provides country information from an environmental perspective, including risk assessment, topography, climate, population, water supply, living and sanitary conditions and pollution.

106. U.S. Dept. of Defense. Central Intelligence Agency. *World Factbook*. Washington DC: U.S. Government Printing Office. Annual. LCCN 81-641760. SUDOCS PREX 3.15: Annual. ALSO on Internet sites and *National Trade Data Bank*.

This factbook has country information from Afghanistan to Zimbabwe, United Nations information, abbreviations for international organizations, and weights and measures. Country information includes: population, birth rate, religion, language, political parties, economic overview, inflation rate, exports, imports and military budget, GNP, telephone, railroads, and telecommunications.

107. U.S. Dept. of State. *Background Notes*. Washington DC: U.S. Government Printing Office SUDOCS S 1.123: Also on *National Trade Data Bank.*

Concise information on a particular country that is updated by the State Department covering: gross domestic product, natural resources, agriculture, trade, membership in international organizations, people, history, economy, government officials, customs, telecommunications, national holidays and foreign relations is included in this source.

108. U.S. Dept. of State. *Post Reports*. Washington DC: U.S. Government Printing Office. SUDOCS S 1.127:.

This series has individual country reports that are periodically updated. There is information on: area, geography and climate; population, public institutions, transportation, radio and T.V., health and medicine, employment for spouses and dependents, small maps of major cities, custom duties and passage, and social life, taxes, and local holidays.

109. U.S. Dept. of the Army. Central Intelligence Agency. *Area Handbook Series*. Washington DC: U.S. GPO. SUDOCS D 101.22:550- ALSO on *National Trade Data Bank*.

This series describes and analyzes an individual country's political, economic, social and national security system. Statistics include: education, employment, foreign trade and investment, and government budgets.

110. *World Development Report*. New York: Oxford University Press. ISSN 0163-5085. LCCN 78-67086. Annual.

This annual looks at major social and economic developments. It has tables on economic indicators for over a hundred countries on population, GNP per capita, and growth of GNP per capita, health expenditure and total flows from external assistance, and growth of consumption and investment, and social insurance in selected countries. Recent issues look at the role of government and of the market in health, government policies, health systems, and investing in public health as the economic development of a country is intimately related to health.

111. World of Information. *World Business & Economic Review*. London: Kogan Page, 1995. ISSN 1351-4725. LCCN sn94033384. Annual -.

This source reviews the economics of the world by looking at world currencies in units per dollar from 1988-1991, population, area, GDP, inflation, GDP real growth and balance of trade. Each country is characterized with key data on population, gross domestic product, consumer prices, agricultural production, imports, exports, balance of trade, external debt, exchange rate, media, domestic economy, and industry.

112. World Trade Press. *Country Business Guides*. San Rafael, CA.: World Trade Press.

These country guides series are for importers/exporters and

people doing business internationally with information on a country's economy, opportunities, investment, business culture and etiquette, political issues, demographics, marketing, and import policies and procedures. SEE ALSO *Singapore Business.*

REGION AND COUNTRY

AFRICA AND THE MIDDLE EAST

Background

SEE ALSO *African Business.*

113. Europa Publications Ltd. *Africa South of the Sahara.* London: Europa Publications Ltd. ISSN 0065-3896. LCCN 78112271. Annual. 1971-.

This annual is like the *Europa World Yearbook* with information on the continent and country surveys for African countries. SEE ALSO *Europa World Yearbook.*

SEE ALSO South African Reserve Bank. *Quarterly Bulletin Kwartaalblad.*

114. United Nations. *African Economic and Financial Data.* New York: United Nations, the World Bank, 1989. 204 p. ISBN 0821312510. LC 89-22481.

This provides data to monitor development programs. The basic indicators include: population, area, GNP per capita (1987), average annual growth rate, life expectancy, consumer prices, and exports.

115. U.S. Department of State. Bureau of African Affairs. *Investment Climate Reports Sub-Saharan Africa.* Washington, DC: U.S. Government Printing Office, 1994. 48 p. SUDOCS S 1.2:C 61.

A one to two page country summary of the investment climate from Angola to Zimbabwe is given with market potential, export opportunities, economic prospects, problems, and business language.

116. World of Information. *The Africa Review*. Essex, U.K.: World of Information. 1991/92 LCCN 85-646255.

Maps, currencies, key indicators, and events of the year arc described in this publication with profiles of countries from Algeria to Zimbabwe.

Guides

117. Greenblum, Jeffrey L. *Africa Guide to Business Finance for US Firms*. U.S. International Trade Administration. Washington DC: U.S. Government Printing Office, 1990. 80 p. LCCN 90-601568. SUDOCS C 61.8:Af8.

This is a guide for American businesses that lists financial sources of U.S. Government agencies, multilateral programs, foreign bilateral programs, and Sub-Saharan African Country development agencies. It includes a description of the program, investment parameters and contact person.

118. Reuvid, Jonathan, ed. *Doing Business in South Africa*. London: Kogan Page, 1993. 302 p. ISBN 0749408782. LCCN G.B. 93053247.

This is a guide for corporations and individuals interested in doing business with South Africa including: economic overview, legal strategies for foreign investment in South Africa, competitive advantage and the promotion of export growth, and an overview of the development regions.

119. Sudarkkasa, Michael E.M. *African Business Handbook: A Practical Guide to Business Resources for US/Africa Trade and Investment*. Washington, DC: International Trade and Development Counseling, 1993. ISSN 1072-0812. LCCN 94-640716. Biennial.

This guide is aimed at U.S. companies interested in exporting to Africa. It has data on African demographics, global economic trends, emerging African communities, U.S. Trade and Investment in Africa, market information, assistance in finance and investment, and America's top African trading partners.

Minerals Industry

120. U.S. Dept. of the Interior. Bureau of Mines. *Minerals Industry of Africa*. U.S. Washington DC: U.S. Government Printing Office. SUDOCS I 28.37:992/v.3/Africa. Annual.

This yearbook covers the mineral industries of Africa from Angola to Zimbabwe with government policy, production, consumption, major companies producing minerals, location of main facility, annual capacity and outlook, and trade throughout Africa.

MIDDLE EAST

SEE ALSO *Middle East Executive Reports*.

121. World of Information. *The Middle East Review: The Economic and Business Report*. Essex, England: World of Information. ISSN 1351-4717. LCCN 82-640110. Annual. 1981-.

This has information on currencies in units per dollar and sterling, population, area, GDP per capita, inflation, GDP real growth, and balance of trade. There is country coverage from Afghanistan to Yemen with key facts: official name, head of state, ruling party, capital, official language, currency, exchange rate, agriculture, industry, mining and a business guide for travelers.

Mineral Industry

122. U.S. Dept. of the Interior. Bureau of the Mines. *Mineral Industries of the Middle East*. Washington, DC: U.S. Government Printing Office, 1992. ISSN 0076-8952. LCCN 33026551. SUDOCS I 28.37:992/v.3/Mid.East. Annual.

This report has location maps, government policies, production, trade, structure of the mineral industry, commodity review on metals, mineral fuels, reserve, infrastructure and outlook from Bahrain to Yemen.

ISRAEL

123. *Statistical Abstract of Israel.* Jerusalem: Government Printer. ISSN 0081-4679. LCCN 52023991. Annual.

This abstract has data on Israel's social, economic, and population developments including: population estimates, geographical distribution, projections of population, tourism, consumer prices, prices of dwellings, labor, wages, and industry.

SAUDI ARABIA

124. U.S. Dept. of Commerce. International Trade Administration. *A Guide to Establishing Joint Ventures in Saudi Arabia.* Washington DC: U.S. Government Printing Office, 1985. 14 p. SUDOCS C 61.8:V56.

This is a brief guide on joint ventures in Saudi Arabia.

ASIA and OCEANIA

Background

SEE ALSO Chapter VI. Regionally Oriented Periodicals. Asia.

125. *Asia Yearbook.* Hong Kong: Review Publishing Co. LCCN 7464128. Annual. 1973-

This annual focuses on regional performance (figures include population, student, workforce, GDP, foreign trade, and public expenditures), Asian markets, commodities, transport, and fishing. There is a chronology of the past year and an overview of events from the *Far Eastern Economic Review.* Also it has a news diary of the current year.

126. Asian Development Bank. *Asian Development Outlook.* Manila, Philippines: Asian Development Bank. ISSN 0117-0481. Annual.

This annual reviews economic developments and policy issues that affect the region examining: economic prospects, policy adjustments and macroeconomic performance, economic trends and prospects in member countries. The member countries include: China, Hong Kong, Korea, Singapore, and Taiwan. Statistical tables include: growth rates of value added in industry and services, and gross domestic savings.

SEE ALSO Dun & Bradstreet Information Service. *Dun's Asia/ Pacific Key Business Enterprises.*

127. Europa Publications. *The Far East and Australasia 1995.* London, Eng.: Europa Publications Limited. LCCN 74417170. ISSN 0071-3791. Annual. 1969-.

This source has country surveys with information on: physical geography, history, economy, industry, mining, and energy; area survey listing population and economic trends; statistics on population, provinces, balance of payment, principal trading partners , directory of government officials and principal dailies. Countries include: Afghanistan to Vietnam.

128. Heginbotham, Erland. *Asia's Rising Economic Tide: Unique Opportunities for the U.S.* Washington, DC: Committee on Changing International Realities, 1993. 138 p. ISBN 0890681228. LCCN 93085951.

The rapid economic integration and growth in East Asia are the focus of this book. It provides business, labor, and decision makers strategies for dealing with the new realities. The study says that although the U.S. enjoys a competitive edge because of its product and technology, this advantage may only be for a few years. U.S. companies are reluctant and less experienced in organizing a national consortia than the Japanese or Europeans because of antitrust constraints and less government support for industry. It includes an overview of the East Asia region, importance of immediate U.S. effort, and Asian advantages and disadvantages.

129. Nemetz, Peter N. *The Pacific Rim: Investment, Development and Trade.* Vancouver: University of British Columbia Press, 1990. 361 p. ISSN 0774803606.

The economic data of the Pacific Rim are integrated and analyzed with attempts to identify issues of trade, investment, and development: their past and future patterns. This analysis is aimed at foreign investors and trading partners. The Pacific Rim policy is examined with a comparison of Hong Kong and Singapore as financial centers; U.S. and Japanese trade policies; and the critical role of energy in the future of the Pacific Rim.

130. Taylor, Robert H., editor. *Asia and the Pacific*. New York: Facts on File, 1991. 1879 p. ISBN 08160182. LCCN 8902337624.

This handbook gives individual country information from Afghanistan to Vietnam including: population, language, religion, constitutional system, history, economy, social services, education, mass media, and biographical sketches. It also gives comparative statistics for the area, population, GNP per capita, economically active population, urbanization, land use (1986), agricultural production indexes, indexes of manufacturing production (1977 and 1987), exchange rates and currencies, debt-service ratios (1985). It cites the original source.

131. Thant, Myo, Min Tang, and Hiroshi Kakazu. *Growth Triangles in Asia: A New Approach to Regional Economic Cooperation.* Quarry Bay, Hong Kong: Oxford University Press for the Asian Development Bank, 1994. 306 p.

Growth triangles are Asia's unique solution for economic cooperation among countries at different stages of economic development with different economic and social systems to attain higher and faster rates of growth. This study focuses on three growth triangles: the Southern China Growth Triangle consisting of Hong Kong, Taipei, China, and South China; the Johor-Singapore-Riau Growth, consisting of Singapore, the southern part of the Malaysian state of Johor, and Riau province of Indonesia operating since 1992; and the third triangle is being planned in the Tumen River Delta area which includes the northern provinces of the People's Republic of China, Siberia in Russia, and the Democratic People's Republic of China.

132. United Nations. *Industrial Development News for Asian and the Pacific.* Bangkok, Thailand: United Nations. Economic and Social Commission for Asia and the Pacific. ISSN 0252-4481. LCCN 91-643114. Annual.

Recent industrial progress in selected developing economies are examined. Data include: average annual growth rates of manufacturing productions, growth rates of manufacturing value added, GDP, inflation, resource gap, and debt service ratio for selected countries. Countries covered: Afghanistan to Myanmar.

133. World of Information. *Asia & Pacific Review*. Essex, UK: World of Information. LCCN 85646180. Annual. 1984-.

Maps, currencies, key indicators, and country coverage from Afghanistan to Vietnam on political system, main city, media, domestic economy and employment are some topics in this review.

Guides

134. Dunung, Sanjyot P. *Doing Business in Asia: the Complete Guide*. New York, NY: Lexington Books, 1995. 621 p. ISBN 0029077613. LCCN 94042226.

This is a guide to doing business with Asia. It includes a map of the countries, brief history, political structure, people, social values, customs, work schedule, making contacts, corporate structure, negotiation, conduct of business in a social setting, gift giving, dress code and useful phrases. It doesn't include products.

135. Engholm, Christopher. *Asia & Japan Business Information Sourcebook*. New York: John Wiley & Sons, Inc, 1994. 422 p. ISBN 0471304662. LCCN 93-47219.

The aim of this source is to provide business information for the Asia-Pacific region. It lists over 1000 sources with descriptions including: periodicals, directories, online sources, indexes and market data.

SEE ALSO Chapter IV. Marketing. Asia.

136. Washington Researchers Publishing. *Asian Markets: A Guide to Company and Industry Information Sources*. Washington, DC: Washington Researchers Publishing, 1991. 410 p. ISBN 1563650029.

This is a guide to government, international, and private sector organizations, publication listings, online databases, country information experts, offices in foreign country, and business associations in the U.S. with name, address, telephone numbers, and a description of the service organization or agency. The emphasis of this guide is on the source of the information, rather than the information itself.

Marketing

137. Euromonitor. *Consumer Asia*. London: Euromonitor (distributed by Gale), 1994. 310 p. ISBN 0863385710.

This source has marketing data on the consumption of various goods. It includes information on the following countries: China, Hong Kong, India, Indonesia, South Korea, Malaysia, Pakistan, Singapore, Sri Lanka, Taiwan, and Thailand. This is a series with analytical surveys of consumer markets. SEE ALSO *Consumer China* and *Consumer Japan*.

138. W-Two Publications. *Consumers in the Four Tigers: Hong Kong, Singapore, South Korea, Taiwan*. Ithaca, NY: W-Two Publications. 1994. 66 p.

This source looks at trends in the Asia-Pacific region, the transition to lower birth rates and longer life spans, and the issues of improving the quality of life. Profiles of Hong Kong, Singapore, South Korea, and Taiwan are included such as: demographics, labor force, and household income. Also there are trading tips, consumer marketing information, media and advertising, and direct marketing information.

Minerals Industry

139. U.S. Dept. of the Interior. Bureau of the Mines. *Mineral Industries of Asia and the Pacific*. Washington DC: U.S. Government Printing Office. SUDOCS. I 28.37: Annual.

This is a mineral industry survey for Asia and the Pacific covering selected mineral commodities. Also there is individual country information on: government policy, program, production, consumption and trade throughout Asia and the Pacific, location maps, and outlook.

AUSTRALIA

140. Austrade. *Australian Exports*. Victoria, Australia: Peter Isaacson Publishing Pty. Ltd. 1993. 691 p. ISSN 1032-2116

This source is divided into trading with Australia and Australian exports. Trading with Australia covers purchasing Australian products and services. There is information on government and private industry organizations, freight services, industry, company, country where companies are exporting, brand name index, and indicator as to whether company is exporter, importer, manufacturer, or distributer of product.

141. Australian Bureau of Statistics. *Year Book Australia*. Canberra, Australia: Australian Bureau of Statistics. ISSN 0810-8633. LCCN 81-644139. Annual.

Text and tables focus on the demographic, social, economic, educational, political and business trends of this island continent. The information includes: industry structure, industry turnover, employment, labor costs, capital expenditure, and foreign investment in manufacturing.

142. Gale Research. *The Australian Business and Investment Guide*. South Melbourne: Longman Professional Publishing. Distributed by Gale Research. 1994. ISSN 0815-9688. 1987-

This guide for doing business in Australia includes information on marketing, economics, investment, business leaders and government.

143. U.S. Dept. of Commerce. International Trade Administration. *The Australia Textile and Apparel Market*. Washington, DC: U.S. Government Printing Office, 1993. 59 p. SUDOCS C 61.2:T 31/4.

This report on the Australian textile and apparel industry includes: a market profile with market consumption and import, textiles and apparel industry trend overview, market analysis, export potential, and market and product requirements including labeling, specifications and standards for textile products, and Australian tariffs.

CHINA

Background and Guides

144. De Keijzer, Arne J. and Allan H. Liu. *China: Business Strategies for the '90s*. Berkeley, CA: Pacific View Press, 1992. 279 p. ISBN 1881896005 LCCN 92-70169.

This is a guide for doing business with China, including reasons China is worth the risk, background information on China, land resources, people, political framework, trade investment strategies, trading system, investment organizations, economic zone, and trends for the 90's with many case studies.

Euromonitor. *Consumer China*. London: Euromonitor. 1994. ISBN 0863385516. SEE Euromonitor. *Consumer Asia* for type of information contained.

SEE ALSO Genzberger, Christine et al. *China Business: the Portable Encyclopedia for Doing Business with China.*

145. Lee, Chung H. and Helmut Reisen. *From Reform to Growth: China and Other Countries in Transition in Asia and Central and Eastern Europe=De la Reforme a la croissance: la Chine et d'autres pays en transition en Asie et Europe centrale et orientale*. Paris: Organisation for Economic Co-operation and Development, 1994. 286 p. ISBN 92-64041184.

Decisions on transforming the Socialist planned economy into a market economy without chaos are the result of the fall of Communism. Different approaches for the transition include "gradualism" or "shock therapy." The differences are striking: China's real GDP growth vs. Russia and the Central Eastern European countries' decline in GDP. These papers discuss the transformation process in these developing countries.

146. Kenna, Peggy. *Business China: a Practical Guide to Understanding Chinese Business Culture*. 1994. 55 p. ISBN 0844235563. LCCN 93042811.

The aim of this etiquette guide is to understand Chinese culture.

It compares the two perspectives: competition (U.S.) vs. harmony (China); individual oriented (U.S.) vs. group oriented (China); and relationships that are short term (U.S.) vs. relationships formed slowly as the Chinese network of relationships gets things done. Patience and persistence are keys to dealing with the Chinese.

147. Murray, Geoffrey. *Doing Business in China: the Last Market.* Great Britain: St. Martin's Press, 1994. 350 p. ISBN 0312116829. LCCN 94013029.

China has a market of 1.2 billion consumers and this guide examines: the economic experiments of the Chinese in capitalism such as special economic zones; foreign investments (the bulk of foreign investment of 7.7 billion dollars in 1992 came from Hong Kong and Macao); Chinese multinationals, finding the right partners, bureaucratic barriers in foreign ventures, joint venture mistakes; and case studies of industries. The appendix includes China's banking system and the law on foreign capital enterprises.

148. *People's Republic of China Year Book.* Beijing, China: PRC Year Book and Hong Kong. Wah Gar Group. distr. Bristol, PA., ISSN 1000-9396. Annual.

This reviews the previous year's events covering history, politics, business, industry, education, special economic zones and statistics.

149. U.S. Congress. House. Committee on Foreign Affairs. Subcommittee on Economic Policy, Trade, and the Environment. *Future of U.S.-China Policy. Joint Hearings before the Subcommittees on Economic Policy, Trade, Environment, International Security, International Organizations, and Human Rights; and Asia and the Pacific of the Committee on Foreign Affairs. House of Representatives, One Hundred Third Congress, First Session.* Washington, DC: U.S. Government Printing Office. 1993. 194 p. SUDOCS Y 4.F76/1:C 44/27.

This hearing examines the U.S. policy towards China and hears arguments for and against extending the MFN status to China. The U.S. has concerns about importing Chinese goods produced by prison inmates and forced labor camps and reviews the human rights issues and the outlook for the U.S. role. It uses the MFN status and foreign policy in trade as a lever for human rights issues. It also has concerns about China's sale of missiles and nuclear technology to developing countries.

150. U.S. Dept. of Commerce. International Trade Administration. *The China Business Guide*. Washington DC: U.S. Government Printing Office. 1994. 52 p. ISBN 0160430917. SUDOCS C 61.8:C 44.

This guide includes information on: the Chinese economy, business operations, foreign trade outlook and system and the Chinese Economic Development Plan for the next ten years. It includes information on: organizations with trading rights, liberalization of the system, methods for pricing, marketing, taxation, foreign export controls, and a listing of key China trade contacts, and Chinese officials in the United States.

SEE ALSO *Understanding the Process of Doing Business in China, Taiwan, and Hong Kong*.

Statistics

151. China Kuo chia tung chi chu. *China Trade and Price Statistics*. Beijing: China Statistical Information and Consultancy Service Centre. LCCN 89656050. 1989-

This source is packed with data on the purchasing power of the Chinese, per capita living expenditures in urban and rural areas, consumption of vegetable oil, pork, fresh eggs, shoes, detergent, tea, poultry, beef and mutton by urban and rural residents.

152. Editorial Board of the Almanac of China's Foreign Economic Relations and Trade. *Almanac of China's Foreign Economic Relations and Trade=Chung-kuo tui wai ching chi mao i nien chien: chung-kuo tui wai ching chi mao i nien chien pien chi wei uyan hut*. Beijing, China: Editorial Board of the Almanac of China's Foreign Economic Relations and Trade. LCCN sn 85061248. Annual. 1984-

This almanac includes laws and regulations in foreign trade, foreign investment, customs, taxation, inspection, quarantine, finance and foreign exchange, statistics on imports/exports, growth rates of imports/exports, total value, and China's export share and ranking in world total exports.

153. Green, Charles E. *China Facts & Figures*. Gulf Breeze, FL: Academic Press. ISSN 0190-602X. LCCN 79640300. 1979- Annual.

This is a compendium of social, economic, demographic, and industrial data on China. There is a chronology of the past year with party information -- family connections of high officials, military statistics, events of population progress, selected province characteristics from Beijing to Xinjian broken down by urban population, illiterate population, GNP per capita, life expectancy, crude birthrate, a chronology of industrial and economic events and statistics on textile production and iron and steel.

154. International Centre for the Advancement of Science and Technology. *China Statistical Yearbook*. Hong Kong: International Centre for the Advancement of Science and Technology: Beijing: China Statistical Information & Consultancy Service Center. ISSN 1052-9225. LCCN 90660279. Annual. 1988-.

Land area, administrative divisions of China, employment, labor force, GNP, investment in fixed assets, industrial production, gross output, value of industry, volume of freight traffic, and investment plans and plan fulfillment are some data presented in this yearbook.

155. Tien-tung, Hsueh et al., ed. *China's Provincial Statistics, 1949-1989*. Boulder, CO: Westview Press, 1993. 593 p. ISBN 0813387329. LC 93-014244.

There are statistics on various aspects of the thirty Chinese provinces covering: income, industry, investment, transport, domestic trade, foreign trade, prices, hospital beds, newspapers, magazines, and investment. The data are in columns with the keys at the beginning and the definitions at the end, an inconvenient arrangement.

HONG KONG

156. Hong Kong. Census and Statistical Dept. *Hong Kong Annual Digest of Statistics*. Hong Kong. Census and Statistical Dept. Distributed by Congressional Information Services. ISSN 1011-4033. LCCN sn 89012750. Annual. 1978-.

157. Trade Media Ltd. *The Company Handbook-Hong Kong*. Hong Kong: Trade Media. Ltd, 1991. 230 p.

SEE ALSO: Trade Media Ltd. *Importing from ... A Buyers Manual for Selecting Suppliers, Negotiating Order and Arranging Methods of Payment for More Profitable Purchasing*. There is one for Hong Kong in this series.

SEE ALSO *Understanding the Process of Doing Business in China, Taiwan, and Hong Kong*.

158. U.S. Dept. of Commerce. International Trade Administration. *Hong Kong*. Springfield, VA: National Technical Information Service. 1993. Order Number PB93-218360/CAU.

This book discusses the opportunities for U.S. exporters and investors in Hong Kong. It is in the fastest growing economic region of the world and it plays a key role in trade with China. Billions of dollars are spent on infrastructures such as airports, improvements in the environment and water supply. These projects provide these opportunities.

INDONESIA

159. Indonesia. Biro Pusat Statistik. *Buku Saku Statistik Indonesia: Statistical Pocketbook of Indonesia*. Jakarta, Indonesia: Biro Pusat Statistik. ISSN 0126-3595. LCCN 78-644313/sa. Annual. 1978- Also available from Greenwood Press in microfiche.

Text in English and Indonesian.

160. Kompass. *Standard Trade & Industry Directory of Indonesia*. Jakarta: Kompass. ISSN 0215-4730. LCCN 83640934.

Sec. I has background information on Indonesia, development of economic sectors, manufacturing industries, imports, commodities, and foreign investment. There is a listing of investment fields and companies alphabetically arranged with name, telephone number, fax, and line of business. Sec. 2 has a directory of Indonesian state functionaries and representatives abroad. Sec. 3 has a list of products alphabetically arranged.

JAPAN

Background and Guides

161. Access Nippon, Inc. *Access Nippon 1994 Business Handbook: How to Succeed in Japan.* Tokyo: Access Nippon, Inc. Distributed by The Reference Press, Inc., 1994. 423 p. ISBN 1878753134. ISSN 0915-4841. LCCN 92657663.

This is a guide for doing business in Japan with useful information on: Japanese industries, Japanese companies, organizational contacts, food, housing, transportation services, and other basics. The company profile includes name, address, brief history, operations, principal overseas offices and subsidiaries, and overseas sales ratio. Industry information includes recent trends and medium and long term prospects.

SEE ALSO Chapter VI. Asia. Japan

Euromonitor. *Consumer Japan.* London: Euromonitor. 1993. ISBN 0863385087. SEE *Consumer Asia* for type of information contained.

162. Euromonitor Publications. *Japan Marketing Handbook.* London: Euromonitor Publications, 1988. 160 p. ISBN 0863382134. LCCN 88-158904.

This handbook presents strategies for gaining access to Japanese markets. It covers: Japanese consumers, technology and markets, competitive position, major growth industries, and consumer spending patterns. Statistics on imports by country of origin, advertising expenditure by media, and trends in medical care facilities are also included.

163. Fingleton, Eamonn. *Blindside: Why Japan Is Still on Track to Overtake the U.S. by the Year 2000.* Boston: Houghton Mifflin Co., 1995. 406 p. ISBN 0395633168.

Japan is on track to become the new world leader. Americans underestimate the Japanese and the changing balance of power in the economic sector. Japanese corporations are the new sales leaders in the industrial sector, and other things being equal, the company with the largest sales can invest more in developing new technologies. Also Japan can buy more political favors because it now outspends the U.S. in foreign aid, and the economic leader sets the rules on trade and economic matters. There are new economic forces at work brought on by technological change. The Japanese have a better understanding of these forces at work.

164. Higashi, Chikara and Peter G. Lauter. *The Internationalization of the Japanese Economy.* 2nd ed., 1990. Boston: Kluwer Academic Publishers. 430 p. ISBN 0792390520. LCCN 89020081.

The evolution of the Japanese economy is remarkable, growth characterized by increasing export activity. The industrial policies reflect the consensus of growth objectives and the continuous improvements in productivity and international competitiveness in a targeted group of industries. Infant industries are protected and no tax is levied on income from small savings accounts. This book gives insight into the Japanese path to economic power. The Maekawa Report is the centerpiece of this internationalization effort and is discussed in this book.

165. *Japan ...Marketing and Advertising Yearbook.* Tokyo, Japan: Dentsu Inc. ISSN 0918-4406. LCCN 92-648226. Annual.

This yearbook includes trends in corporate advertising and marketing, activities, and advertising expenditures in Japan by media. For 1991 it examines Japan society and culture as seen through television with seven crucial points to understanding the Japanese consumer including: overpopulation, lack of space that affects Japanese life, "Tokyo is the center of the Universe" thinking, difference among equals, image consciousness, quasi-affluence, and extreme quality consciousness.

166. *Japan: the Electronic Tribe*. Northbrook, IL.: Coronet Film & Video, 1987.

This is a 57 minute video that gives the cultural background of the Japanese people. It explores its history, religion, and geography and shows how its collective thinking has translated into a highly efficient and productive work force and different management style.

167. Kennedy, Eric. *Destination Japan: A Business Guide for the 90's*. Washington, DC: U.S. Government Printing Office, 1991. 67 p. LCCN 92-187072. SUDOCS C 61.8:J 27.

This exporting guide to Japan provides data on Japan including: population, religion, trade, foreign supplier, share of imports, import policy, foreign ownership restrictions and relevant publications list. It recommends best export prospects covering industries such as pharmaceutical, telecommunications industrial chemicals, aircraft and aircraft parts.

168. Morgan, James C. and J. Jeffrey Morgan. *Cracking the Japanese Market*. New York, NY: Toronto: The Free Press, 1991. 295 p. ISBN 4478300364

The emphasis of this book is on marketing to the Japanese. American companies can succeed by producing the right product and employing the proper strategy for Japan's unique market. It means understanding the "Japanese Way" including: the group-oriented society; the Japanese market covering: keiretsu -- the business elite, soga shosha -- Japan's commercial elite that dominate trade; and the Japanese Company (the customer is God): kaisha -- the corporate family, consensus management, service as a religion; the Japanese acquisition of investments in American companies, the Japanese strategy of attacking the underserved markets, then moving to more sophisticated and competitive markets. The appendix has statistics on: selected foreign subsidiary performance in Japan and Japanese corporations with the most potential for growth in the 1990s.

169. *Nippon 1989: JETRO Business Facts and Figures*. Tokyo: JETRO, 1989. 159 p. ISBN 482240448X.

This statistical booklet is packed with information on: the

Japanese economy, industry, corporations, labor and life. There are statistics on energy demand, rates of dependence on foreign energy, sources by major nations and types of energy used, Japanese automobile production, vehicles exported, value of parts procured abroad by major automobile manufactures, electronics industry production forecasts, production and sale of semiconductors, integrated circuits, and machine tool production and exports. Text is in English and Japanese.

170. Rowland, Diana. *Japanese Business Etiquette: a Practical Guide to Success with the Japanese*. New York: Warner Books, 1993. 286 p. ISBN 0446395188.

Rules of etiquette are essential to conducting business with the Japanese. This informative guide has advice on where to take your guests, seating behavior, guidelines for receiving guests in your office, business card etiquette, negotiating and basic concepts for understanding the Japanese.

171. Trade Media Ltd. *Exporting to Japan: A Practical Guide to Strategies and Procedures for More Profitable Selling*. Hong Kong: Trade Media Ltd, 1992. 204 p. ISBN 962713841X.

This guide provides a step-by-step approach to the Japanese market such as: researching a trip, finding a special company, and discussing the distribution and legal system. It lists companies by industry, and includes a directory of government organizations, industrial machinery associations, and a glossary of transport and trade terms.

Industry

172. Chao, Sheau-yueh J. *The Japanese Automobile Industry: An Annotated Bibliography*. Westport, CT: Greenwood Press, 1994. 188 p. LCCN 93-35797.

This is a listing of books, documents, monographs and articles covering the history and development of the Japanese automobile industry, the relationship of the U.S. and Japanese auto industries, and Japanese transplants in the United States. It also has a listing of periodicals that cover the automotive industry.

Economics and Statistics

173. *Economic Survey of Japan*. Tokyo: Japan Times. ISSN 0021-1833. LCCN 5106135.

This survey analyzes the Japanese economy by looking at patterns, problems, and cycles. Charts and tables include economic indicators, changing patterns in capital flows, export growths and investment in plants and equipment.

174. Keizai Koho Center. *Japan: An International Comparison*. Tokyo: Keizai Koho Center. ISSN 0389-3502. LCCN 84-642095. Annual.

This booklet is packed with statistics and comparisons on population, foreign trade, trends in customs, duty ratios, exports and imports by commodity and country, Japan's merchandise trade by area, Japan's leading trading partners, and total energy requirements.

175. Nihon Kokusei Zue. *Nippon: A Charted Survey of Japan*. Tokyo: Kokusei-sha Corporation. ISSN 0300-0004. LCCN 1754207. Annual. 1927-

This annual describes the Japanese society with statistics, charts and tables on population, principal commodities, total value of machinery, labor, and national income. It covers household budget, food, clothing, foreign trade broken down into automobile and magnetic tapes etc., and trade with U.S., E.C., and China.

176. Statistics Bureau. *Nihon Teokei Nenkan=Japan Statistical Yearbook*. Tokyo: Statistics Bureau. ISSN 0389-9004. LCCN sn85-19225. Annual. 1949-

This yearbook is both in English and Japanese. It covers social, economic, demographic and political data such as: consumer price indexes by city groups, households, household members, and area of floor space per person, total expenditure for social security, persons covered by social insurance, and value of exports.

KOREA

Doing Business in Korea. SEE ALSO Price Waterhouse. *Price Waterhouse Information Guide.* Series.

SEE ALSO Chapter VI. Regionally Oriented Periodicals. Asia. Korea

177. Hynson, Larry M., Jr. *Doing Business with South Korea: A Handbook for Executives in the Public and Private Sectors.* New York: Greenwood Press, 1990. 287 p. ISBN 0899305091. LCCN 90030015.

This is a handbook for executives conducting business with South Korea. It contains: an export checklist, products that sell, the Korean economy, Korean import market characteristics, and Korean business etiquette, U.S. trade, and trade policies,

178. Korean Overseas Information Service. *A Handbook of Korea.* Seoul, Korea: Korean Overseas Information Service, 1993. 592 p. ISBN 89737500210.

This handbook covers the Korean people, its history, religion, customs, tradition, government, finance, economy, industry and social development with a chronology of the South-North dialog, statistics on exports and imports by commodity groups, composition of export and import markets by principal country, and major economic indicators.

179. Saccone, Richard. *The Business of Korean Culture.* Elizabeth, NJ: Hollym Corporation Publishers. 1994. 187 p. ISBN 1565910338. LCCN 94-77532.

This is a cultural guide to Korea. It includes geography, history, and cultural contrasts such as individual vs. group. Understanding relationships, interpersonal communications, the importance of face saving, and kibun (the essence of the Korean spirit) are keys to success.

180. Yonham New Agency. *Korea Annual* Seoul, Korea: Yonham New Agency. LCCN 64-6161. Annual. 1964-

Some highlights of this annual include: chronology of the past year, government events, economy, manufacturing, construction, energy, population, transportation, who's who, telephone and telegraph services.

MALAYSIA

Trade Media Ltd. *Importing from Malaysia: A Buyer's Manual for Selecting Suppliers, Negotiating Orders and Arranging Methods of Payment for More Profitable Purchasing*. Hong Kong: Trade Media Ltd. 1990. 219 p. ISBN 9627138134. SEE ALSO *Importing from... A Buyer's Manual for Selecting Suppliers* for description.

MONGOLIA

181. Rana, P.B. *Mongolia: A Centrally Planned Economy in Transition*. Oxford University Press, 1992. 250 p. ISBN 019585893X. LCCN 92038236.

This is revised from an earlier economic report on economic conditions and policy in Mongolia.

NEW ZEALAND

182. New Zealand. Dept. of Statistics. *New Zealand Official Yearbook*. Wellington, New Zealand: New Zealand, Dept. of Statistics. ISSN 0078-0170. Annual. 1893-.

This is a statistical annual.

SINGAPORE

183. Genzberger, Christine. *Singapore Business: the Portable Encyclopedia for Doing Business with Singapore*. San Rafael, CA.: World Trade Press, 1994. 310 p. LCCN 93045979.

This is a guide for doing business in Singapore with information on Singapore's economy, trade, leading exports and imports by commodity, trading partners, importing and exporting opportunities, special trade zones, foreign investment, investment policy, statistics on export commodity, import policy and procedures, and industry review sources.

184. Singapore, Dept. of Statistics. Chief Statistician. *Yearbook of Statistics, Singapore*. Singapore: Singapore, Dept. of Statistics Chief Statistician. ISSN 0583-3655. Annual. 1967-

TAIWAN

185. Chen, Min and Winston Pan. *Understanding the Process of Doing Business in China, Taiwan, and Hong Kong: Guide for International Executives*. Lewiston, New York: E. Mellen Press, 1993. 257 p. ISBN 28889442. LCCN 93029328.

The understanding of the shared political and economic changes in China, Taiwan, and Hong Kong gives insight in dealing with the Chinese. This guide is written for executives interested in doing business with China, Taiwan, and Hong Kong. It surveys the historical, geographical, political, and economic developments of China, Taiwan, and Hong Kong. The second part examines the practical aspects of doing business and investing in China, Taiwan, and Hong Kong.

186. Council for Economic Planning and Development. *Taiwan Statistical Data Book*. Republic of China: Council for Economic Planning and Development. ISSN 1016-2224. LCCN 74641255. Annual. 1974-

This source includes social, economic and demographic data, such as: area, population, labor force statistics, employment by industry and average monthly working hours for Taiwan.

187. Directorate-General of Budget Accounting and Statistics. *Statistical Yearbook of the Republic of China*. Taipei, Taiwan: Directorate-General of Budget Accounting and Statistics, Executive Yuan, Republic of China. ISSN 0256-7857. LCCN 77-64803. Annual. 1975-

Taiwan's economic and social development are reflected in this yearbook with chapters on: land and climate, population, health and environment, industry, commerce, productions of major manufactured goods, and commercial censuses.

188. Klintworth, Gary, ed. *Taiwan in the Asia-Pacific in the 1990s*. St. Leonard, NSW, Australia: Allen & Unwin: Canberra, ACT, Australia: Dept. of International Relations, Australian National University, 1994. 291 p. ISSN 1863735941.

This is a conference held in Taiwan. It analyzes Taiwan's recent transition to democracy by looking at its political, institutional, and economic changes. The growing economic strength of Taiwan has changed its role in the Asia-Pacific region. There are tables on the characteristics of the Taiwan economy for 1961-1992, education, vital statistics, transportation, communications, consumer durables, per capita GNP, population and area of East Asia in 1989, and percent of investment in GDP, and trade between Taiwan, Mainland China, and Hong Kong.

THAILAND

189. Atkinson, Karen Gritzmacher. *Thailand Business Basics*. Bangkok, Thailand: Standard Chartered Bank. Tilleke & Gibbons, 1991. ISBN 9748868729.

This is a loose-leaf volume that is packed with cultural, business, and social information such as: living in Thailand, managing business relationships, business cards, gifts and criticism, confrontation, global and regional trade relations, investments in Thailand, calculating operating costs, marketing and identifying suppliers, and intellectual property rights. Statistics have been compiled from *Board of Trade Bulletin, Business in Thailand*, and *Bank of Thailand Quarterly Bulletin*.

VIETNAM

190. Quinlan, Joseph P. *Vietnam: Business Opportunities and Risks*. Berkeley, CA: Pacific View Press, 1994. 174 p. ISBN 1881896102. LCCN 94-67837.

There are opportunities and risks in Vietnam, which is considered to be the next Asian dragon. This guide includes: Vietnam's background, political landscape, economic overview, major economic sectors such as mining, textiles, construction, transportation projects, and emerging sectors of growth.

191. Robinson, James W. *Doing Business in Vietnam.* Rocklin, CA: Prima Pub., 1995. 288 p. ISBN 1559585919. LCCN 94-13044. 288 p.

Opportunities await those willing to take risks in Vietnam. This guide covers: country, risks, political and economic profile, understanding Vietnamese business culture, the problems and pitfalls, directory of helpful organizations, and a list of firms operating in Vietnam.

EUROPE

192. Balachandran, M. ed. *Encyclopedia of Business Information Sources: Europe.* Detroit, MI: Gale Research Co., 1994. 877 p. ISBN 0810384590. LCCN 92010924.

This encyclopedia is alphabetically arranged with 450 subjects. There are more than 11,000 entries from the abrasives to the zinc industry including almanacs, dictionaries, directories, periodicals, and associations. Industries are broken down by European country and region. Very extensive and useful for periodicals on specific industry outlook.

193. Buckley, Peter J. and Pervez N. Ghauri, eds. *The Economics of Change in East and Central Europe: Its Impact on International Business.* London; San Diego: Academic Press, 1994. 418 p. ISBN 0121391655.

The liberalization of Eastern and Central Europe offer great opportunities. The task is difficult because these countries do not have the social or political structure to establish democratic institutions and the telecommunications and transport sectors are inadequate. This book deals with country specific issues; with facts and forecasts on GDP, real GDP growth, personal consumption, comparison of market conditions in Eastern and Western Europe; business and management strategy for Western companies in trade with Eastern Europe; tables of foreign retailers in Eastern Europe by country of origin (1991); and export tariff tables.

SEE ALSO *Doing Business in Eastern Europe.*

194. Dudley, James W. *1992 Understanding the New European Market*. Dearborn, MI: Financial Publishing Inc., 1991. 430 p. ISBN 0793102650.

This guide for managers concentrates on strategies for the changing conditions in the European Community. It looks at: the single market environment that will affect business in terms of legal issues, trends and opportunities; the European Community; strategies adopted by the "blue chip" Japanese companies; and marketing research.

195. Economist. *The Economist Atlas of the New Europe*. New York: H. Hold, 1992. 1 atlas. 288 p. ISSN 0805019820. LCCN 92010565/Map.

This is more than an atlas with a wealth of information on: history, communications, business, finance, international relations, environment, and country analysis for the New Europe. The business chapter includes data on car registrations for Europe and Japan (1990), productivity questions, sales strategy, shares of world spinning capacity (1990), EC's leading textile suppliers (1990), European chemical sales (1990), and advertising spending. The international relations chapter has information on U.S. imports and exports, the relationship between Europe and Latin America, and new patterns of the Commonwealth of Independent States, comparisons for Europe and Asia on average wage, trade balance, inflation, and main imports and exports to the U.S.

SEE ALSO *EuroMarketing: A Strategic Planner for Selling into the New Europe*.

196. Euromonitor. *The Book of European Forecasts*. London: Euromonitor, 1992. 311 p. ISBN 0863384013. LCCN 92-231744.

This source covers: the European economy, the single market, corporate outlook, demographic trends, industrial development, trade, market and consumer expenditure, and advertising. There are forecasts on: GDP growth 1988-2000; market forecasts for various industries such as data processing equipment and electric goods; consumer expenditures; world population by region from 1989-2025, and macroeconomic trends. Some concerns are: the opening of Eastern Europe, the reunification of Germany, the fragmentation of the USSR, and the European Monetary

Union. Some problems Americans may face are: Europe's market leaders will defend local dominance, and the distribution system differs dramatically from country to county.

197. Euromonitor. *The Book of European Regions: Key Facts and Figures for Business*. London: Euromonitor, 1992. 473 p. ISBN 0863384285. LCCN 93-173951.

This handbook is for marketers with regional statistics on Europe and coverage of economic conditions and bibliographical references.

Euromonitor. *Consumer Eastern Europe*. London: Euromonitor, 1994. 392 p. ISBN 0863385532. SEE *Consumer Asia* for type of information contained.

SEE ALSO Euromonitor. *Consumer Europe*.

Euromonitor. *Consumer* Southern Europe. London: Euromonitor. 1993. ISBN 086338515X. SEE *Consumer Asia* for type of information included.

198. Euromonitor. *European Business Planning Factors: Key Issues for Corporate Strategy in the 1990's*. London: Euromonitor, 1992. 450 p. ISBN. 0863384412. LCCN G.B. 92-477769.

This source looks at significant issues and industrial trends that companies operating in Europe need to be aware of and the effects these issues will have on their business activities.

199. Europa Publications Ltd. *Eastern Europe and the Commonwealth of Independent Dates 1994*. London: Europa Publications. 1994. 783 p. ISSN 0962-1040. LCCN 93648651.

This source looks at 27 countries in central and eastern Europe, the Caucasus, and Central Asia. Country information includes: geography, chronology, history, economy, statistical survey, directory, bibliography, and a statistical survey. It is similar to *Europa World Yearbook*.

SEE ALSO Chapter VI. Regionally Oriented Periodicals. Europe.

200. Humbert, Marc, ed. *The Impact of Globalisation on Europe's Firms and Industries*. London: Pinter Publishers. 1992. 266 p. ISBN 1855671131. LCCN 93-016879.

This is a collection of papers from industrial economists on the impact of globalization on Europe's firms and industries. It attempts to define globalization and discuss the globalization myth in the car industry because no automaker is entirely global although Toyota and Nissan have the best international production structure. European automakers are especially vulnerable in terms of production and marketing. The papers include: strengthening the ESPRIT (European Strategic Programme for Research in Information Technology) for industrial competitiveness and recommending a European industrial policy.

201. Newman, Oksana and Allan Foster. *European Business Rankings: Lists of Companies, Products, Services and Activities Compiled from a Variety of Published Sources*. London: Gale Research International, 1992. 437 p. ISBN 1873477007. LCCN gb92-34965.

This has an encyclopedic arrangement of subjects with rankings on areas from absenteeism to the Zurich Stock Exchange. The original source of the rankings is cited. Some rankings include: leading advertising firms in countries from Austria to the United Kingdom; airports; top baby product brands; most valuable companies in (name of country); the top ten French Chemical companies; biggest merger and acquisitions and leading advertisers of main pet food brands.

SEE ALSO *OECD Economic Outlook*.

202. Office for Official Publication of the European Communities. *Enterprises in Europe: Second Report*. Luxembourg: Office for Official Publication of the European Communities, 1992. 367 p. ISBN 92-82646092.

The European Community Commission recognizes the importance of small businesses for economic growth and the conditions under which they flourish. This statistical report describes enterprises in the European Community with comparative analysis of the population of SME (small and medium size enterprises) and large enterprises in the EC, Japan and the

U.S.; activities by size of enterprises, size class predominance by activity, analysis of labor productivity, and analysis by country.

203. Organisation for Economic Cooperation and Development. *Foreign Direct Investment Relations Between the OECD and the Dynamic Asian Economies*. Dialogue with the DAE's. Paris: Organisation for Economic Cooperation and Development, 1993. 197 p. ISBN 9264138501.

Business leaders from the OECD and the Dynamic Asian Economies (DAE) of Hong Kong, Korea, Malaysia, Singapore, Taiwan, and Thailand agree that foreign direct investment (FDI) can contribute to growth, employment, technology transfer, and stimulate local company efficiency. This report looks at trends and prospects for international direct investment in the DAE, investment policy issues, and measures that promote foreign direct investment. Statistical (FDI) tables on FDI inflow by sector and inflow by country (in millions of dollars) are included.

204. Poullier, Jean-Pierre. *OECD Health Systems*. Paris: Organisation for Economic Cooperation and Development, 1993 2 vols. ISBN 9264138005.

Volume 1 has facts and trends from 1960-1991 including total health and hospital spending for OECD countries. Volume 2 covers total population, wage and salaried employment, employment in manufacturing, employment in services, GDP, and female participation rates.

SEE ALSO *Resource Guide to Doing Business in Central and Eastern Europe*.

205. Szajkowski, Bogdan. *Encyclopaedia of Conflicts, Disputes, and Flashpoints in Eastern Europe, Russia, and the Successor States*. Harlow, Essex, U.K.: Longman Group, 1993. 489 p. ISBN 058221002X. LCCN 94113996.

The author arranges the Eastern Europe conflicts, places, and ethnic groups alphabetically from Akkahazia to Zemlyak. He identifies over 70 ethno-territorial conflict in Central and Eastern Europe and 204 in the former Soviet Union. Yugoslavia has a chronology of U.N Security Council Resolutions for their conflicts.

206. Washington Researchers. *European Markets: A Guide to Company and Industry Information Sources.* IVth ed. Washington, DC: Washington Researchers Publishing, 1992. 598 p. ISBN 1563650126. ISSN 1044-9280. LCCN 82-62886.

This is an annotated guide to European industry information from U.S. government, European, and international organizations and agencies, published sources, online databases, and country information. The summary includes the industry area of the agency, some of its functions, its publications and country experts in the U.S. Government and their specialties. This refers to sources of information rather than the information itself. It is similar to *Asian Markets: A Guide to Company and Industry Information Sources.*

207. Winters, Alan L. and Zhen Kun Wang. *Eastern Europe's International Trade.* Manchester; New York: Manchester University Press. Distributed in USA and Canada by St. Martin's Press. 189 p. 1994. ISBN 0719042763. LCCN 93040662.

The focus of this source is the liberalization effects of international trade on Eastern European countries. It looks at: (1) extent and direction of Eastern Europe's international trade (2) the trading relationship between the EC and East European Countries (3) the factors influencing the composition of Eastern Europe. The authors use the gravity model to estimate Eastern Europe's potential trade, discuss the data used, and present the results and alternative models. The trading potential of Central and Eastern Europe is great, but to expand its imports to help the Central and Eastern European countries, the West must accept their cheap and low quality exports for a time.

208. World of Information. *The Europe Review.* Essex, U.K.: World of Information. ISSN 0269-3852. LCCN 86-649411. Annual. 1986-

Currencies, key indicators such as population and inflation, maps of Europe, country profiles from Albania to the former Yugoslavia, and survey of the region are the topics included in this review.

EUROPEAN UNION OR COMMUNITY

209. Economist Intelligence Unit. *The EIU European Yearbook.* London: Economist Intelligence Unit, 1993. 1 vol. LCCN 94648516. Annual. 1993-

This is a guide to understanding the way the EU works, the status of the EU directives, and the agenda for 1994. It also discusses the Maastricht Treaty and the implications for businesses, reviews the past year and previews developments in the coming year. This is a complement to *European Trends* and *Business Europe.* (Description of 1993 issue)

210. Egan, Colin and Peter McKiernan. *Inside Fortress Europe: Strategies for the Single Market.* London: Economist Intelligence Unit, 1994. 227 p. ISBN 020159384X. LCCN 93244460.

Global markets are undergoing rapid political, economic and technological changes. The authors take a historical approach by understanding the process of change in European markets. They begin with the origins of the single market. They investigate the strategies of non-European firms in preparing for the single market including the Japanese. The Japanese are successful because they: plan globally and have long term perspectives; understand cultural contrasts as opposed to their Anglo-American rival's "cultural myopia"; internationalize their research and development by establishing fundamental research facilities outside of Japan; drive for market share; include employee planning involvement and have a dedicated management. Also included are case studies of corporate preparations, experiences, and expectations for the single market.

211. Euromonitor. *1992: The Single Market Handbook.* London: Euromonitor Publications Limited, 1990. 222 p. ISBN 0863383556. LCCN 90-194489.

The effects of the single market in economics and social sectors including financial services, trade and the media are discussed in this handbook. The decision making process of the European Commission and legislation extracts are covered with their implications. Statistics on the single market effects include economic projections, projected GDP changes, tariff barrier removal on construction products, price reductions in telecommunications equipment, and deregulation in automobile sales.

212. Miller, Debra L., ed. *EC 1992: A Commerce Department Analysis of European Community Directives*. U.S. Department of Commerce. International Trade Administration. Washington, DC: U.S. Government Printing Office, 1989. 3 v. LC 89-602373. SUDOCS C 61.2 :Eu 7/vol.

This is a Commerce Dept. analysis of EC directives. Volume 1 analyzes the 66 European Community directives and regulations on the removal of trade barriers in 1992 and their impact on U.S. market access. The directives deal with technical barriers to industrial trade and services. Volume 2 analyzes 54 directives and regulations, primarily on product safety and environmental protection. Appendix B lists the directives that constitute the EC's 1992 program and indicates whether they are being reviewed by the Department of Commerce. Also notice is given regarding the adoption and implementation of the directives.

213. Purcell, Susan Kaufman and Francois Simon. *Europe and Latin America in the World Economy*. London: Lynne Rienner Publisher, 1995. 215 p. ISBN 1555874983. LCCN 94-14627.

The creation of a Single European Market affects the relationship between Europe and Latin America (LA), as well as the trilateral relationship of the U.S., Latin America, and Europe. This source examines the impact of this union and includes: the economic relationship of Europe and LA, and the impact of regional integration on Europe and LA relations.

214. Stitt, Iaian P.A. and John J. McGonable, Jr., eds. *The Arthur Anderson European Community Sourcebook*. Chicago: Triumph Books, Inc., 1991. 489 p. ISBN 0962443646. LCCN 90-71573.

This is a sourcebook to the single market with an overview of the European community and the single market program. It includes a summary of the business climate in EC member states; the need to balance the concerns of the EC and its 12 member states, and profiles of member states with background, population, currency and exchange controls, authorizations for establishing a business, investment incentives, key elements of taxable income, social security taxes, and withholding taxes.

215. U.S. Congress. House. Committee on Foreign Affairs. Subcommittee on International Economic Policy and Trade. *Europe and the United States: Competition & Cooperation in the 1990's*. Washington, DC: U.S. Government Printing Office, 1992. 408p. ISBN 0160387159. SUDOCS Y 4.F 76/1: Eu7/40.

In the post cold war era, the European Community is emerging as an economic power. This study examines the effects of an assertive Europe on U.S. interest and whether the U.S.- European relationship will be one of cooperation or competition. It includes: the Maastricht Treaty, EC enlargement, EC economic, social, and agricultural policies, the Single European Market, and the challenge of Eastern Europe and the former Soviet Union.

216. U.S. Dept. of Commerce. International Trade Commission. *Effects of Greater Economic Integration within the European Community on the United States: Fifth Follow Up Report*. Washington, DC: U.S. Government Printing Office, 1993. 1 v. SUDOCS C 61.2:E 7/3 microform.

217. U.S. Executive Office of the President. *EC 1992: An Assessment of Economic Policy Issues Raised by the European Community Single Market Program*. Washington, DC: U.S. Government Printing Office, 1990. 33 p. LCCN 92-203399. SUDOCS PrEx 9.2: As7.

The goal of the European Community is to create a single market by adopting directives that will be implemented into law by the twelve EC members. The program harmonizes the rules and regulations. This report discusses the implications, challenges, and opportunities facing the U.S.

218. Winters, L. Alan, ed. *Trade Flows and Trade Policy after '1992'*. Cambridge, England; New York: Cambridge University Press, 1992. 294 p. ISBN 0521440203. LCCN 92027968.

The aim of this scholarly work is to quantify and estimate the possible effects of the European Community's Single Market Program on the European economy and the rest of the world. Many tables are included on the expected changes in employment, trade, and production.

Marketing Data

SEE ALSO Euromonitor. *The Book of European Forecasts*.

219. Euromonitor. *Consumer Europe 1994.* London: Euromonitor ISBN 0863385281. 503 p.

This provides market information and consumer trends for Europe. It covers food, drink, tobacco, household cleaning, health care, paper products (toilet tissues), cosmetics and toiletries, home furnishing, and consumer electronics. The uneven coverage is due to data availability. The original source of data is cited.

220. Euromonitor. *European Advertising Marketing and Media Data: A Directory and Media Data.* London: Euromonitor. Distributed by Gale Research. LCCN 93-6410510. Annual. 1990-

This compendium has tables of useful information with trends indicated for a range of years. Individual countries are covered with key indicators with numbers on population, consumer spending trends, advertising and marketing trends. There is also a listing of advertising agencies by country, and media information.

221. Euromonitor. *The European Compendium of Marketing Information*. London: Euromonitor, 1st ed. 1992. 421 p. ISBN 0863384404. LCCN 92-231842.

This provides a summary and analysis of market data and consumer trends across Europe including: ownership of large domestic appliances 1990, car ownership 1980/1985/1990, Japanese sales penetration of cars 1990, pharmaceutical -- trade 1988, large kitchen appliances -- comparable market sizes 1989, musical instruments -- apparent consumption 1985-1990, and cigarettes -- consumption 1985-1989 and consumer electronics.

222. Euromonitor. *European Directory of Consumer Brands and Their Owners*. London: Euromonitor, distr. by Detroit: Gale, 1992. 823 p. ISBN 086338465X.

This arranges European brands alphabetically and then by

country. The directory is divided by: brands and their owners by products and European firms alphabetically arranged with their brands. Each entry includes: name of company, address, telephone, telex, and fax number and a brief summary of recent financial performance.

223. Euromonitor. *European Directory of Marketing Information Sources*. London: Euromonitor. ISSN 0950-565X. LCCN 88-652001. Annual. 1987-

The information provided is a listing of official sources, business contacts, companies, associations, journals, and research organizations relevant to specific industries and topics, and socio-economic profiles of countries which include population, religion, manufacturing, income per capita, and domestic private consumption, and major dailies.

224. Euromonitor. *European Marketing Data and Statistics*. London: Euromonitor Publications. ISSN 0071-2930. LCCN sn 84-44066. Annual. 1962-.

This is a compendium of statistical information on Western and Eastern European countries. Sec. 1 has country data on population, land area, religion, and head of state. Sec. 2 has demographic trends and forecasts. It also lists key European marketing sources covering trends in consumer and food prices, costs of consumer goods, retail sales of clothing and footwear, white goods, electronics, consumer market sizes, advertizing patterns, media access, per capita consumption of bakery products, and cleaning products.

225. Euromonitor. *Market Research Europe*. London: Euromonitor Plc. ISSN 0308-3046. LCCN sn 83-11759.Monthly. 1983-.

Each monthly includes a different market research report on European industries such as: skincare, pet foods, books, beer, entertainment software, foods, cigarettes, television & video products, and car products. Key trends, total market size, sources of supply and purchasing patterns for industries and countries are also included. Beginning with September 1995 there are tables on key economic indicators including inflation, unemployment, balance budget, exchange and interest rates.

SEE ALSO Chapter IV. Marketing. Europe.

226. Newman, Oksana and Allen Foster, eds. *European Market Share Reporter: A Wide-Ranging Compilation of Statistics from Journals and Limited Circulation Publications*. London: Distributed by Gale Research International, 1993. 361 p. ISBN 187347735X.

The European Market is moving closer to a Single market and this source gives information on market share, products, and industries with statistics using SIC codes and including data on consumption, sales, market, production and end use. (Similar to the *Market Share Reporter* which has U.S. data.) It also lists original source.

Industry and Statistics

227. Organisation for Economic Co-operation and Development. Tourism Committee. *Tourism Policy and International Tourism in OECD Member Countries*. Paris: Organisation for Economic Cooperation and Development, LCCN 74648130. 1974-

This source has useful information on the tourist industry including: OECD member country policy and actions, international tourist flow in member countries, the economic importance of international tourism in OECD countries and tables on international tourist trends.

228. U.S. Congress. Office of Technology Assessment. *U.S. Telecommunications Services in European Markets*. Washington, DC: U.S. Government Printing Office, 1993. 220 p. ISBN 0160481895X. LCCN 93-246890. SUDOCS Y 3.T 22/2:2T 23

U.S. telecommunications firms can compete effectively in the Europe and there is a need for this service. Technological trends, issues, European telecommunications market, European activities, user's perspectives, views of U.S. services exporters, R & D telecomunication expenditures in selected countries, and some U.S. strategies are examined.

229. U.S. Dept. of Commerce. International Trade Administration. *U.S. Trade with Eastern Europe: 1988-1992 Highlights and Outlook for 1993*. Washington, DC: U.S. Government Printing Office, 1993. 42 p. SUDOCS C 61.2:T 47/11/993

These are mostly tables on trade statistics with Eastern Europe.

230. U.S. Dept. of the Interior. Bureau of the Mines. *Mineral Industries of Europe and the Central/Eurasia*. Washington, DC: U.S. Government Printing Office, 1995 . SUDOCS I 28.37:993 v.3/Europe/U.S.S.R. Annual.

This book reviews the mineral industry of forty-six countries including Western Europe, Eastern Europe, and Central Eurasia. It includes information on: the production of selected minerals including iron, steel, ferroalloying materials, aluminum, copper, lead, zinc, and mineral fuels. Government policies, production, trade, and outlook are given for countries from Albania to the former Yugoslavia.

BULGARIA

231. Touche Ross, Sinclair Roche & Temperly. *Doing Business in Bulgaria*. London: Kogan Page, 1993. 248 p. ISBN 0749406895. LCCN 93155871.

This guide explores trade and investment opportunities in Bulgaria. It looks at the political, legal, and economic transformation of Bulgaria including its external debt, its market potential, its transportation infrastructure, its industrial production, business culture, joint venture, commercial outlook, trading partners, restrictions on investment, types of investment vehicle, taxes, excise duty, and export regulation.

COMMONWEALTH OF INDEPENDENT STATES

232. Batalden, Stephen K. and Sandra L. *The Newly Independent States of Eurasia: Handbook of Former Soviet Republics*. Phoenix, AZ: Oryx, 1993. 205 p. ISBN 0897747631. LCCN 93-26307.

This handbook provides a statistical profile for each of the former

Soviet Republics encompassing: population, ethnic groups, religion, urban centers, education, birth and mortality rates, number of hospital beds, principal products, and per capita GNP. It includes: a history, description of each state and contemporary issues that affect each, such as the aftereffects of Chernobyl, political changes, and military security.

233. Touche Ross & Co., KPMG Peat Marwick, Frere Cholmely Bischoff. *Doing Business in Russia.* Lincolnwood, IL.: NTC Business Books, 1994. 284 p. ISBN 0844235628. LCCN 93043079.

Russia is undergoing a business, economic, and political transformation. The marketing infrastructure is unpredictable. This handbook includes: sources of law, Russia's trading partners, business culture, banking information with a directory of Russian commercial banks with a general license, privatization issues, foreign investment, accounting regulations, taxes on resident companies, and value added taxation (VAT).

234. U.S. Central Intelligence Agency. *Defense Industries of the Newly Independent States of Eurasia.* Springfield, VA: National Technical Information Service, 1993. 27 p. LCCN 93-676828/Map. Order Number PB93-928104/CAU.

This report provides a general overview of the defense industrial base in each of the newly independent states of the Soviet Union. Formerly these establishments were centrally controlled, but after the breakup of the Soviet Union, these independent states are now establishing their own defense industries on the former facilities.

235. U.S. Central Intelligence Agency. *Measuring Russia's Emerging Private Sector: New Economic Institutions Branch.* Springfield, VA: National Technical Information Service, 1992. 15 p. Order number PB93-928101/CAU.

This report attempts to measure private sector size in Russia. The program is moving some 60 percent of shops, restaurants, service establishments into private hands. However, the sales are going poorly.

236. U.S. Congress. Joint Economic Committee. *Global Economic and Technological Change*. Washington, DC: U.S. Government Printing Office, 1991. ISBN 0160448603. LCCN 95-184783. SUDOCS Y 4.EC 7:G 51/4/pt.4.

This report covers economic and technological changes for the Soviet Union, Eastern Europe, and China. It sees the Soviet Union as having: an economy in turmoil, a system in crisis, a deterioration in economic performance, regional fragmentation, and cutbacks in investment

237. U.S. Dept. of Commerce. Office of General Counsel. Legal Text Service. *Legal Text Service from Central and Eastern Europe and Russia and Independent States*. Springfield, VA: National Technical Information Service, 1993. 1 v. Order Number PB93-218378/CAU.

The rapidly evolving commercial legislation of Central and Eastern Europe, the Baltics and the Independent States are updated by this Legal Text Service in order to aid the business community and government agencies. The laws pertain to foreign investment, privatization, monetary policy, securities, and environmental protection.

DENMARK

238. Denmark. Statistiske Departement. *Statistisk Arbog=Statistical Yearbook*. Kobenhavn: Danmarks Statisik. ISSN 0070-3567. LCCN 83-643178. Annual.

This is a statistical yearbook for Denmark.

239. Ebeling, Mogens and Bernhard Gomard. *Corporations and Partnerships in Denmark*. Deventer, Netherlands: Kluwer Law and Taxation Publishers, 1993. 250 p. ISBN 9065447407.

The focus of this source is on corporations and partnerships in Denmark. It includes: geography, political system, population, employment statistics, and company and partnership statistics. It gives a historical background of companies and partnerships. It defines the structure of

240. *Export Directory of Denmark*. 1993/94. Copenhagen, Denmark: Kraks Forlag, AS. LCCN 27007552.

A business guide, organization directory, consular service listing, and a company directory are some of the subjects covered in this source.

FINLAND

241. Finland. Tilastollinen. *Suomen tilastollinen vuosikirja. Statistisk arsbok for Finland. Statistical Yearbook of Finland.* Helsinki: Tilastokeskus. ISSN 0081-5063. Annual. 1879-

242. Helsinki. Ministry of Finance. Dept. Economics Dept. *Economic Survey... Finland.* Helsinki. Ministry of Finance. Economics Dept. LCCN sn 85021852. Annual 1984-

FRANCE

243. France, Institut National de la Statistique et des Etudes Economiques. *Annuaire Statistique de la France*. Paris: Institut National de la Statistique et des Etude Economiques. ISSN 0060-3654. LCCN 07039079. Annual 1878-

244. International Herald Tribune. *French Company Handbook: A Guide to the Companies in the SBF 120 Index*. Paris: International Herald Tribune. Distributed by The Reference Press, 1993. 198 p. ISBN 290543709x.

This handbook is updated annually and it includes information on: the state of the French economy, foreign trade, trading partners, trade surpluses, foreign investment trends, industry evaluations, and key company profiles. The profiles include information on: company history and operations, address, phone and fax numbers, number of employees, officers, and financial information.

SEE ALSO Kompass. *Kompass France*.

GERMANY

245. Germany, Statistisches Bundesamt. *Statistisches Jahrbuch...fur das vereinte Deutschland.* Stuttgart, Germany: Metzler-Poeschel. LCCN 92-640026. Annual. 1991-

This is a statistical yearbook for Germany.

246. Kopka, Reinhard, et al. *Doing Business in Germany's New Federal States.* Cologne: Federal Office of Foreign Trade Information, 1991. 216 p. LCCN93-139833.

This guide discusses the conversion of the new German states to a free market economy covering poor transport infrastructure in the new states, development projects in transport and communications, expansion of telecommunications (a key to Germany's economic recovery,) data on GDP, the number of jobs classified by industry, and coverage of industry, food, beverage, iron and steel, and taxation.

HUNGARY

247. Budapest. Hungarian Central Statistical Office. *Hungarian Statistical Yearbook. Hungarian Central Statistical Office.* Budapest. Hungarian Central Statistical Office. ISSN 0237-1901. LCCN 92-641912. Annual. 1991-

248. U.S. Dept. of Commerce. International Trade Administration. *Investment Guide to Hungary.* Washington, DC: U.S. Government Printing Office, 1991. 40 p. SUDOCS C 61.8:H 89.

Information for entrepreneurs on investment opportunities and challenges in Hungary is provided. It looks at the Transformation Act that established the legal framework for state owned companies to transform themselves into corporations which can be sold to Hungarians or foreigners. The U.S. is a leading investor in Hungary with small manufacturing companies. The best areas for investors are listed with Hungarian organizations and U.S. agencies for assistance. The name of the organization, telephone and fax number, and contact person are given.

NETHERLANDS

249. *Statistical Yearbook...of the Netherlands*. Hague, Netherlands: Central Bureau of Statistics. ISSN 0303-6448. LCCN 75-640878. Annual.

Population, mining, manufacturing, international economic relations, and prices are some topics included in this yearbook. Prices include: consumer price index, producer price indices of domestic sales by industry class.

NORWAY

250. Norway. Statistisk sentralbyra. *Statistisk arbok=Statistical Yearbook of Norway*. Norway: Statistisk Sentralbyra. ISSN 0377-8908. Annual. 1964-

SWEDEN

251. Sweden. Nordic Council. *Yearbook of Nordic Statistics. Nordisk statistisk Arsbok.* Sweden: Nordic Council. ISSN 0078-1088. LCCN 65001336. Annual. 1962-

Text is in Swedish and English.

252. Sweden. Statistiska Centralbyran. *Staistik Arsbok foer Sverige/Abstract of Swedish Statistics*. Stockholm: Statistiska Centralbyran. ISSN 0081-5381. 1914-

This is a statistical abstract for Sweden.

UNITED KINGDOM

253. Dennis, Geoff, ed. *Annual Abstract of Statistics*. London: HMSO Central. ISSN 0072-5730. Annual.

This is a statistical abstract for the United Kingdom with about 350 tables on area, demographics, death by cause, social trends, law enforcement, education, regional trends, employment, manufacturing, energy and food supplies.

254. H.M. Stationery Office. *Britain.* London: H.M. Stationery Office. ISSN 0068-1075. LCCN 50014073. Annual.

This is a handbook on Britain. It includes: England, Northern Ireland, Scotland and Wales with information on population, GDP, total employment, percentage of employees in the service and manufacturing industry, unemployment rate, early history, construction industries, overseas trade such as exports, imports, and natural resources.

255. Kenna, Peggy and Sondra Lacy. *Business U.K.: A Practical Guide to Understanding British Culture.* Lincoln, IL: Passport Books, 1994. 53 p. ISBN 0844235601. LCCN 94-17745.

This is an etiquette guide for doing business with the British. It includes business practices, protocol, understanding the culture, communication style, and organizational structure.

256. Oliver, Nick and Barry Wilkinson. *The Japanization of British Industry.* Oxford, UK: New York, NY: Blackwell, 1992. 366 p. ISBN 063118676X. LCCN 92-5453.

The globalization of industry results in importing successful manufacturing techniques and implementing them at home. This book is about some United Kingdom companies applying Japanese production methods. The chapters include: a review of industrial practices in Japan, comparing and contrasting British situations; production methods based on successful management of high dependency relationships; experiences of both U.K. and Japanese companies in the U.K.; and the implications of Japanization for trade unions; and the likely consequences of Japanization.

THE CARIBBEAN AND LATIN AMERICA

CARIBBEAN

257. Caribbean Pub. Co. *Caribbean Basin Commercial Profile.* Washington, DC: Caribbean Pub. Co. LCCN 94663009. Annual. 1994-.

This source profiles Caribbean and Latin America countries from

Anguilla to Venezuela including: climate, foreign exchange, transport, contacts, NAFTA, and interim trade programs for the Caribbean Basin. Country information contains data on: population, currency, GDP, GDP growth rates, exports, imports, external debt, debt as a percentage of GDP, list of business firms, and trade and investment incentives.

258. Rauner, Julia M. *Caribbean Basin*. Washington, DC: U.S. Government Printing Office, 1992. 110 p. SUDOCS C 61.8:19/2.

This is a guide to financing trade and investment in Central America and the Caribbean. It provides information for over 75 financing mechanisms and institutions for domestic and foreign investment.

259. R.W.T. *Caribbean Business Directory*. Grand Cayman Island: R.W.T. Distributed by Caribbean Imprint Library Services. LCCN sn 85-24458. Annual. 1985-.

This annual has country and company information with names of shipping agents, air cargo, and banking services. The country information includes an economic summary, profile, government, key economic indicators, trade and investment incentives, tax information, foreign firms with operations in the Caribbean country, business hours, holidays, tourist information, official language, population, adult literacy and GDP.

260. Tirado de Alonso, Irma. *Trade Issues in the Caribbean*. Philadelphia, PA: Gordon and Breach, 1992, 231 p. ISBN 2881245501. LCCN 92015396.

This book explores the trade issues of the Caribbean Islands examining: trade trends and flows, structure of trade, economic integration among the Caribbean Basin countries, and export manufacturing. Some findings: most trade occurs with the U.S. and the European Community.

261. U.S. Dept. of Defense. Central Intelligence Agency. *Cuba: a Handbook of Trade Statistics. Directorate of Intelligence*. Washington, DC: The Agency. Distributed by National Technical Information Service, 1994. 108 p. Order Number PB93-927901/GAR.

This has trade statistics for Cuba covering the period 1985-92 derived primarily from Cuba's trading partners. Tables include Cuba's total trade by countries and commodities.

262. U.S. Dept. of Commerce. International Trade Administration. *Caribbean Basin Exporter's Guide*. Washington, DC: U.S. Government Printing Office, 1992. 84 p. SUDOCS C 61.8:C 19/3.

This guide defines the Caribbean Basin Initiative (CBI), compares the Generalized System of Preferences (GSP) with the CBI, discusses basic steps for exporting from the US to the Caribbean Basin, government programs for business development, customs procedures, documentation and safeguards.

263. U.S. Dept. of Commerce. International Trade Administration. *Caribbean Basin Investment Survey 1990*. Washington, DC: US Government Printing Office, 1990. 1v. SUDOCS C 61.2:C 19/3.

Information on investment registration, investment size, employment generated, products produced, country profiles, and company listings are included in this source.

264. U.S. Dept. of Commerce. International Trade Administration. *Guide to the Caribbean Basin Initiative*. Washington, DC: U.S. Government Printing Office. 1994. LCCN sn 95-27244. SUDOCS C 61.8/2: (microfiche).

The Caribbean Basin Initiative (CBI) is a program to promote economic development in Central America and the Caribbean Islands. Its goal is to expand foreign and domestic investment by diversifying the country's economy and increasing imports. The program includes: duty free entry to the United States, U.S. economic assistance to the region, tax deduction for companies that hold conventions in qualifying CBI countries. Appendix A lists U.S. organizations involved with CBI.

LATIN AMERICA

Background and Guide

265. Euromonitor. *Consumer Latin America*. London: Euromonitor, 1994. Distributed by Gale Research Inc. ISBN 0863385737. SEE *Consumer Asia* for type of information included.

266. Inter-American Development Bank. *Economic and Social Progress in Latin America*. Washington, DC: Inter-American Development Bank. ISSN 0095-2850. LCCN 74648164. Annual. 1972-.

This annual looks at the economic and social progress in Latin American with data on gross domestic product for over 10 years, macroeconomic trends, balance of payment for Latin America, policy considerations, real exchange rates, money supply, inflation and outlook. Individual country profiles are included with economic trends, indicators, and outlook. Each year covers a special topic such as: Manufacturing Exports (1992), Social Security (1991), and Working Women (1990).

267. Inter-American Development Bank. *Latin America in Graphs: Demographic, Economic & Social Trends, 1994-94 ed.* United States: Inter-American Development Bank. Johns Hopkins University Press, 1995. 200 p. ISBN 0940602792. LCCN sn95-29123.

This source shows trends in Latin American countries and the Caribbean in graph form broken down by population, vital statistics, education, national accounts, balance of payments, energy, and external debt.

SEE ALSO Chapter VI. Regionally Oriented Periodicals. Latin America.

268. U.S. Dept. of Commerce. International Trade Administration. *Guide to Computer Hardware and Software Markets in Latin America. 1990.* Washington, DC: Distributed by NTIS. Order Number PB90-163197/CAU.

This report covers 22 countries in South and Central America and the Caribbean for companies that want to sell computers in the region with information on: market and trade, export regulations, market indicators, investment policies, and tariffs.

269. U.S. Dept. of Commerce. International Trade Administration. *Guidebook to the Andean Trade Preference Act, ATPA*. Washington, DC: U.S. Government Printing Office, 1992. 53 p. LCCN 92-249454. SUDOCS C 61.8:An 2. (also a Spanish edition).

The Andean Trade Preference Act (ATPA) promotes economic development in Bolivia, Colombia, Peru, and Ecuador by allowing duty-free entry into the United States for certain products. This guide provides contacts and advice such as: conducting market research, tariff and non-tariff regulation, the factor of pricing, quality and quantity in the marketing and distribution of a product. Appendix A lists the top products eligible for duty free or duty reduction under the ATPA.

270. Washington Researchers Publishing. *Latin American Markets: A Guide to Company and Industry Information Sources*. Washington, DC: Washington Researchers Publishing, 1993. ISSN 1067-0408. LCCN 93-657703.

This is a guide to government, international, and private sector organizations, publication listings, online databases, country information experts, offices in foreign countries. Provides a list of information sources rather than the information itself.

271. World of Information. *The Americas Review*. Essex, U.K.: World of Information. LCCN 90-661425. Annual.

Currencies, key indicators such as population, inflation, GDP real growth, and balance of trade are some topics covered. North America, Latin America and the Caribbean are the regions included. Profiles for countries from Anguilla to U.S. Virgin Islands with information on: head of state, official language, political system, trade, bank and newspapers.

Industry

272. U.S. Dept. of Commerce. International Trade Administration. *Guide to Telecommunications Markets in Latin America.* Washington, DC: U.S. Government Printing Office, 1993. 157 p. LCCN 93-127474 SUDOCS C 61.8:M 34.

This summarizes information on the telecommunication authorities, the networks, and the expansion plans of the telecommunication industries of the Latin countries, and lists key industry contacts with phone numbers and addresses.

273. U.S. Dept. of the Interior. Bureau of Mines. *Mineral Industries of Latin America and Canada.* Washington, DC: US Government Printing Office, 1995. 291 p. SUDOCS I 28.37:995/v.3/Latin. Annual.

This document examines the mineral economy of Latin America including production, trade, mineral reserves, and principal producing corporations. The areas include: Central America, the Caribbean, Mexico, and South America. Mineral industries are defined to include fuel and non-fuel sectors, the extractive mining industries, smelting and refining.

Investment and Trade

274. Bradford, Colin I. ed. *Mobilising International Investment for Latin America.* Paris: Organisation for Economic Cooperation. 1993. 252 p. ISBN 92-64138374.

Direct investments are essential to economic development as they are a source of financing for Latin American industries without incurring debt. They provide opportunities for transferring technology to gain productivity. These papers look at opportunities and risks for companies.

275. U.S. Dept. of Commerce. International Trade Administration. *Latin American Trade Review: A United States Perspective*. 1989. Washington, DC: U.S. Government Printing Office, 1990. 65 p. LCCN sn93-27478. SUDOCS C 61.38: Annual. 1984-.

This source provides information on United States trade with

Argentina, Bolivia, Brazil, the Caribbean Basin, Chile, Colombia, Ecuador, Mexico, Paraguay, Peru, Uruguay, and Venezuela. It includes a regional overview, the economy, exports, imports, trade balance, and trends.

276. U.S. Dept. of Commerce. International Trade Administration. *U.S. Exports to Latin America and the Caribbean: A State by State Overview 1987, 1992, 1993.* Washington, DC: U.S. Government Printing Office, 1995. 70 p. SUDOCS C 61.2:EX 7/23.

This provides industry-level statistics on individual states' merchandise exports to Latin America and the Caribbean (LAC). Some highlights are: U.S. merchandise exports to LAC grew from 34.5 billion in 1987 to nearly $78 billion in 1993. Some tables included are: export sales to LAC by industry sectors, states and regional exports to LAC by region, increasing or decreasing dollar amounts in state export sales to LAC:1987-93 (ranked by dollar changes) and individual state profiles.

ARGENTINA

277. Buenos Aires. INDEC. *Statistical Yearbook, Republic of Argentina.* Buenos Aires: INDEC. ISSN 0328-0055. LCCN 95663012. Annual.

278. U.S. Dept. of Commerce. International Trade Administration. *The Argentina Textile and Apparel Market.* Washington, DC: U.S. Government Printing Office, 1993. 52 p. LCCN 94-147219. SUDOCS C 61.2: T 31/5.

This document enumerates the opportunities for U.S. textile and apparel producers including the following products: denim jeans and active sportswear. It also gives an economic and demographic profile, market size, consumption trends, and an apparel industry overview.

BRAZIL

279. *Brazil Company Handbook.* Austin, TX: The Reference Press, Inc. 1993. 172 p. ISSN 0103-3921. LCCN 89-661487. Annual.

Information on Brazil's economy, investment climate, and company profile with financial information including: name, address, ticker symbol, year established, balance sheet data, income statements, ratios, and per share data are included in this handbook.

MEXICO

280. Bolsa Mexicana de Valores. *Mexico Company Handbook.* Tonala, Mexico: International Company Handbook. Distributed by The Reference Press, 1994. 133 p. ISBN 187875372x.

This handbook has information on: the Mexican economy, economic indicators, securities market, service institutions, foreign investment in the Mexican stock market, accounting principles and practices, and company investment information. The information on companies includes: main raw materials, sales breakdown, earnings per share, balance sheet, income statement, total dividends paid and ratios.

281. Bonime-Blanc, A. and W. E. Mooz Jr. *Doing Business in Mexico.* Ardsley on Hudson, NY: Transnational Juris Publication Inc., 1995. 1v.

This is a source for doing business in Mexico. It looks at its legal system, the economy, Mexico and the U.S. trade and investment relations, Mexican law concerning contractual and procedural formalities, intellectual property and the transfer of technology.

282. Brothers, Theresa and Holly Gallo, eds. *Investing in Mexico.* New York: The Conference Board, 1992. 39 p. LCCN 92-191522.

The Salinas government in Mexico has dramatically turned the Mexican economy around by positive government action and policies. This conference report reflects the views of senior executives and government officials and includes: Mexico's economic and investment climate, financial outlook, investment potential, joint venture problem, protection of intellectual property rights, tax laws, and regulations for private investments.

283. Cambridge Data & Development. *Access Mexico: Emerging Market Handbook & Directory*. Arlington, VA: Cambridge Data & Development, 1992-93. 624 p. ISSN 1064-928X.LCCN 94-642105. Also available on computer disk.

This handbook/directory provides profiles of the Mexican states and information on business and marketing, a directory, and an overview of the North American Free Trade Agreement.

284. Jessup, Jay and Maggie. *Doing Business in Mexico: Your Guide to Exporting, Investing, and Manufacturing*. Rocklin, CA.: Prima Pub., 1993. 276 p. ISBN 1559582774. LCCN 92030484.

The guide furnishes exporting, importing, investing, and marketing information on Mexico. It includes business etiquette, a checklist to get started, and emerging opportunities.

285. Kent, Kara and Aaron Schilhaus, ed. *The U.S.-Mexico Trade Pages: Your Single Source for Transborder Business, 2nd ed.* Washington, DC: The Global Source, 1992. 329 p. ISBN. 0963367013.

This has a directory of contacts for U.S. and Mexican government agencies, export finance companies, banks, accounting firms, marketing specialists, transportation companies, and publications to aid executives, marketers, importers, and exporters doing business with Mexico. It also includes information on export and import profiles between the U.S. and Mexican states.

286. Matthew Bender & Co. *Doing Business in Mexico*. New York, NY: Matthew Bender & Co. 1994. 1 vol. LCCN 80051896.

The legal aspect of doing business in Mexico is the emphasis of this guide with information on government, legal system, cultural considerations, economic system, business environment, constitution, regulation of foreign investment, taxation, import-export, contracts, property, real estate, intellectual property, and franchising.

287. McKinniss, Candace Bancroft and Arthur Natella, Jr. *Business in Mexico: Managerial Behavior, Protocol, and Etiquette*. New York: Haworth Press, 1993. 156 p. ISBN 1560244062. LCCN 93023222.

This is an etiquette, communication, and corporate culture guide for doing business in Mexico. It includes bibliographical references.

288. Newman, Gray and Anna Szterenfeld. *Business International's Guide to Doing Business in Mexico*. New York: McGraw-Hill, 1993. 281 p. ISBN 0070093393. LCCN 92022656.

This guide examines changes in Mexico's business and regulatory environment, their implications for multinational companies; and Mexico's economic recovery and trends to the 90's. It includes: strategy of multinationals in anticipation of NAFTA with case studies. Its sector profiles include: agricultural reforms, the automotive and petrochemical industry, computers, maquiladora, and opportunities in services.

289. Nolan, James. *Mexico Business: the Portable Encyclopedia for Doing Business with Mexico*. San Rafael, CA: World Trade Press, 1994. 488 p. ISBN 096318640X. LCCN 94-15696.

This is a guide for doing business with Mexico. It contains exporting, importing, and investing information. The information covers: NAFTA, import/export policy and procedures, industry reviews, and a listing of trade associations, directories and periodicals.

290. Pick, James and Edgar W. Butler. *The Mexico Handbook: Economic and Demographic Maps and Statistics*. Boulder, CO: Westview Press, 1994. 422 p. ISBN 081336774. LC 94-12195.

Population, social characteristics, the economy, labor force, and politics are subjects included in this source on Mexico. Industry information covers crude oil, natural gas production (1988), beverage and automobile production, number of corporations per 1,000 population (1988), location of Mexico's "Fortune 500" corporations, maquiladora employment, work force and value of new mortgages.

291. Tuller, Lawrence W. *Doing Business in Latin America and the Caribbean: Including Mexico, the U.S. Virgin Islands, and Puerto Rico, Central America, South America.* New York: AMACON, American Management Association, 1993. 348 p. ISBN 0814450350. LCCN 93-9247.

This is a guidebook for conducting business in the Latin American area.

292. U.S. Dept. of Commerce. International Trade Administration. *U.S. Exports to Mexico: State by State Overview.* Washington, DC: U.S. Government Printing Office, 1993. 1v. LCCN sn95-35227.

Major trends in states exports are highlighted. U.S. exports to Mexico in 1991 were 3.3 billion dollars. The top five exports totalled 20 billion dollars. The exports included: industrial machinery and computers, chemical, rubber and plastic products, electric and electronic equipment, and transportation equipment.

293. U.S. Dept. of Commerce. International Trade Administration. *US-Mexico Trade: Pulling Together or Pulling Apart.* Washington, DC: U.S. Government Printing Office, 1992. 225 p. ISBN 0160380968. LCCN 92-243125. SUDOCS Y 3.T 22/2:2 M 57.

This report states that market forces are not the only considerations in implementing the NAFTA. Other fundamental changes in the relationship among government, industry and labor are needed if both countries are to go forward, and it expounds on these changes.

294. Winsor, Anita. *The Complete Guide to Doing Business in Mexico.* New York: Amacom, 1994. 256 p. ISBN 0814402119. LCCN 93-30311.

This guide for Americans interested in business opportunities in Mexico includes information on geography, population, government, language, business customs, economy, foreign investment, importing regulations, and the impact of NAFTA.

PUERTO RICO

295. Government Development Bank for Puerto Rico. *Puerto Rico Economic Indicators*. San Juan, Puerto Rico; New York: Government Development Bank for Puerto Rico. LCCN 86-656694. Monthly.

This monthly includes information on: labor force, manufacturing employment, employment sectors, tourism, electric energy consumption, construction, cement, external trade including exports and imports.

SEE ALSO *Puerto Rico Business Review*.

VENEZUELA

296. *Company Handbook, Venezuela* 1992-1993. Caracas: IC International Company Handbook. Distributed by The Reference Press, Inc., 1993. 74 p. ISBN 187853126. LCCN sn93-35564. Annual. 1991-.

This informative handbook has information on Venezuela's economy, investment climate, opportunities, and company profiles with information on company, address, fax and phone, background, main officers, major stock holders, assets and liabilities, income statement data, ratios, per share data, sales breakdown, and main raw materials.

NORTH AMERICA

CANADA

Background and Guides

297. Asian Sources Media Group. *Exporting to Canada*. Hong Kong: Asian Sources Media Group, 1992. 256 p. ISBN 9627138444.

This guide includes information on: negotiating in Canada, current Canadian trade and buying patterns, marketing environment, demographics, shipping, transportation, investing and banking.

298. Brown, Barbara E., ed. *Canadian Business and Economics: A Guide to Sources of Information.*Ottawa: Canadian Library Association, 1992. 675 p. ISBN 0888022565. LCCN cn92-90721.

This guide has an extensive listing of Canadian business and economic sources. It includes: bibliographies, atlases, directories, periodicals, online sources, statistics, banking and finance, industries such as beverage industry, computers, and energy and transportation. Text is mostly in English with some French sources.

299. *Canada Facts*. Ottawa: Prospectus Publications. ISSN 0848-8681. LCCN cn90030542. Annual. 1989-.

This annual is packed with facts on the Canadian population, economy, competitiveness, average cost of office space, natural gas delivered price, consumer price index, relative export price of manufacturers markets, foreign investment, finance and banking.

300. *Canadian Economic Observer = L'Observateur Economiques Canadian*. Ottawa: Statistics Canada. ISSN 0835-9148. LCCN 89-648300. Monthly. 1988-.

This is a summary of the Canadian economy and includes statistics.

CANCORP. Canadian Financials is an online database that has information on over 8,000 Canadian companies with text on management, the president's letter, 150 of the most recent filings with the Ontario securities and mergers and acquisitions. SEE *DIALOG* File 491.

301. Financial Post Information Services. *Canadian Markets*. Toronto: Financial Post Information Service. ISSN 0832-2503. LCCN cn87039031. Annual. 1986-.

This presents Canadian buying power indices by province, economic region, and census division including population, number of households, per capita income, retail sales, and forecasts for the Canadian economy.

302. The Financial Post. *The Canadian Trade and Investment Guide*. Toronto, Ontario: The Financial Post. ISSN 0846-4332. LCCN cn89-33677. Annual. 1989-.

This guide describes the business environment, government relations, the Canadian economy, competitiveness, leading Canadian corporations, and the entrepreneurial climate.

303. Matthew Bender & Co. *Doing Business in Canada*. New York: Matthew Bender & Co., 1993. LCCN 84-71749.

This loose-leaf guide looks at doing business in Canada from a legal aspect with information on: government, legal and political system, economic and business environment, constitution, regulations on foreign investment, taxation, import-export, contracts, property, real estate, intellectual property and franchising.

304. Southam Information and Technology Group. *Corpus Almanac & Canadian Sourcebook*. Don Mills, Ontario: Southam Information and Technology Group. ISSN 0823-1133. LCCN 83-647236. Annual.

This almanac has information on: natural resources, people, religion, education, communication, business periodicals, associations, and societies in Canada, government departments, consulates and trade commissions in Canada, industry, trade, and an overview of the economy.

305. Statistics, Canada....*Canada Yearbook*. Ottawa: Statistics Canada, 1994. 707 P. ISBN 0660151863. LCCN cn90030542. Annual. 1984- (Also available on compact disk).

This yearbook is divided into five chapters: land, people, nation, economy, arts and leisure with numbers on employment and unemployment, total imports, exports and trade balance, and imports into Canada from all countries.

306. Statistics, Canada. Consumer Income and Expenditure Division. *Income Distributions by Size in Canada. Repartition du Revenue au Canada selon la talbe du revenu.* Ottawa: Statistics Canada, Consumer Income and Expenditure Division. ISSN 0575-8750. LCCN 73644155. 1971-

This is a statistical source that breaks down the income of Canadians by size, family type, marital status, sex and age. It summarizes the Canadian income for the previous year. It also gives breakdown for low income families by province.

UNITED STATES

Basic Statistics

307. U.S. Dept. of Commerce. Bureau of the Census. *County and City Data Book.* Washington, DC: U.S. Government Printing Office. SUDOCS C 3.134/2: Also available on compact disk.

This irregularly issued document covers topics such as: U.S. education, labor force, and manufacturing and breaks them down by counties and cities covering earnings, number of establishments, number of employees, value of shipments and new capital expenditures.

308. U.S. Dept. of Commerce. Bureau of the Census. *Statistical Abstract of the United States* Washington, DC: U.S. Government Printing Office. ISSN 0081-4741. LCCN 04-18089. SUDOCS C 3.134: Annual. 1878- Also available on compact disk.

This annual is a frequently used source for social, demographic, economic, business, industry, and financial data in the United States. It compiles the numbers and gives the original source. (For historical data, consult *Historical Statistics of the United States*).

Business, Industry, and Labor

309. Darnay, Arsen J. ed. *Economic Indicators Handbook: Time Series, Conversion, Documentation*. Detroit, MI: Gale Research, Inc., 1992. 1056 p. ISBN 081038400. LCCN 92-13545.

This handbook has statistical time series indicating the health of the United States economy with data on gross national product (actual dollars, personal consumption expenditures, durable goods, non-durable goods, gross private domestic investment, and fixed investment), business cycle indicators (average weekly hours in manufacturing, average weekly initial claims for unemployment insurance, manufacturer's new orders, index of stock prices, S & P 500 common stocks, money supply M2, cyclic indicators, and economic series).

310. Graham, Edward M. and Paul R. Krugman. *Foreign Direct Investment in the United States*. Washington, DC: Institute for International Economics, 1991. 195 p. ISBN 0881321397. LCCN 90-23526.

The source analyzes the issues in foreign direct investment in the U.S. and develops new approaches for dealing with them. The first edition assesses the nature, extent, and cause of foreign direct investment and its effect on the economy and political process. This second edition updates the analysis to include more current data.

311. Matsumura, Wilfred and Paul Ryscavage. *Dynamics of Economic Well-Being: Labor Force and Income 1990 to 1992*. Washington, DC: U.S. Dept. of Commerce, Economics and Statistics Administration. Bureau of the Census, 1994. 1 vol. SUDOCS C 3.186:P-70/2/40.

This document looks at the dynamics of the U.S. labor force and income in the 1990 to 1992 period to measure the overall health of the economy and the economic well being of persons and households. Some findings are: after a decade of rising employment and income levels, the number of nonfarm payroll jobs fell from a monthly average of 109.4 million in 1990 to 108.5 million in 1992; the nation's monthly civilian unemployment rate rose to 7.4% in 1992; and the economy's inability to create jobs was part of the reason for the falling incomes.

312. Standard & Poor's Statistical Service. *Standard & Poor's Statistical Service. Basic Statistics* New York, NY: Standard & Poor's Statistical Service. ISSN 0147-363X. LCCN sn87017037. Kept current with updates.

Current statistics on U.S. banking, finance, production, labor, price indexes, income, trade, metals, transportation, textiles, chemicals, paper, security price record, New York Stock exchange, Dow Jones averages, and business failures are some data covered in this monthly.

313. U.S. Dept. of Commerce. Bureau of the Census. *County Business Patterns*. Washington, DC: U.S. Government Printing Office. SUDOCS C 3.204/4: Also available on a compact disk. Annual.

This annual has data for each state, and a U.S. summary on establishments, employees, and payroll, by 4 digit SIC industry groups for each county.

314. U.S. Dept. of Commerce. Economics and Statistics. *U.S. Jobs Supported by Goods and Services*. Washington, DC: U.S. Government Printing Office, 1995. 45 p. LCCN 95-216013. SUDOCS C 1.93:1-95.

The U.S. economy and standard of living are interdependent with major economies of the world through international trade, capital flows, and technology. There is an intimate relationship between international trade, goods and services, and U.S. employment and wages. This report explores the relationship of export supported jobs to the size of labor force and unemployment, U.S. trade's largest and rising importance to the U.S. economy, and goods exports that support high paying jobs.

315. U.S. Dept. of Labor. *Report on the American Workforce*. Washington, DC: U.S. Government Printing Office, 1995. 221 p. ISBN 0160483492. LCCN 95-27827. SUDOCS L 1.2:AM 3/6/995.

This report examines U.S. labor market trends, the structure of earnings and working conditions by analyzing long term economic, social, and demographic changes that influence the structure of the labor force, employment and unemployment. It studies the influences of secular and cyclical changes that affect the level and distribution of worker's earnings. Tables on employment cost index for wages and salaries and average weekly pay are included.

316. U.S. Dept. of Labor. Bureau of Labor Statistics. *Compensation and Working Conditions. CWC.* Washington, DC: U.S. Government Printing Office. (U.S. GPO) LCCN 91-656642. SUDOCS L 2.44: Monthly.

This monthly reports on U.S. employment compensation wages, salaries, benefits and working conditions, negotiated changes in wages and benefits, major agreements expiring, major work stoppages, and occupational injuries, and illnesses.

317. U.S. Dept. of Labor. Bureau of Labor Statistics. *Employment Cost Indexes and Levels, 1975-1994.* Washington, DC: U.S. GPO, 1994. 149 p. ISBN 016045199X. SUDOCS L 2.3:2447. Annual.

In the U.S. the two measures of employee compensation are: employment cost index (ECI) and employer costs for employee compensation. This publication reviews recent trends in compensation cost changes and examines the structure of these costs with data on: employer costs for employee compensation broken down by civilian workers, private industry, components of compensation costs, cost levels by industry group, occupation by group, within industries, establishments, employment size, part time and full time status. It provides historical data on the ECI from 1975-1994. Tables include: total compensation for civilian, state, local government, and private industry.

318. U.S. Dept. of Labor. Bureau of Labor Statistics. *Employment, Hours, and Earnings, United States.*Washington, D.C.: U.S. GPO, 1995. ISSN 1047-059X. LCCN 92-649503. SUDOCS L 2.3:2465

This document presents statistics on employment, hours, and earnings by industry including women employees, production workers in mining and manufacturing, construction workers, and private production of non-supervisory workers.

319. U.S. Office of the President. *Economic Report of the President Transmitted to the Congress*. Washington, DC: U.S. GPO. ISSN 0193-1180. LCCN 47-32975. SUDOCS PR 42.9: Annual.

This economic report of the President transmits to Congress the health of the U.S. economy with its trends, developments, and statistical tables relating to income and product accounts, employment, production, foreign transactions, corporate profits and finance, common stock prices and yields.

320. U.S. Dept. of Treasury. Internal Revenue Service. *Statistics of Income. SOI Bulletin*. Washington, DC: U.S. Government Printing Office. ISSN 0730-0743. LCCN sn86-15853. SUDOCS T 22.35/4: Quarterly. 1981-.

This publication reports on annual financial statistics obtained from various types of tax and information filed from corporate returns. Recent issues have information on international companies such as: corporate foreign tax credit: a geographic focus on large U.S. corporations, and domestic corporations controlled by foreign persons. For 1990, Canada, the U.K., Japan and West Germany were the leading source of foreign income for large U.S. corporations.

Economic Censuses -- Government

The economic censuses provide primary data on the structure and function of the nation's economy for government, business, industry and the public. The economic censuses have been taken every five years since 1967 and are supplemented by the annual surveys. The data include: selected operating ratios for the industry such as payroll per employee, production workers as a percent of total employment, annual hours of production workers, average earnings of production workers, cost of materials as a percent of value shipment, and industry statistics.

321. U.S. Dept. of Commerce. Bureau of the Census. *Annual Survey of Manufactures. Geographic Manufacturers: Geographic Area Statistics*. Washington, DC: U.S. G PO. LCCN 87-658326. SUDOCS C 3.24/9-9: Annual.

322. U.S. Dept. of Commerce. Bureau of the Census. *Annual Survey of Manufactures. Statistics for Industry Groups and Industries (including Capital Expenditures, Inventories, and Supplemental Labor, Fuel, and Electric Energy Costs.)* Washington, DC: U.S. GPO. LCCN sn88o-33689. SUDOCS C3.24/9-7: Annual.

This annual has statistics for U.S. manufacturing establishments including auxiliaries, employment statistics for operating manufacturing establishments, and industry groups. The industry groups are: food and kindred products, textile mill products, apparel and other textile products, chemical and allied products, rubber, and primary metals.

323. U.S. Dept. of Commerce. *Census of Manufacturers. Geographic Area Series*. Washington, DC: U.S. GPO, 1993. SUDOCS C 3.24/3-no:MC 92-. Also available on compact disk.

324. U.S. Dept. of Commerce. *Census of Manufacturers. Industry Series*. Washington, DC: U.S. GPO, 1993. SUDOCS C 3.24/4 -no:MC 92- Also available on compact disk.

The series include a census for each state and surrounding areas.

325. U.S. Dept. of Commerce. *Census of Retail Trade: Geographic Area Series*. Washington, DC: U.S. GPO, 1992. SUDOCS C 3.255/2: RC 92-A. Also available on compact disk.

This is a series with information for each state and the entire U.S. on: the kind of business, number of establishments, sales, annual payroll, first quarter, and paid employees for payroll period. It is published every 5 years.

326. U.S. Dept. of Commerce. ...*Census of Service Industries. Geographic Area Series*. Washington, DC: U.S. GPO, 1994. SUDOCS C 3.257/2: SC92- A.

There is a service industry census for every state and a U.S. total with the kind of business operation, number of establishment, receipts, annual payroll, first quarter payroll, and paid employees for pay period.

327. U.S. Dept. of Commerce ...*Census of Service Industries. Industry Series*. Washington, DC: U.S. GPO, 1994 SUDOCS C 3.256/2:WC 92-A.

328. U.S. Dept. of Commerce ...*Census of Wholesale Trade. Geographic Area Series*. Washington, DC: U.S. GPO, 1994. SUDOCS C 3.256/2: WC-92-A- .

There is one for each state and a total for the U.S. There are summary statistics by state for wholesale trade broken down by types of operation, number of establishments, sales, annual payroll, paid employees, operating expenses, and end of the year inventories.

329. U.S. Dept. of Commerce. Economics and Statistics Administration. *Current Industrial Reports: Manufacturing Profiles 1993*. Washington, DC: U.S. Government Printing Office, 1995. LCCN 95-640609. SUDOCS C 3.158/4:992. Annual. 1992-.

This publication compiles the data in the *Current Industrial Reports* program for the year 1992. It covers food products, textiles, apparel, footwear, building materials, chemicals and related products, glass products, primary metals, electronics, consumer durables, industrial equipment, heavy machines and aerospace including: manufacturers' shipments (quantity), exports of domestic merchandise with quantity and value, percent exports to domestic production, and imports for consumption with quantity and value.

330. U.S. Dept. of Commerce. Economics and Statistics Administration. *Current Industrial Reports: Manufacturing Technology: Factors Affecting Adoption,* 1991. SUDOCS C 3.158/3: 991.

Marketing and Advertising

SEE ALSO *Advertising Age.*

331. Ambry, Margaret. *Official Guide to Household Spending: the Number One Guide to Who Spends How Much on What.* Ithaca, NY: New Strategist, 1993. 428 p. ISBN 0962809233.LCCN 93226477.

This guide tracks U.S. consumer spending trends with breakdowns by age for food & alcoholic beverages, shelter & utilities, apparel, household operations, transportation, health care, and entertainment .

332. Ambry, Margaret and Cheryl Russell. *The Official Guide to the American Marketplace.* Ithaca, NY: New Strategist Publications and Consulting, 1993. p. LCCN sn93-26986.

This guide examines characteristics and attitudes of Americans including trends on: population, households, spending, wealth , and labor force.

333. Conroy, Thomas F., ed. *Markets of the U.S. for Business Planners: Historical and Current Profiles of 183 U.S. Urban Economies by Major Section and Industry with Maps, Graphics, and Commentary.* Detroit, MI: Omnigraphics, 1996. 2 vol. ISBN 0780800192. LCCN 95021392.

This two volume set presents personal income data for 183 area markets ranging from Bangor, Maine, to Honolulu, Hawaii. The data include composition of counties, most dynamic industries, income history, economic base, minerals industry, manufacturing, transportation, utilities, and growth projections for selective industries for 1995 and 2000.

334. Darnay, Arsen J., ed. *Market Share Reporter.* Detroit, MI: Gale Research, Inc. ISSN 1052-9578. LCCN 91-649704. Annual. 1991-.

This is an annual with numbers on market share with over 2,000 entries. They are broken down by: (1) general interest and broad topics (2) Standard Industrial Classification Code with product and service description, pie charts, and original source. Examples are: information on U.S. exports to China by percent, joint ventures in Hungary by nationality and top 15 television brands.

335. Euromonitor. *Consumer USA*. London: Euromonitor. ISSN 0952-9543. LCCN 89-643932. Irregular. 1998-

This is a Euromonitor perspective on USA consumer markets with an overview of U.S. markets, profiles of states with population, race, major cities, income per capital, total tax collections per capita, trends in personal consumption expenditure by category such as: food and tobacco, clothing, personal care, housing, transport and recreation. Also various industries are covered such as: market for bottled water by sector, manufactures share for soft drinks, market for air fresheners and insecticides by sector, and penetration of households by audio product, and market for home computers and processors.

336. *Rand McNally... Commercial Atlas & Marketing Guide*. Chicago: Rand McNally. 1996. LCCN 90657419. Annual. 1983-

This oversize annual includes: maps of U.S. cities, counties, and states with income and buying power for retail and wholesale, manufacturing with quintile grouping of counties and independent city according to total value added by manufacture. It also includes information on current population, income and sales data for metropolitan statistical areas, and major military installations. (Description based on 1994).

337. Russell, Cheryl and Margaret Ambry. *The Official Guide to American Incomes: A Comprehensive Look at How Much Americans Have to Spend: with a Special Section on Discretionary Income*. Ithaca, NY: New Strategist Publications & Consulting, 1993. 343 p. ISBN 0962809225. LCCN 93-218899.

American incomes in various forms are scrutinized such as: income trends, household, personal and, discretionary income, household income projections and personal savings.

338. *Sourcebook of Zipcode Demographics*. Arlington, VA: CACI Marketing Systems, 1995. 1v. ISBN 0918417562. Annual.

Recent demographic information on U.S. households, families, income, race, market potential for various products, investments, loans, travel, sporting goods, electronics, and home improvements are included in this source. The data are divided by ZIP codes.

339. Standard Rate and Data Service. *The Lifestyle Market Analysts: A Reference Guide for Consumer Market Analysis*. Oak Brook, IL: Standard Rate and Data Service. ISSN 1067-182x LCCN 89-644773. Annual. 1989-

This guide has market profiles from Abilene, TX to Zaneville, OH with life style profiles, consumer segment profiles, consumer magazine, and direct mail lists. It analyzes markets at a local, regional, and national level, breaking down the American population geographically.

340. Standard Rate and Data Service. *Lifestyle ZIP Code Analyst: A Reference Guide for Consumer Market Analysis*. Oak Brook, IL: Standard Rate and Data Service, 1993. ISSN 1057-8080. LCCN 91-649786. Annual. 1991-

Americans are profiled demographically and their lifestyle data are collected, presented, and analyzed for market researchers for targeted promotion in coupons, mailing, radio spots, and advertisements. Some lifestyle data are: good life activities such as: cultural/ art events, career oriented activities, foreign travel, real estates investments and stock/bond investments.

341. U.S. Bureau of Labor Statistics. *Consumer Expenditure Survey*. Washington, DC: U.S. Government Printing Office, 1995. 245 p. LCCN 0160420164. SUDOCS L 2.3:2462.

This report provides data on the buying habits of American consumers for use in economic research and in periodic revisions to the Consumer Price Index. For 1993, the largest increase in spending is for health care.

Import/Export/ Trade Statistics

342. U.S. Bureau of Labor Statistics. *U.S. Import and Export Price Indexes*. Washington, DC: U.S. Government Printing Office. LCCN sn85061440. LCCN sn85-061440. SUDOCS L 2.60/3: Monthly 1988-.

This monthly records percent changes in import and export price indexes by end use category, import and export price indexes by SITC, import and export price indexes by Harmonized System, and U.S. international price indexes by Harmonized System. The use of the indexes is to deflate trade statistics.

343. U.S. Dept. of Commerce. Bureau of the Census. *Exports from Manufacturing Establishments: 1988 and 1989*. Washington, DC: U.S. Government Printing Office. LCCN 91-648396. SUDOCS C 3.24/9-12: Annual. 1985-.

This publication estimates the value of manufactured exports and export-related employment. Estimates are by state, industry group (two and three digit SIC), total value of shipments and total employment.

344. U.S. Dept. of Commerce. Bureau of the Census and U.S. Dept. of Labor. *Trade and Employment* Washington, DC: U.S. Government Printing Office. LCCN sn92-23410. SUDOCS C 3.269: Quarterly. 1984-1995.

This document measures changes in U.S. imports and employment; shows average percent change in the value of the top 20 SIC import commodity groups and the average percent change in exports for selected industries based on top 20 SIC import commodity groups; and has data on imports for consumption by two to four digit SIC based commodity groups.

345. U.S. Dept. of Commerce. Bureau of the Census. *U.S. Exports. Harmonized Schedule B Commodity by Country*. Washington, DC: U.S. Government Printing Office. LCCN sn92-40989. SUDOCS C 3.164: 447. (microfiche) Annual. 1989-

SEE ALSO U.S. Dept. of Commerce. Bureau of the Census. *U.S. Exports of Merchandise.*

346. U.S. Dept. of Commerce. Bureau of the Census. *U.S. Exports & Imports by Harmonized Commodity: Six Digit Harmonized Commodity by Country.* Washington, DC: U.S. Government Printing Office. LCCN sn95-27854. SUDOCS C 3.164:947. Annual.

347. U.S. Dept. of Commerce. *U.S. Imports for Consumption. Harmonized TSUSA Commodity by Country.* Washington, DC: U.S. Government Printing Office. LCCN 92-040987. SUDOCS C 3.164: 247/. (microfiche) Annual. 1989-.

SEE ALSO U.S. Dept. of Commerce. *U.S. Imports of Merchandise.*

348. U.S. Dept. of Commerce. Bureau of the Census. *U.S. Merchandise Trade: Exports, General Imports and Imports for Consumption. FT 925. Standard International Trade Classification Revision 3. Commodity by Country.* Washington, DC: U.S. Dept. of Commerce. LCCN sn92-23904. SUDOCS C 3.164:925/(microfiche) Monthly. 1989-.

349. U.S. Dept. of Commerce. Bureau of the Census. *U. S. Merchandise Trade: Seasonally Adjusted Imports and Exports.* (microfiche) Washington, DC: U.S. Government Printing Office. SUDOCS C 3.164:900/. Monthly.

This monthly keeps a running tab of exports and imports and the merchandise trade balance (trade deficits). Supplements include exports, imports, and merchandise trade balance by selected SIC based product code.

350. U.S. Dept. of Commerce. Bureau of the Census. *U.S. Trade: Selected Highlights. FT 920.* Washington, DC: U.S. Government Printing Office. LCCN sn92-23331. SUDOCS C 3.164:920 (microfiche). Monthly.

351. U.S. Dept. of Commerce. Bureau of the Census. *U.S. Trade with Puerto Rico and U.S. Possessions*. Washington, DC: U.S. Government Printing Office. LCCN sn93-28280. SUDOCS C 3.164: 895. Annual. 1982-.

352. U.S. Dept. of Commerce. Bureau of the Census. *U.S. Waterborne Exports and General Imports*. Washington, DC: U.S. Government Printing Office. LCCN 74-69895. SUDOCS C 3.164:985- (microfiche).

353. U.S. Dept. of Commerce. International Trade Commission. *The U.S. Automobile Industry Monthly Report on Selected Economic Indicators*. Washington, DC: U.S. International Trade Commission. LCCN sn92-23580. SUDOCS ITC 1.16/3: Monthly. 1983- (microfiche).

This microfiche includes: statistics for new passenger automobiles on: retail sales of domestic production, production, inventory, day's supply and employment; imports by principal sources, exports of domestic merchandise by principal markets, and retail price changes in the U.S. market. The statistics are about a year old.

354. U.S. Dept. of Commerce. International Trade Administration. *U.S. Foreign Trade Highlights*. Washington, DC: U.S. GPO. ISSN 0884-3171. LCCN 85-643059 SUDOCS C61.28/2: Annual.

This annual has data on: U.S. merchandise trade, U.S. total exports and imports to individual countries, major trends in imports and exports, U.S. manufacturers exports to individual countries, annual U.S. exports: two digit SITC product groups, annual U.S. imports: two digit SITC product groups, and U.S. commodity trade by geographic area (list of commodities that we import from other countries) and top 50 partners in total U.S. trade.

355. U.S. Dept. of Commerce. Social and Economic Statistics Administration. *U.S. Commodity Exports and Imports as Related to Output*. Washington, DC: U.S. GPO 1994. ISBN 0501-7793. SUDOCS C 3.229: Annual. 1958-.

This report looks at the relationship between U.S. domestic output (production of goods and services) and U.S. exports and imports based on the Standard Industrial Classification Code. The value of exports, imports, and import duty is shown at the commodity classification level and compared to output for the following industries: agriculture, minerals, and manufacturing. Tables include: exports, imports, and calculated import duty by SIC based commodity division from 1958-1991.

ADDITIONAL INFORMATION

CULTURAL

356. Alston, Jon P., compiler. *The Social Dimensions of International Business: An Annotated Bibliography*. Westport, CT: Greenwood Press, 1993. 312 p. ISBN 0313280290. LCCN 92-29466.

This is an annotated bibliography of over 1300 citations of cultural and social dimensions of international business covering: business-related behavior, managerial behavior, superior-subordinate relationships, negotiating strategies, and business communications, and comparison of behavior among different nationalities.

357. Andersson, Thomas. *Managing Trade Relations in the World Economy*. New York: Routledge, 1993. 182 p. ISBN 0415095689. LCCN 93-9831.

This book looks at perspectives important for trade relations in the new world economy. It looks at the changing positions of countries in the new economy, the large trade deficits of Western countries, and foreign investment and country characteristics.

358. Axtell, Roger E., ed. *Do's and Taboos of International Trade: A Small Business Primer Around the World*. New York: Wiley & Sons, Inc., 1994. 312 p. ISBN 0471007609. LCCN 94008586.

This is an easy-to-read primer on international trade opportunities and an etiquette book on protocol, hand gestures, body language, gift giving and receiving, business cards, and jargon for Europe, Africa, Asia, and the Americas. It is a revised edition of *Do's and Taboos Around the World*.

359. Costa, Janeen Arnold and Gary J. Bamossy. *Marketing in a Multicultural World: Ethnicity, Nationalism and Cultural Identity.* Thousand Oaks, CA: Sage Publications, 1995. 341 p.

Marketing in a Multicultural World looks at the effects of cultural identity on marketing by examining research, trends and data.

360. DeVries, Mary Ann. *Internationally Yours: Writing and Communicating Successfully in Today's Global Marketplace.* Boston, MA: Houghton Mifflin Co., 1994. 352 p. ISBN 0395670268. LCCN 93-49439.

This is a guide on ways to communicate successfully and avoid costly errors in the global marketplace. It includes: differences between domestic and international correspondence, the art of formatting international messages, effective writing style, and saying what you mean, avoiding slang and jargon, and respect for other people.

361. Gale Research Inc. *Peoples of the World.* Detroit, MI: Gale Research Inc. 1989-1993. 7v.

This source includes cultural groups inhabiting the area with geographical setting, historical background, culture, language, and religion. It looks at people from an ethnological perspective.

362. Levinson, David, ed., *Encyclopedia of World Cultures.* Boston, MA: GK Hall, 1991. 10v. ISBN 08168840X. LCCN 90-049123.

This is a multivolume cultural encyclopedia of the world from an ethnological perspective. It includes, demographics, linguistic affiliation, history and cultural relations, economy, kinship groups, and social and political organizations.

363. Moran, Robert T. and Jeffrey D. Abbott. *NAFTA: Managing the Cultural Differences.* Houston: Gulf Pub. Co, 1994. 198 p. ISBN 0884155005. LCCN 94012482.

This source explores the cultural values of the U.S., Canada, and Mexico, including corporate culture, the historical evolution and chronology of the agreement beginning with the Free Trade Agreement and the North American Free Trade Agreement covering the period from 1895 -- January 1, 1994. It is the first agreement by industrial countries that includes intellectual property, labor rights, and the environment. The agreement is divided into eight parts: 1) general 2) trade in goods 3) technical barriers to trade 4) government procurement 5) investment services 6) intellectual property 7) administrative and institutional provisions, 8) other provisions. NAFTA's future and all its benefits depend on the U.S., Canada, and Mexico, corporate executives, and companies bridging these cultural differences and making human relationships work.

364. Randlesome, Collin and William Brierly et al.. *Business Cultures in Europe,* 2nd ed. Oxford: Butter-Heinemann, 1993. 373 p. ISBN 0750608722. LCCN gb93035888.

This is a guide to understanding the major business cultures of the EC including: Germany, France, Italy, the United Kingdom, Spain, and the Netherlands. It focuses on the business culture of the late 1970's to 1990's. It looks at the relationship of business, government, the economy, law, finance, labor market, trade unions, education and the EC's Single Market.

365. Salacuse, Jeswald W. *Making Global Deals*. Boston: Houghton Mifflin, 1991. 193 p. ISBN 0395533651. LCCN 91000292.

Effective negotiation is the key to making international business deals. This book gives strategies for overcoming obstacles, discussing negotiating environment, culture, ideology, foreign bureaucracies, foreign labor laws, multiple currencies, and instability.

366. United Nations. Dept. of Economic and Social Affairs, Statistical Office. *Demographic Yearbook. Annuaire Demographique*. New York: United Nations. LCCN 5000641. ISSN 0082-8041. Annual.

This book answers population questions such as: the world population rate increase, birth and death rates, population by sex, surface area and density for each country, vital statistics rates, and natural increase. There is a summary of basic demographic statistics, followed by a table on the size distribution and trends in population, natality, fetal mortality, and general mortality.

367. United Nations. *World Investment Report.* New York, NY: United Nations. Annual. 1991-.

Each issue has a distinctive title and covers foreign investment and its effects on countries and the way companies do business. See next entry.

368. United Nations. *World Investment Report 1994: Transnational Corporations, Employment and the Workplace.* New York, NY: United Nations, 1994. 446 p. ISBN 9211044359.

Foreign investment has intensified competition internationally and transnational corporations (TNC) are adapting new structures and strategies to deal with it. This UN report examines global trends of TNC, regional trends, and the role of TNC as employers generating employment opportunities directly and indirectly. The evolution towards a more integrated economy has resulted in slower economic growth and the rise of unemployment in developed countries.

369. U.S. Dept. of Commerce. Bureau of the Census. *World Population Profile: 1994 With a Special Chapter Focusing on HIV/AIDS.* Washington, DC: U.S. Government Printing Office, 1994. LCCN 87647992. ISSN 0895-3341. SUDOCS C 3.205/3:WP-94/maps.

Some data from this report are: World population is about 5.6 billion in 1994 and is expected to increase to 7.9 billion by the year 2020. Population growth rates remain highest in Sub-Saharan Africa -- about 2.9% in 1994. The World Health Organization estimates that 14 million people are infected with the HIV virus as of mid-1993.

370. U.S. Dept. of State. *National Negotiating Styles: Assessing the Negotiating Styles of China, the Soviet Union, Japan, France, Egypt, and Mexico* (1987). Washington, DC: U.S. Government Printing Office, 1987. 147 p. LCCN 87-619801. SUDOCS S 1.114/3:N 31/3.

Negotiating styles have their roots in the country's culture, history, political system and position in the world. This source contrasts the negotiating styles of China, the (former) Soviet Union, Japan, France,

Egypt, and Mexico. Understanding a country's negotiating style may increase the chances of making a better deal.

371. U.S. Dept. of State. *U.S. Department of State Indexes of Living Costs Abroad, Quarters Allowance, and Hardship Differentials.* Washington, DC: U.S. Government Printing Office ISSN 91640691. LCCN 1058-0018. SUDOCS S 1.76/4: Quarterly.

This cost of living information is used by business and private firms. The countries covered are Algiers to Zimbabwe.

ENVIRONMENTAL

372. Darnay, Arsen. *Statistical Record of the Environment.* Detroit, MI: Gale Research, 1992. 855 p. ISBN 0810383748. LCCN 91030214.

This presents a statistical record of environmental concerns in the United States with data on: air, water, land pollutants, and wastes; effects; costs, budgets and expenditures; tools, methods, and solution; pollution control industry, general industry and government data. The industry data include: beverage cans by U.S. market share, beverage containers by types, common thermoplastic resin sales by type, leading states with reinforced plastic plants, and plastic consumption worldwide by end uses.

373. Newman, Oksana and Allan Foster. *European Environmental Statistics Handbook.* London: Gale Research International, 1993. 436 p. ISBN 1873477600. LCCN 95-160923.

Some areas covered by this handbook are: European environmental statistics on air, water, land, pollution; general industry, laws, regulations, and pollution control industries. There is also coverage of specific European countries such as: the environmental protection investments in the manufacturing sector of the German Republic and the cost of enhancing the rural and marine environment in the United Kingdom.

374. U.S. President. *The NAFTA, Report on Environmental Issues.* Washington, DC: U.S. Government Printing Office, 1993. 153 p. ISBN 0160429811. LCCN 94-129591. SUDOCS PREX 1.2:N 82/2.

The North American Free Trade Agreement will create the world's largest market composed of 370 million people and a $6.5 trillion worth of production. This report addresses some concerns including: NAFTA's environmental provisions, Mexico's pollution control regime, recent developments in the U.S. Environmental relationship, potential environmental effects of NAFTA, and product standards, pesticides, and food safety.

375. World Resources Institute. *World Resources: A Report by the World Resources Institute and the International Institute for Environment and Development.* NY: Oxford University Press. ISSN 0887-0403. LCCN 86-659504. Annual. 1986-.

This covers natural resource consumption: social and historical patterns, population, the environment, population trends and projection, women and sustainable development of the world. The regional focus covers a specific region, conditions, and trends. Data include: GNP, external debt indicators, imports and exports for food, raw materials, manufacturers and services, official development assistance, and world commodity indexes and prices.

LABOR AND EMPLOYMENT

376. International Labour Office. *Year-book of Labour Statistics.* Geneva: International Labour Office: the Office. ISSN 0084-3857. LCCN 136-130. Annual. 1936-.

This covers the labor statistics for countries of the world with data on the economically active population, employment breakdown by industry and occupation, manufacturing, mining, construction, unemployment by age group, by industry and occupation, hours of work, wages, labor cost, occupational injuries, strikes and lockout.

377. Organisation for Economic Co-operation and Development. *Labour Force Statistics: Statistiques de la Population Active.* Paris: Organisation for Economic Co-operation and Development. ISSN 0474-5515. LCCN 78-231497. Annual. 1961-

This source includes statistics for 24 OECD member countries. Part I contains historical time series which indicate trends in: total population, labor force, employment, civilian employment, and civilian employment by industry. Part II has country tables covering the topics listed in Part I. Part III has participation rates and unemployment rates of OECD countries from Canada to the United Kingdom.

378. Organisation for Economic Co-operation and Development. *OECD Employment Outlook.* Paris: Organisation for Economic Development. LCCN 85650534. Annual.

This publication provides an assessment of OECD labor market development and prospects for member countries with an analysis of labor market trends, short term outlook, and key labor market developments.

379. Organisation for Economic Co-operation and Development. (OECD) *Quarterly Labour Force Statistics.* Paris: Organisation for Economic Co-operation and Development. ISSN 0304-3312. LCCN sc83008311. Also available in electronic format.

This quarterly publishes the basic statistical series in the annual *Labour Force Statistics*. It includes: total labor force, civilian labor force, unemployment total, civilian employment and unemployment rate for member OECD countries.

380. OECD. *The Tax Benefit Position of Production Workers = La Situation des ouvriers au regard de l'impot et des transferts sociaux.* Paris: Organisation for Economic Cooperation and Development. LCCN 85650227. Annual. 1984-.

This annual report has the tax/benefit position of an average production worker of an OECD country. The text is in English and French. It includes: personal income taxes, employee's social security contributions paid, and cash transfers received by household units at the average earnings level of a production worker. There are tables on personal tax at the income level of an average production worker (APW), impact of non-standard tax reliefs on the personal income tax.

381. Scarpetta, Stefano. *The Regional Dimension of Unemployment in Transition Countries: A Challenge for Labour Market and Social Policies—La Dimension regionale du chomage dans les pay en transition: un defi pur le marche du travail et les politiques sociales.* Paris: Organisation for Economic Co-operation and Development, 1995. 533 p. ISBN 9264044434.

There are wide disparities in the way labour markets are evolving in transition economies. This source attempts to explain the reasons behind the disparities to assist policy makers in implementing and evaluating the adequacy of labour market and social policies. One explanation for regional differences in unemployment being long lasting may be due to different economic structure, nature, and pace of the regions. Some countries covered in this source are: Russia, Czech and Slovak Republics, and Eastern Europe.

382. U.S. Dept. of Labor. Bureau of Labor Statistics. *Hourly Compensation Costs for Production Workers in Manufacturing: 31 Countries or Areas: All Manufacturing, 1975 and 1983-94: 39 Other Manufacturing Industries, 1975 and 1982-94.* Washington, DC: U.S. Government Printing Office (U.S. GPO), 1995. LCCN sn92-23658. SUDOCS L 2.2:C 73/8/995.

This document covers hourly compensation costs for production workers for 31 countries in manufacturing and then a breakdown by: food, beverages and tobacco (U.S. SIC 20 and 21; ISIC 31); textile, apparel, and leather products (U.S. SIC 22, 23 & 31; ISIC 32); lumber, wood products, & furniture (U.S. SIC 24; ISIC 33); paper, printing & publishing (U.S. SIC 26 & 27; ISIC 35); stone, clay and glass products (U.S. SIC 32 and ISIC 36); primary metal (U.S. SIC 33 and ISIC 37; and fabricated metal products, machinery and equipment (U.S. SIC 34-38 and ISIC 38).

383. U.S. Dept. of Labor. Bureau of Labor Statistics. *International Comparisons of Hourly Compensation Costs for Production Workers in Manufacturing*. Washington, DC: U.S. GPO. LCCN sn94-28552. SUDOCS L 2.130: Annual.

This annual compares levels and trends in hourly compensation costs for production workers in 29 countries covering the years 1975-992 in the 1992 edition.

384. U.S. Dept. of Labor. Bureau of Labor Statistics. *International Comparisons of Manufacturing Productivity and Labor Cost Trends*. Washington, DC: U.S. GPO. LCCN sn87042303. SUDOCS L 2.120/2-6: Annual. 1984-.

This source has international comparisons of manufacturing productivity and unit labor costs for selected countries including output per hour, output, hours, employment, average hours, hourly compensation, national currency, U.S. dollars and exchange rates.

385. U.S. Dept. of Labor. Bureau of Labor Statistics. *International Labor Comparisons Among G-7 Countries*. Washington, DC: U.S. GPO, 1995. 123 p. LCCN 95-216861. SUDOCS L 2.71:890.

This chart book examines the U.S. economic performance with the G-7 countries to evaluate its position in foreign trade. The data focuses on trends covering 1970-1994 including comparisons of population, labor force, employment, unemployment, education of labor force, hourly compensation costs in manufacturing, labor productivity, and unit labor costs, and the percent of distribution of civilian employment by economic sector for 1970-1993.

386. U.S. Dept. of Labor. *Foreign Labor Trends*. Washington, DC: U.S. Government Printing Office, SUDOCS L 29.16:.

These publications examine and analyze labor developments, labor-management relations, trade unions, employment and unemployment, wages and working condition, and international labor activities. Each issue is country specific. For example, the 1991-92 Australia publication has data on civilian employment, employment in industry, agriculture, unemployment rate, labor productivity, and work related accident, and average monthly earnings by major industry, and minimum wage rate per year.

387. U.S. Dept. of Labor. *Labor Shortages, A Growing Dilemma in East Asia, 1990*. Washington, DC: U.S.GPO, 1991. 8 p. ISBN 0160313635. SUDOCS L 29.16:AS 4.

This document discusses labor shortages in Japan, Taiwan, Singapore, South Korea and Hong Kong in 1990.

CHAPTER IV

GUIDES AND BIBLIOGRAPHIES

The guides and bibliographies in this chapter are: business, exporting, importing/trade, and marketing guides.

The business information guides give methods for researching and finding information; some have explanations for concepts while others list information sources.

This selective list of exporting, importing, and trade guides helps explore decisions to export or not. Some give an overview, provide step-by-step instructions, identify government agencies for assistance and cover various aspects of overseas marketing. Others cover legal documentation and services, custom duties, import policy, financial statistics, and country and cultural information.

The marketing guides include marketing plans, setting up the venture, funding, and obtaining assistance from government sources. Some are by region such as *Business Opportunities in the Far East*. International expansion can take many forms such as joint ventures, export trading companies and strategic alliances. Because marketing guides take time to compile they may not have the most current information, and a newspaper or periodical is needed to complement this information. Any country-specific marketing guide will be listed under the name of the country.

BUSINESS

388. Argenti, Paul, ed. *The Portable MBA Desk Reference: An Essential Business Companion*. New York: J.Wiley. 1994. 688 p. ISBN 0471576816.LCCN 93-32666.

Part I has a dictionary of business terms and topics. Part II has an annotated listing of business sources including international business.

389. Daniells, Lorna M. *Business Information Sources, 3rd ed.* Berkeley, CA: University of California Press, 1993. 725 p. LCCN 92-41827. ISBN 0520081803.

This is a classic business reference source with methods of locating facts, comprehensive listings of the business sources, U.S. business and economic trends, foreign statistics, corporate finance and banking, a good index and descriptive annotations.

390. *Findex*. Bethesda, MD: NSA Directories. ISSN 0273-4125. LCCN 80-645160. Annual. 1979-

This is a listing describing over 12,000 marketing research reports, studies, and some surveys arranged by industry classification. The reports tend to be expensive.

391. Freed, Melvyn N. and Virgil P. Diodata. *Business Information Desk Reference*. New York: Macmillan Publishing Co., 1991. 513 p. ISBN 0029106516. LCCN 90-38996.

Asking the "right questions," looking in appropriate places, listing printed and online sources for business resources, corporate operations, officials, and international business transactions are some of the subjects included in this source.

392. Gale Research Co. *Business Organizations, Agencies, and Publications Directory*. Detroit, MI: Gale Research Co. 1993. ISSN 0888-1413. LCCN 0749-0801. Annual. 1986-

This annual publication has more than 26,000 entries covering business information sources with chapters on U.S. and international organizations, business and commercial associations, foreign trade zones, world trade centers, international research centers, incorporating information in a foreign country, and financial backing information for a new venture.

393. Godin, Seth, ed. *The 1996 Information Please Business Almanac & Desk Reference*. Boston, MA: Houghton Mifflin Co., 1995. 745 p. ISBN 0395643848. LCCN 93006268.

This is a useful handbook covering: business, law, government, industries attracting foreign buyers by number of transactions, foreign buyers of U.S. companies by number of transactions by countries, regulatory agencies, government assistance, number of business failures by industry and international mailing and internet sources.

394. Hawbaker, A. Craig and Judith M. Nixon. *Industry and Company Information: Illustrated Search Strategy and Sources*. Ann Arbor, MI: Pierian Press, 1991. 172 p. ISBN 0876502877. LCCN 93-122971.

A search strategy flowchart, search strategy objectives, overview, periodical articles, associations and directories, ratio analysis, CD-ROM database searching, and ways to look for statistics are explained clearly with examples from the sources themselves in this handy guide on finding industry and company information.

395. Lavin, Michael R. *Business Information: How to Find It, How to Use It*. Phoenix, AZ: Oryx Press, 1992. 499 p. ISBN 0897745556. LCCN 91-28129.

This source helps locate experts, and find business and investment information by searching directories, reference sources, journals, newspapers, news services, and corporate finances. Basic business concepts and foreign trade statistics have clear explanations.

396. Levine, Sumner and Caroline Levine, eds. *The Business One Irwin International Almanac*. Homewood, IL.: Business One Irwin, 1993. 742 p. ISSN 1068-0942. LCCN 93-000091.

Each almanac focuses on a different aspect of investing. The 1993 issue looks at country profiles from *The World Factbook*, economic and financial trends for the major developed countries, international investing, international stock market performances, and top international companies. The 1994 issue looks at industry and industry trends.

397. Mackenzie, Leslie, ed. *The Directory of Business Information Resources*. Lakeville, CT: Grey House Pub. 1994. 887 p. LCCN 92-038430.

This has a listing of associations, newsletters, journals, and trade shows with subjects alphabetically arranged from accounting to wholesaler, retailer & services businesses.

398. Pagell, Ruth A. *International Business Information: How to Find It, How to Use It*. Phoenix, AZ: Oryx Press. 1994. 371 p. ISBN 0897747364. LCCN 930449000.

Pagell's practical guide is for researchers and librarians with publications and database listings. It has, for example, information on the keiretsu (business alliances) of Japanese companies. The contents include general sources for business research such as accounting standards, company information, marketing, and industrial and economic statistics.

399. Rasie, Larry. *Directory of Business Information*. New York: J. Wiley. 1995. 612 p. ISBN 047159816X. LCCN 94040077.

This directory lists business sources such as: indexes, online databases, periodicals, newspapers, directories, and bibliographies. It also gives industry overviews with the general status, the global situation and outlook, phone numbers for specialists in the field, bibliographies and periodicals for the industry, associations, and leading companies.

400. Schlessinger, Bernard S. and Rashelle S. Karp. *The Basic Business Library: Core Resources*. Phoenix, AZ: Oryx Press, 1995. 371 p. ISBN 0897747399. LCCN 94022809.

This is an annotated list of 200 business sources including authority and scope, evaluation of reference sources, periodicals, government documents and online databases.

401. Special Libraries Association. *Directory of Business and Financial Services*. New York: Special Libraries Association, 1994. ISBN 087114208. LCCN 25-4599.

The 1994 directory is arranged alphabetically by title with descriptive abstracts of business and financial services that are available in print, online, and compact disk format. It includes a publisher's index, master title and subject index.

402. Woy, James, Inc. *Encyclopedia of Business Information Sources*. Detroit, MI: Gale Research, Inc., 1993. ISSN 0071-0210. LCCN 84643366.

There are 1,100 business, financial and industrial subjects from the abrasive to zinc industry with references to encyclopedias, abstracting and indexing services, handbooks and manuals, online databases, price sources, statistic sources, and trade associations. SEE ALSO *Encyclopedia of Business Information Sources: Europe*.

EXPORTING

403. Douress, Joseph, ed. *Exporter's Encyclopaedia, 2nd ed.* New York, NY: Dun & Bradstreet, 1993. ISBN 1-56203-305-5. ISSN 8755-013x. LCCN 84647135.

Country profiles with information on population, language, gross domestic product, best U.S. export prospects, principal trading partners, principal banks, legal system, electric current, overseas telephone service, international telephone rates, key contacts, documentation, customs tariff, taxes, value added tax, value for duty, foreign investment patents and country- specific trademarks are some topics covered by this encyclopedia.

404. *Exporting from the United States*. Rocklin, CA: Prima Publishing and Communications, 1993. 175 p. LCCN 93-009897. ISBN 1559583282.

This is a more expensive reprint of the government publication *Basic Guide to Exporting*.

405. Gordon, John S. *Profitable Exporting: A Complete Guide to Marketing Your Products Abroad*. New York: John Wiley and Sons, 1993. 388 p. ISBN 0471575143. LCCN 92-14983.

This guide provides an overview of the export business including: reasons for exporting, critical factors, mistakes of new exporters, decision factors in market entry, market preparation, pricing, and export financing.

406. *International Trade Reporter: An Export Reference Manual*. Washington, DC: Bureau of National Affairs, Inc. ISSN 1043-5670. LCCN 89-7389.

The arrangement of this export loose-leaf reference manual is alphabetically by country. It includes mail information with addressing, documentation, fees, insurance, international business supply service, weight limits; country information with population, currency, major banks; government information offices, holidays and business hours, consulates in the U.S.; and tariff systems with specific duties, ad valorem duties, customs surcharges, indirect taxes and fines and penalties.

407. Nagel, Walter H. and Gaston Z. Ndyajunwoha. *Export Marketing Handbook*. New York: Praeger, 1988. 149 p. ISBN 0-275-92949-3. LCCN 87-82237.

This export guide is aimed at medium-sized corporations, entrepreneurs, and college students. It presents: an overview with a step-by- step approach to successful exporting of products and services with the most potential, best U.S. export opportunities, products to be avoided, pricing procedures, and export challenges such as political risk and culture, regulatory forces, technology and nontariff barriers.

408. *North American Trade Guide*. Philadelphia, PA: North American Pub. Co., 1993. ISSN 1071-958X. LCCN 94-657068. Annual.

This is a guide and directory for doing business in the United States, Canada, and Mexico with a listing of: contacts, sources, statistics, tariff schedule, port listings, air and sea port descriptions and a directory of wholesalers, distributors, legal carriers and brokers.

409. *Official Export Guide*. Glen Cove, NY: Budd Publications, Inc. 400 p. ISSN 0278-6389. LC 81-645762. Annual. 1981-

This guide includes information on: export aid and support from agencies; country profiles, trade data, duties, non-tariff barriers, policies, agent distribution, patents and trademarks; directory of ocean carriers; Schedule B contents; and export documents such as: samples of bank draft, transmittal letter, bill of lading, certificate of origin, and letter of credit.

410. U.S. Dept. of Commerce. International Trade Administration. *Basic Guide to Exporting* Washington, DC: U.S. GPO, 1992. 173 p. ISBN 0160361222. LCCN 92-25560408. SUDOCS C 61.8:Ex 7/3/.

This guide provides information to export profitably. It outlines an export plan, gives market research advice, and lists agency support, such as the U.S. and Foreign Commercial Service and banks, Chambers of Commerce, trade associations, and a list of desk officers.

411. U.S. Dept. of Commerce. International Trade Administration. *The Environmental Technologies Export Handbook/Joint Project of the U.S. and Oklahoma Departments of Commerce*. Washington, DC: U.S. G PO, 1995. 139 p. SUDOCS

The handbook provides information to suppliers of environmental products and services to identify export opportunities, sources of assistance and financing. It includes an environmental market summary for most countries listing promising products, environmental contacts, and tables with best market, import market, and receptivity to U.S. products.

412. U.S. Dept. of Commerce. International Trade Administration. *Export Programs: A Business Directory of U.S. Government Resources*. Washington, DC: U.S. Government Printing Office. 1993. 70 p. LCCN 93-649567. SUDOCS C 61.2:Ex 7/21.

This source briefly describes its export programs such as: counseling, contact points for market information and expertise, trade leads, overseas activities, and financial assistance. It also includes: Business Information Service for the Newly Independent States (BISNIS), Eastern Europe Business Information Center (EEBIC), Japan Export Information Center (JEIC) and Latin America/Caribbean Business Development Center and U.S. and Foreign Commercial Service. Phone and fax numbers are included.

413. U.S.. Dept. of Commerce. International Trade Administration. *Export Trading Company Guidebook.* Washington, DC: U.S. Government Printing Office. 1987. 151 p. ISBN 0160003369. LCCN 89-601167.SUDOCS C 61.8: EX 7/4/987

This source presents the advantages and risks in forming an export trading company (ETC). It covers: objectives of the Export Trading Act of 1982, government help, and financial considerations in forming an ETC such as flow of goods and element of cost and a check list for Federal Reserve approval.

414. U.S. Small Business Administration. *Exporters Guide to Federal Resources for Small Business*. Washington, DC: U.S. Government Printing Office. 1993. ISBN 0160215. LCCN 94-35008. SUDOCS SBA 1.19: Ex7/3/993.

This guide includes federal programs to assist small business entrepreneurs in exporting goods and services. Field contacts for district offices are listed by state and phone numbers. Country desk officers are listed by countries.

415. Wells, L. Fargo and Karin B. Dulat. *Exporting from Start to Finance*. Blue Ridge, PA: Liberty Hall Press, 1991. 522 p. ISBN 0830637915. LCCN 91-21411.

This book covers: pros and cons of exporting, market procedures for products, market research, export operations, staying out of trouble, financing an export business, government assistance programs and finance.

416. Weiss, Kenneth. *Building an Import/Export Business: Revised and Expanded*. New York: John Wiley & Sons, Inc., 1991. 278 p. ISBN 0471536261. ISBN 047153627X. LCCN 90-29113.

This source begins by asking 20 essential questions to determine if a company should consider importing or exporting. It discusses setting up the business, opening a bank account, obtaining financing, importing, exporting, choosing markets, making credit payments, and shipping. The volume contains a business plan outline and trade contacts.

417. Zodl, Joseph A. *Export Import: Everything You and Your Company Need to Compete in World Markets*. Cincinnati, OH: Betterway Books. 1995. 151 p. ISBN 1558703888. LCCN 95-3449.

This guide for importers and exporters gives rationale for exporting and includes advice on: finding markets for products abroad, finding help, terms of sale, ins and out of getting paid, and samples of documentation such as commercial invoice, packing slip, NAFTA certificate of origin, and export vessel movement summary sheet.

IMPORTING/TRADE

418. Entrepreneur Magazine. *Starting an Import/Export Business*. New York: John Wiley & Sons. 1995. 256 p. ISBN 047110590. LCCN 95-16999.

This guide provides basics of starting an import/export business with information on understanding the world market, forming an import/export service, writing a business plan, marketing plan, understanding regulations and maintaining records.

419. Estell, Kenneth. *World Trade Resources Guide: A Guide to Resources on Importing from and Exporting to the Major Trading Nations of the World*. Detroit: Gale Research Inc. 1992. ISSN 1058-1618. LCCN 92-659025.

This is a foreign trade directory listing 11,000 contacts and information sources on 80 of the largest and most significant trading nations of the world. Information begins with a country profile on: population, language, capital, GDP, total exports, imports, major trading partners, principal commodities imported, statistical sources, air cargo carriers, freight forwarders, and shipping agents. It also includes organizations and agencies, banks and financial institutions, government agencies, and research centers.

420. Goldsmith, Howard R. *Import/export: A Guide to Growth, Profits, and Market Share*. Englewood Cliffs, N.J.: Prentice Hall. 1989. 484 p. ISBN 0134518659. LCCN 88-18021.

This guide targets small and medium sized companies new to international trade by presenting a step-by-step directive. It covers: chances of success in exporting/importing, setting up business with the right image, filing system, identifying a product to market and the importance of market research. It also looks at trade and economic statistics, product potential checklist, foreign patent protection, treaties and national laws, export help such as a foreign freight forwarder who assists in documentation, shipping schedule, insurance warehousing, and best method of transportation.

421. *Importing into the United States, Revised Second Edition*. Rocklin, CA: Prima Publishing, 1991. 86 p. LCCN 91-42149. ISBN 1-55958-177-8.

This is a more expensive version of the government publication, *Importing into the United States*. SEE ENTRY 425.

422. Moran-Lever, Tery, ed. *U.S. Custom House Guide*. Philadelphia: North American Pub. Co. 1600 p. ISSN 0891-1517. LCCN 88-10187. Annual.

This annual lists U.S. customs ports of entry. Ports are arranged alphabetically by city, then Puerto Rico, Virgin Islands, and Canada. The port profiles include: address, telephone numbers for customs, Department of Commerce Office, airports, seaports and Chamber of Commerce. It describes airport and seaport facilities. Foreign trade zone information is included. Service directories supply information on international air cargo carriers, ocean carriers and banks, software, hardware, and computer commercial invoice, prohibitions, restrictions, and other agency requirements. The text of customs regulations is included. There are updates to this source.

423. Nelson, Carl A. *Import/Export: How to Get Started in International Trade*. New York, NY: McGraw- Hill, Inc., 1995. 246 p. ISBN 0070472763. LCCN 95-16132.

This is a guide for getting started on international trade with information on importing/exporting, the opportunities, marketing and research plans, tips and traps of culture, negotiations, documentation, and the ten commandments of starting an overseas business.

424. Trade Media Ltd. *Importing from...: a Buyers Manual for Selecting Suppliers, Negotiating Orders and Arranging Methods of Payment for More Profitable Purchasing*. Hong Kong: Trade Media Ltd.

Each guide in this series is country specific with information on selecting suppliers, negotiating techniques, business style, free trade zone, banking and finance, shipping and infrastructure, settling trade disputes, and setting up an office. Brazil (ISBN 9627138274), China (ISBN 962-7138460), Hong Kong (ISBN 962713824X), India (ISBN 9627138096), Malaysia (ISBN 9627138134), the Philippines (ISBN 962713807X), South Africa (ISBN 962738479), Vietnam (ISBN 962-7138-19-3) are some of the countries included in this series.

425. U.S. Dept. of the Treasury. Customs Service. *Importing into the United States, Customs Publication Service No. 504.* Washington, DC: U.S. Government Printing Office, 1993. 86 p. ISBN 0160227240. LCCN 91-42149. SUDOCS T 17.17:

There are many procedures and legal requirements before goods can enter the United States. This source covers importing procedures to assure that imports are processed quickly and accurately; listings of ports of entry by state; suggestions to exporters for faster customs clearance; right to make entry (merchandise must be entered by owner purchaser); examination of goods, packing of goods, foreign trade zones, assessment of duty, and frequent invoicing errors.

426. World Trade Press. *Importers Manual U.S.A.* San Rafael, CA: World Trade Press, 1992. 960 p. ISBN 0-9631864-1-8. ISSN 1065-5158. LCCN 94-648197. 1992-

This handy guides cites reasons for importing or not importing, key elements of a successful import operation, easy import products, top fifty suppliers of imports, international law, visas and work permits. It includes specifics such as: Saudi Arabian Islamic law, international banking, packing, shipping, and insurance, and a commodity index.

MARKETING

Asia

427. Chimerine, Lawrence, ed. *Business Opportunities in the Far East: The Complete Reference Guide to Practices and Procedures*. Homewood, IL: Dow Jones-Irwin, 1990. 611 p. ISBN 1556231970. LCCN 89-23542.

This is a resource to help American, Canadian, and European companies compete effectively in the Far East. It includes: the problems and opportunities in the Far East, business aspects of trading with Japan, Korea, Taiwan; operating a business in Japan, Korea, Taiwan; financial and tax considerations in Japan, Korea, Taiwan and other Asian markets.

428. Enderlyn, Allyn and Oliver C. Dziggel. *Cracking the Pacific Rim: Everything Marketers Must Know to Sell into the World's Newest Emerging Markets*. Chicago: Probus Publishing. 1992. 252 p. ISBN 1557382549.

The Pacific Rim is the area of emerging opportunities. This guide's aim is to aid Westerners in cracking this market. Countries include Hong Kong, Indonesia, Japan, South Korea, Malaysia, the Philippines, Singapore, Taiwan, and Thailand with data on demographics, politics, economics, commodities, and investment climate.

Europe

429. Arons, Rick. *EuroMarketing: A Strategic Planner for Selling into the New Europe*. Chicago, IL: Probus Publishing Co. 1991. 278 p. ISBN 1557382018. LCCN 91-30334.

The problems of rebuilding Eastern Europe provide opportunities for American business to set the foundation for the future in the economy of the European Community. This guide covers the seven rules of strategic alliance; modification of American marketing tools for European markets, coverage of the following European industries: transportation, telecommunications, computer and software, pharmaceutical, insurance, fiberoptic, and broadcasting. It includes a directory of European information sources and a "Eurospeak" glossary.

430. Danton de Rouffignac, Peter. *Doing Business with Eastern Europe: A Handbook for the 1990s*. London: Pitman. 1991. 237 p. ISBN 0273032941.

This handbook is for doing business in Eastern Europe. There are opportunities and pitfalls. The history and role of Comecon (Council for Mutual Assistance); the structure of foreign trade in centrally planned economies; patterns of trade, sales promotion and research are some areas covered by this marketing handbook. The countries included are: Bulgaria, Czechoslovakia, GDR, Hungary, Poland, Romania, and the USSR.

431. Dudley, James W. and Hans Marten. *1993 and Beyond: New Strategies for the Enlarged Single Market.* London: Kogan Page. 1993. 456 p. ISBN 0749408405.

This manager's guide focuses on the impact of the political and economic integration of Europe and formulates strategies for the changing business environment in the European Community. These changes provide opportunities and risks for companies. It gives background for the Single European Act, the Paolo Cecchinis report, comparison between EC and Japanese industrial strategies, and the European monetary cooperation and the Maastricht Treaty.

432. Euromonitor. *World's Emerging Markets: Business Opportunities in the World's Fastest Growing Regional Economies.* London: Euromonitor. 1992. 212 p. ISBN 0863384277.

This is a marketing guide to the world's emerging markets that includes: Eastern and Southern Europe, Central Asia, Latin America, Africa and the Middle East. It gives a regional overview, current issues, constraints, market potential, market access, and current economic outlook.

433. Faulkner & Gray Inc. *1995 European Business Directory: A Comprehensive Resource Guide for Doing Business Throughout Europe and the Former Soviet Union States.* 1994. 44 p. ISBN 1881393275.

This source includes: profile of European countries with population, area, currency, inflation rate, tax rates, value added tax rates, GDP, and best prospects for U.S. business, business contacts, economic and trade profile, infrastructure, investing, taxation, forms of business organization, distribution and sales channel, advertising and market research.

434. Lynch, Richard. *European Marketing: A Strategic Guide to New Opportunities*. New York: Irwin Professional Publishing, 1994. 304 p. ISBN 1-55623-757-X. LCCN 93-25794.

The U.S. can view the new Europe as an opportunity or competitor. This guide discusses the definition of Europe, European markets and culture, common currency in Europe, (EMU -- European monetary union) the decision making process of the European Commission, European marketing research, and Europeans as customers. Tables and graphs on: share of world exports, Europe's major industries by sources of sales, etc. are included.

SEE Price Waterhouse Information Guide Series. *Doing Business in Eastern Europe*.

435. U.S. Dept. of State. *Resource Guide to Doing Business in Central and Eastern Europe*. Washington, DC: U.S. Government Printing Office, 1991. 38 p. SUDOCS S 1.71/5:Eu 7/2

Marketing information on Bulgaria, the former Czechoslovakia, Hungary, Poland, Romania, and the former Yugoslavia is included in this guide. U.S. government programs to encourage these countries to move towards a market economy are other areas covered.

436. William, Robert and Mark Tegan. *World's Largest Market: A Business Guide to Europe*. New York, NY: AMACON, American Management Association, 1993. 280 p. ISBN 0814477747.

Managers are provided with information on the European Community such as: the aim of the European Community (EC) to become a single market, the progress towards this aim and the implications for American business. It looks at background information on the EC, its institutions, legal process and outlook for business by industrial sector. A four step approach for companies for 1992: (1) perform industry analysis (2) factor the 1992 EC into your strategy (3) examine the implications of the EC directives on your industry (4) generate specific action steps.

437. Zonis, Marvin and Dwight Semler. *The Eastern European Opportunity: The Complete Business Guide and Sourcebook.* New York: Wiley. 1992. 438 p. ISBN 0471547344. LCCN 92000992.

The Eastern European countries included in this guide are: Poland, the former Czechoslovakia, Hungary, Romania, Bulgaria, and the former Yugoslavia with information on politics, history, government, and current state of the economy. Statistics are from many sources and include: communications and transport, economic profile, GNP per capita in dollars (1990), GNP per capita as a percentage of OECD average, consumer spending, number of radio and telephone stations, pipelines, airports, number of passenger cars and basic structure of industry. The original statistical source is cited.

The Caribbean and Latin America

438. Enderlyn, Allyn and Oliver C. Dziggel. *Cracking Latin America: A Country by Country Guide to Doing Business in the World's Newest Emerging Markets.* Chicago: Cambridge, England: Probus. 1994. 403 p. ISBN 1557384320. LCCN 94-120592.

This guide covers doing business in Latin America and includes: Argentina to Venezuela including Guyana and Jamaica. The information includes: population, main urban area, language, best hotel, political condition, key economic indicators, political/institutional infrastructure, principal U.S. exports (1991), principal U.S. imports (1991), trade and investment policies and climate, commercial environment, demand for goods and services, and implications for U.S. exporters..

439. Tuller, Lawrence W. *Doing Business in Latin America and the Caribbean: Including Mexico, the U.S. Virgin Islands, and Puerto Rico, Central America, South America.* New York: AMACOM. American Management Association. 1993. 348 p. ISBN 0814450350. LCCN 93009247.

Many doors are being opened in Latin America and the Caribbean. This marketing guide points to opportunities and risks of doing business in the area. It gives market specifics for individual countries in the area and practical information for investing, exporting and importing.

International

440. Business International Corp. *FFO: Financing Foreign Operations* New York: Business International Corp. LCCN 66-24791.

This is a loose-leaf volume with a country by country analysis on the political and economic environment, important financial events, currency considerations, foreign exchange regulations, monetary system, sources of capital, short term and long term financing techniques.

441. Business International Corporation. *Investing, Licensing, & Trading Conditions Abroad.* New York: Business International Corporation. 1991. 3 vol. LCCN 34102138.

This loose-leaf volume has information on doing business by area with a regional overview, then individual country coverage, the different organizations that concern investors, political events that affect the area, requirements for establishing a company, and rules of competition. The three volumes are divided by region: Africa, Asia, and North America.

442. *Ernst & Young Resource Guide to Global Markets.* New York: Wiley. ISSN 1059-3098. LCCN sn91-004533. Annual.

This book focuses on issues of global expansion, including trade, markets, demographics, and trends. Chapter I gives an overview of the major markets: North America, European Community, and Southeast Asia. It evaluates the opportunities in the Middle East, the General Agreement on Tariffs and Trade, and intellectual property protection.

Euromonitor. *Consumer International.* London: Euromonitor. 1995. ISBN 0863385508. SEE *Consumer Asia* for type of information included.

443. Kirpalani, V.H. (Manek), ed. *International Business Handbook.* New York: Haworth Press. 1990. 667 p. ISBN 086656862x. LCCN 89-26682.

Doing business internationally requires successfully crossing cultures, business customs, methods of entries and global strategies. This practical guide covers doing business in the Andean countries, Great Britain, Central America, China, and Egypt.

444. Maggiori, Herman J. *How to Make the World Your Market: The International Sales and Marketing Handbook.* Los Angeles, CA: Burning Gate Press. 1992. 463 p. ISBN 1878179063. LCCN 91-73712

This guide includes: developing a marketing and sales plan, defining the differences between domestic and international markets, starting export operations, selecting a distributor, negotiating the distributor contract, and filling out export and shipping documents.

445. Morrison, Terri, Wayne A. Conaway, and George A. Borden. *Kiss, Bow, or Shake Hands: How to Do Business in Sixty Countries.* Holbrook, MA.: B. Adams. 1994. 438 p. ISSN 155850443. LCCN 94-24539.

This marketing guide looks at country information from Argentina to Venezuela and includes: country background, business practices, appointments, negotiations, entertaining and dress, and gift giving.

446. Nelson, Dr. Carl A. *Global Success: International Business Tactics for the 1990s.* Blue Ridge Summit, PA: Liberty Hall Press. 1990. 487 p. ISBN 0830635068. LCCN 90-30037.

Entrepreneurs, managers and decision makers are the target audience of this business manual. It presents a plan to compete effectively; to be aware of the interdependency of nations, make long term commitment of resources to maintain competitive edge, plan company's position in the market place, global sourcing, and examine trade barriers and exportable services. He has tips for women in international trade and a country by country breakdown of do's and taboos for facilitating business transactions.

447. Paliwoda, Stanley J., ed. *New Perspectives on International Marketing*. London and New York: Routledge, Chapman and Hall Inc. 1991. 374 p. ISBN 0415053447. LCCN 90-37092.

This scholarly work analyzes and challenges the literature on international marketing practices. It combines empirical study with critical theory and is aimed at readers with prior knowledge of international marketing. It begins from a European standpoint because international trade in European nations is the most important economic activity in the creation of national wealth whereas in the U.S., foreign trade constitutes 10% of national income. It presents: fifty studies identifying success factors of export marketing, management contracts being the predominant form in industrial cooperation, and a study of product development in an industrializing country -- Indonesia.

448. Renner, Sandra L. and W. Gary Winget. *Fast-Track Exporting*. New York, NY: AMACON. 1991. 275 p. ISBN 0814450091. LCCN 90-56192.

The aim of this book is to help companies internationalize through fast track exporting providing a step-by-step approach for entering trial run export markets, proceeding to market penetration and export profits. There are worksheets and case examples -- tools for jumping over hurdles encountered on the export track. Phase I includes: select the trial product, multiply your resources, set up an export center, select the trial run market and export market entry method, assess the company's readiness to export and finalize the trial run plan.

449. Rodkin, Henry H. *The Ultimate Overseas Business Guide for Growing Companies*. Homewood, IL: Dow Jones-Irwin. 1990. 201 p. ISBN 1556233000. LCCN 89-29372.

This marketing guide discusses successful marketing covering product differentiation, customer service and distribution, and price is not the only consideration. Research and knowledge are necessities in selling products overseas. Seeking answers are only possible if you know the "right" questions. He advises: be American overseas, register your trademarks, and maintain records of your products. There is also a listing of government agencies for export problems.

450. Shawnee Mission. *International Marketing: Breaking Down the Great Wall.* videorecording. Shawnee Mission, KS: distributed by RMI Media Productions.

This 30 minute videotape on international marketing relates the experience of Fluor, an engineering service company. The marketing principles are the same: build credibility and trust by delivering on your promises. The differences are cultural and the variables are the changing markets.

451. Tuller, Lawrence W. *Going Global: New Opportunities for Growing Companies to Compete in World Markets*. Homewood, IL: Business One Irwin, 1991. 334 p. ISBN 1556234120. LCCN 90046849.

This guide offers an overview: (1) decisions on going global, (2) prioritizing global markets with an overview of major developed markets such as Japan, Europe, and Canada; and developing markets such as the Caribbean, Latin America, Middle East, Pacific Basin, Asia and Africa (3) financing global trade, and (4) marketing in a global economy. The appendix has a documentation checklist for letters of foreign credit and major foreign banks with offices in the United States, etc.

452. Tuller, Lawrence W. *The World Markets Desk Book: A Region by Region Survey of Global Trade Opportunities*. New York: McGraw-Hill, 1993. 334 p. ISBN 0070654786. LCCN 92-24524.

This publication analyzes over fifty countries to recommend exporting and direct investment opportunities and to avoid certain countries. The recommendations are specific for each country and include tips to foreign traders and investors, foreign direct investment, future outlook, and specialized niche markets.

453. U.S. Dept. of Commerce. *International Business Practices*. Washington, DC: U.S. Government Printing Office, 1993. 297 p. ISBN 0160422566. LCCN 92-203487. SUDOCS C 1.2:B 96/9.

International Business Practices orients the exporter with information on: finance export transactions, export management companies, trading companies, foreign sales corporation, Foreign Corrupt Practices Act, drafting international sales, and agent distributor agreements. Country specific data on business organizations, exporting, commercial policies, foreign investment, intellectual property rights, and taxation are included.

454. U.S. International Trade Administration. *The Big Emerging Markets: 1996 Outlook and Sourcebook*. Lanham, MD: Bernan Press in conjunction with the National Technical Information Service, 1995. 476 p. ISBN 0890590532. LCCN sn96-17137.

This sourcebook focuses on the "ten big emerging markets" (BEM) for U.S. exporters which are expected to account for 40% of the total world imports and growth for the next 15 years. Some topics included are: ASEAN strategy, ways to increase U.S. market share in the BEM, strengthen relationships and conditions in the BEM. It looks at risks and opportunities. It gives specifics for each country with information on economics, emerging sector opportunities, market access, government policies, competition, and openness to foreign investment.

455. U.S. Small Business Administration. *International Trade: A Golden Opportunity*. Washington, DC: U.S. Government Printing Office, 1993. 16 p. SUDOCS SBA 1.32/2:T 67.

This booklet gives pointers on doing business overseas by: researching the market, exporting versus foreign production, methods of export distribution, testing the market, pricing and promoting the product, transporting and distributing the product, financing the overseas operations, developing an export plan, and being cautious.

456. Walmsley, John. *Development of Overseas Markets*. London and Boston, MA: Graham & Trotmen. 1989. 222 p. ISBN 1853332798. LCCN 89-33464.

The author discusses the development of international markets against the background of world trading patterns. He examines the factors causing the change in the world patterns and the opportunities that arise in these areas of change. He also covers: incentives and risks, problems and advantages of international expansion, research, overseas partner selection, exporting and agents, and joint ventures. Also there is a table on treaties and pacts.

457. Walter, Ingo and Tracy Murray, eds. *Handbook of International Business*. New York, NY: John Wiley & Sons. 1988. 677 p. ISBN 0471842346. LCCN 87-35545.

The handbook covers issues that companies need to consider in international marketing such as: reasons for international trade, protectionism, role of exchange rates, international financial markets, political environment of multinational corporations, and cultural issues in doing business overseas.

CHAPTER V

INDEXES AND ABSTRACTS

The indexes in this chapter provide access to information from journals, government publications, statistical sources, and newspapers. Access is useful for information on a country, business environment, industry trend, product, and market forecast. Indexes allow subject, author, and keyword access. The abstracts describe the article content. Computerized indexes allow rapid searching and the linking of terms such as marketing, country, and product to limit the information to journals with those parameters, whereas the paper indexes such as *Business Periodicals Index* have more comprehensive coverage.

The periodicals indexed by *F & S Index Europe* and *PROMPT* are different from *ABI/Inform* and *Business Periodicals Index* as they tend to be precise indexes for product and industry information because they use a modified Standard Industrial Classification (SIC) code. They also index more technical and trade journals and not many scholarly journals.

American Statistics Index (ASI) and *MARCIVE* (a computerized index) allow access to government publications. *ASI,* a printed index, looks mostly at statistics from government sources, while *MARCIVE* covers a broader area and is not limited to statistical information.

BUSINESS

458. Information Access Co. *F & S Index Europe*. Foster City, CA: Information Access Co. ISSN 0270-4536. LCCN sf 94-34006 . Monthly with quarterly cumulations. Also available on compact disk from Silver Platter, Norwood, MA.

This monthly covers product, company, market data and industry information for over 750 financially related periodicals, newspapers, trade magazines, and special reports. This index includes the following areas: the European Community, Scandinavia, East European Countries, Russia and the Commonwealth of Independent States. Vol. 1 has industry and product information. Vol. 2 uses the standard industrial classification code to classify products and related industries and arranges them by country. Vol. 3 is alphabetically arranged by the name of the company.

459. Information Access Co. *F & S Index International.* Foster City, CA: Information Access Co. ISSN 0270-4528. LCCN sf 94-34001. Monthly with quarterly cumulations. (Annual is ISSN 0277-9692) 1980-

This source gives precise market and product data for the international area. The information coverage is similar to *F & S Index Europe* except the international version excludes the U.S. and Europe. SEE next Entry.

460. Predicasts, Inc. *Predicasts F & S Index. United States.* Cleveland: Predicasts, Inc. ISSN 0270-4544. LCCN sn80-1069. Monthly. 1980- Also on compact disc and online database.

This monthly with quarterly cumulations and an annual gives detailed coverage of business, industrial, product, financial, market, and company information for the U.S. It indexes over 750 publications. In the more recent editions, Vol. 1 (the green pages) has product and industry information arranged by the SIC code (Standard Industrial Classification Code). There is a Predicasts product code guide at the beginning to identify the SIC number. Vol. 2 (the white pages) lists articles by companies.

461. Predicasts, Inc. *PROMPT Predicasts Overview of Markets and Technology*. Cleveland: Predicasts, Inc. ISSN 0161-8032. LCCN 78-646645. Monthly. Also on compact disc and online database. SEE ALSO *DIALOG*, Entry 628.

This source includes international industry news, mergers, acquisition, production and sales, market information in the areas of food & agriculture, packaging & paper, polymers & polymer products, drugs & toiletries, chemicals, electronics, transportation, and energy. The industry news chapter gives a summary of industry news, effects of various legislation, and research and development in spending.

462. University Microfilm. *ABI/Inform Ondisc*. [compact disk]. Ann Arbor, MI: University Microfilm. ISSN 1062-5127. LCCN 92-644430. Monthly. 1986- ALSO *DIALOG* File 15 and BRS.

This computerized database (compact disk) indexes and abstracts over 800 North American, European, Asian, and Australian journals including information on companies, products, industry trends, marketing, management, telecommunications, economics, and finance.

463. H.W. Wilson Co. *Business Periodical Index*. New York: H.W. Wilson Co. ISSN 0007-6961. LCCN sn79-5237. Monthly.

This is an index with a monthly, quarterly and annual cumulations that deals with business, communication, computers, economics, finance, management, and marketing information. There is some overlap with *ABI/Inform*. It has book reviews and lists periodicals indexed at the beginning of each issues. It goes farther back in time than *ABI/Inform*.

464. H.W. Wilson Co. *Wilson Business Abstracts* [compact disk]. New York: H.W. Wilson Co. ISSN 1057-6533. LCCN 93660578. 1991-.

This is the computerized version of the *Business Periodical Index* with coverage from 1982. SEE ALSO above entry.

GOVERNMENT

465. Congressional Information Service, *American Foreign Policy Index*. Bethesda, MD: Congressional Information Service, 1994. Annual. LCCN 94033266.

This index identifies key foreign policy and related publications, describes the contents, indexes and abstracts the information and reproduces the information with an accompanying microfiche set with the full text of the publication identified in the index. It includes information on marketing, most-favored nation principle, trade agreement, industrial productivity, and Asian and European information.

466. Congressional Information Service. *American Statistics Index*. Washington, DC: Congressional Information Service. ISSN 0091-1658. LCCN 73-82599. 1973-

This monthly with annual cumulations indexes U.S. government publications by identifying the statistical data published by the federal agencies by providing comprehensive bibliographic information about the publications, and by announcing new publications, including over 5,000 book titles and 600 periodicals.

467. Congressional Information Service. *Index to International Statistics*. Bethesda, MD.: Congressional Information Service. ISBN 0886923192. Annual.

This is an index to statistical publications of intergovernmental organizations covering population, business, foreign trade, economic, and demographic characteristics.

468. Marcive, Inc, *MARCIVE GPO CAT/PAC*. [compact disk] San Antonio, TX: Marcive, Inc. ISSN 1064-9921. LCCN 92-644645. 1986-.

This computerized index covers government publications from 1976 to current. It is the *Monthly Catalog...* (see *Monthly Catalog of the United States Government Publication*) computerized. It is searchable by title, agency, subject, keyword, or SUDOC number. It is user friendly and versatile.

469. U.S. Government Printing Office. *Monthly Catalog of United States Government Publication*. (*MOCAT*) Washington, DC: U.S. Government Printing Office. ISSN 0362-6830. SUDOCS GP 3.8: Also available on *DIALOG* File 66 and Websites.

This is the most comprehensive index to government publications although there is no one index that covers all government information. Access is by title, subject, agency, serial, and keywords. The printed version is cumbersome and time consuming. SEE ALSO *MARCIVE GPO CAT/PAC*.

NEWSPAPER

470. Dow Jones & Co. *Wall St. Journal Index*. New York: Dow Jones & Co. ISSN 0099-9660. LCCN 76-641311. Daily.

The paper index is divided into two parts: (1) corporate news that is alphabetically arranged by company and (2) subject index. Also available online. SEE ALSO Entry 473.

471. Newsbank. *Business Newsbank*. [compact disk] New Canaan, CT: Newsbank. LCCN 94-26018. System requirements: IBM PC or compatible; 640K; 3.0 DOS or higher; 2MB hard drive; CD-ROM drive.

This compact disk contains company and industry news and provides access with full text from smaller newspapers such as: *The Oregonian, News-Times* (Danbury, CT), and *Akron Beacon Journal* (Akron, OH). It is useful for finding information on smaller companies that are not indexed elsewhere.

472. New York Times Co. *New York Times*. New York: The New York Times Co. ISSN 0147-538X. LCCN 13-13458. Daily.

This index provides coverage on news, editorial matter, special features in the daily and Sunday papers. Entries are by subject whenever possible with geographic names cross referenced to the subjects. (Monthly with annual cumulations) Index also available on a compact disk through University Microfilms, Ann Arbor, MI. SEE ALSO Entry 473.

473. University Microfilms International. *Newspaper Abstract Ondisc*.[compact disk] Ann Arbor, MI: University Microfilms International. ISSN 1064-993X LCCN 92-644642.

This is a computerized database that indexes the larger circulating newspapers such as: *New York Times, Wall St. Journal, Atlanta Constitution, Los Angeles Times, and Boston Globe.*

OTHER BASIC INDEXES

474. Congressional Information Service. *Statistical Reference Index*. Washington, DC: Congressional Information Service. ISSN 0885-6834. Monthly. 1980-.

This source is the counterpart to *American Statistics Index*. It covers statistics other than government publications with a subject index to authors, tables, groups of tables on data by states, industry, or by age. Some categories by foreign country include: agriculture and food, banking and finance, communications, energy resources and demand, and industry and commerce. It includes trade, state, and other commercially produced publications.

475. Public Affairs Information Service. *PAIS International in Print*. New York: Public Affairs Information Service, Inc. ISSN 0898-2201. LCCN sn86-21739. SEE ALSO *DIALOG* File 49.

This is a monthly with every fourth issue being cumulative. It indexes 1600 periodicals including: policy issues in economics, political science, public administration, international law, the environment and demography. (Also available on compact disk and online)

476. H.W. Wilson. *Applied Science and Technology Index*. New York: H.W. Wilson Co. ISSN 0003-6986. LCCN sn79-2989.

This is a cumulative index that is alphabetically arranged by subject covering: aeronautics and space science, chemistry, computers, construction, energy, research engineering, fire, oceanography, petroleum, gas, physics and plastics. It is also available on a compact disk through the H.W. Wilson Co.

477. H.W. Wilson. *Reader's Guide to Periodical Literature*. New York: H.W. Wilson Co. ISSN 0034-0464.

This is a cumulative subject and author index to English language periodicals, indexing about 200 periodicals on popular topics and general interest. This is also available on a compact disk and online (Wilsonline).

478. University Microfilms. *Periodical Abstracts Ondisc.*[compact disk] Ann Arbor, MI: University Microfilms. SEE ALSO *DIALOG* File 484.

This monthly began in 1986 and it indexes articles from over 1,000 journals covering both popular and research topics. It covers: business economics, communications, education, history, literature, religion, social sciences, and philosophy. The years included are 1986-current.

CHAPTER VI

PERIODICALS AND NEWSPAPERS

This chapter begins with periodical directories for information on subscription, indexing, description, and particular topics. Then it is divided into: regionally oriented periodicals such as the *Asia Week* or *Business China*; import/export and trade periodicals such as *Business America*; international; and newspapers such as the *Journal of Commerce and Commercial* which has trade leads and shipping schedules; financial newspapers and newspapers with broad international or regional coverage.

PERIODICAL DIRECTORIES

479. BiblioData. *Fulltext Sources Online*. Needham Heights, MA.: BiblioData. ISSN 1040-8258. LCCN 90-656152. Semiannual. 1989-

This is a handy source for people with computers because it lists periodicals, newspapers, and newsletters on topics of science, business, legal environment, health and industry that are available full text online. Timeliness of the vendors is also covered.

480. Bowker. *Ulrichs International Periodicals Directory*. Midland, GA: R.R. Bowker. ISSN 0000-0125 LCCN 32-16320. Biennial. Also available on compact disk and *DIALOG*.

This biennial lists periodicals for over 500 subject headings with frequency, price, and circulation data.

481. EBSCO. *Serials Directory: An International Reference Book*. Birmingham, AL: EBSCO. ISSN 0886-4179. LCCN 86-645169. Annual 1986-

This directory lists the name of the serial, price, address of publisher, telephone, and brief description of the publication, circulation, and where it is indexed.

482. Oxbridge Communications. *Standard Periodical Directory*. New York: Oxbridge Communications. ISSN 0085-6630. LCCN 64-7498. Annual. 1964-

This annual has a subject arrangement of periodicals published in the U.S. and Canada with title, address, frequency, subscription rates, circulation, name of publisher, advertising director, and description.

483. Standard Rate & Data Service. *Business Publication Advertising Source*. Oak Brook, IL: Standard Rate and Data Service. ISSN 0038-948X. Monthly. 1993-

This source lists periodicals from an advertiser's perspective. It includes: publisher, address, telex, personnel, and general rate for black and white and color advertising. It comes in three parts. Part III has international periodicals. Some other titles in this series are: *SRDS Consumer Magazine Advertising Source* (ISSN 1071-4537) and *Newspaper Advertising Source* (ISSN 1071-4529).

484. Wyckoff, Trip. *Directory of Business Periodical Special Issues*. Austin, TX: Reference Press, 1995. 162 p. ISBN 1878753605.

These are special issue periodicals that provide information such as the "Fortune 500 companies," rankings, and the best exporters. It includes: name of the periodical, where indexed, and brief content. Some specials are: the June *Canadian Business* has Canada's Corporate 500 and next 250; and *Euromoney's* January issue has the world's 100 best banks.

REGIONALLY ORIENTED PERIODICALS

Africa and the Middle East

485. IC Magazines. *African Business*. London: IC Magazines. ISSN 0141-3929. LC 80-649165. Monthly. 1978-

Business, economic development and planning, economic aid, corporate information, trends, industry, and country happenings for the

African countries are some areas covered in this journal.

486. Middle East Executive Reports. *Middle East Executive Reports*. Washington, DC: Middle East Executive Reports, Ltd. ISSN 0271-0498. LCCN 85-646003. Monthly. 1971-

This monthly keeps executives informed of business, industry, marketing, tax, and economic issues that affect companies in the Middle East Region. It updates them on political and economic policies.

487. South African Reserve Bank. *Quarterly Bulletin Kwartaalblad*. Pretoria, South Africa: South Africa Reserve Bank. ISSN 0038-2620. Quarterly. 1966-

This has economic information on South Africa which includes: statistical tables on the South African Reserve Bank: liabilities and assets, money market and related interest rates, capital market and related interest rates and government finance. Text in Afrikaans and English.

Asia

488. American Chamber of Commerce, Japan. *The Journal of the American Chamber of Commerce in Japan*: ACCJ. Tokyo: ACCJ. ISSN 0002-7848. LCCN sn90021069. 11 issues/year. 1964-

Issues in bilateral relations between the United States and Japan are included with information on business, trade, the economy, trends, and industry. "Legal briefs" is a section that discusses changes in US tax laws and other legal areas.

489. Asiaweek. *Asiaweek*. Hong Kong: Asiaweek Ltd. ISSN 0224-95360. LCCN 77648713. Weekly. 1975- It is also available on a web site.

Asiaweek covers Asia's economic, social, political, and business issues. "Vital signs" has numbers on people per telephone, population growth, infant mortality, literacy rate, and people per doctor. The "Good Earth" has prices for rice, maize, wheat, oil, propane, platinum, zinc, sugar etc. It also lists exchange rates for about 34 currencies. The special issue called "Asia 1000" covers the larger Asian companies.

490. Business International. *Business Asia*. Hong Kong: Business International Asia/Pacific Ltd. An Economist Intelligence Unit Publication. ISSN 0572-7545. LCCN sn87-18955. Weekly. 1970-

It looks at trends, corporate strategy, business outlook, executive watchlist, and regulations that affect business in Asia.

491. Business International. *Business China*. Hong Kong: Business International. LCCN sn84-11058. 1979-

This is a weekly update for managers covering topics on trends, marketing information, corporate profiles, currency, taxation, industry, corporate strategy in China.

492. China Books and Periodicals. *Beijing Review=Pei-ching chou pao*. San Francisco: China Books and Periodicals. ISSN 1000-9140. LCCN 79-646655. Weekly. 1979-

This weekly analyzes events and trends in China which include: highlights of the business week, trade, culture and sciences, society and people, and trade perspectives.

493. Chonguk Kyongjein Yonhaphoe. *Korean Business Review*. Seoul, Korea: Federation of Korean Industries. ISSN 0585-89860. LCCN sn8602229. Monthly 1984-

Economic trends, forecasts, business prospects, major economic indicators, money supply, CPI, wholesale price, import/export price, and major Korean companies profiles are the subjects covered by this monthly.

494. Euromoney Publications. *AsiaMoney*. London: Euromoney Publications. ISSN 0958-9309. LCCN sn93-020378. 10/year. 1993-

This periodical includes topics on: money matters, the banking and financial services industry, investments, emerging capital markets, and stock markets in the Asia and Pacific Region.

495. Far East Trade Press. *Asian Business*. Hong Kong: Far East Trade Press. ISSN 0254-3729. LCCN 80-645868. Monthly. 1979-

This periodical looks at market conditions, trends, investments, products, emerging markets, entrepreneurship, and social change in Asia.

496. Fuji Ginko. *Fuji Economic Review*. Tokyo: Fuji Research Institute, International Research Division. ISSN 0916-1937. LCCN 89-649273. Bimonthly. 1988-

This periodical has economic indicators with tables on GDP, production, inventory, prices, employment, wholesale prices, consumer prices, nominal wage index, number of unemployed, foreign trade, balance of payments, and interest rates for Japan.

497. National Council for U.S. *China Business Review*. Washington, DC: National Council for US. ISSN 0163-7169. LCCN 77-641609. Bimonthly. 1977-

This bimonthly has business and economic information on China and Hong Kong including business climate, press reports of contracts, negotiations, and trends.

498. Nihon Ginkeo Teokeikyoku. Research and Statistics Dept. *Keizai Teokei Geppo: Economics Statistics Monthly*. Tokyo: Nihon Ginkeo Teokeikyoku. Research and Statistics Dept., the Bank of Japan. LCCN 79-649020. Monthly. 1979-

This monthly covers Japanese currency in circulation, money supply, changes in money supply, personal savings, flow of funds, exports and imports by country, exports and imports by commodity, and indexes of foreign trade, gold, and foreign exchange reserve.

499. Nihon Kogyo Shimbum. *Business Japan*. Tokyo: Nihon Kogyo Shimbun. ISSN 0300-4341. LCCN 73-643236. Monthly. 1971-

This periodical takes the pulse of the Japanese industry by monitoring business trends, international finance, and economic conditions.

500. Nihon Kogyo Shimbun. *Japan 21st*. Tokyo: Nihon Kogyo Shimbun. ISSN 0916-877X. LCCN 92-659599. Monthly. 1992-

Industry data and news, economic growth, company information, country development, and corporate planning are some areas included.

501. Review Publishing Co. *Far Eastern Economic Review*. Hong Kong: Review Publishing Co. ISSN 0014-7591. LCCN 51033412. Weekly. 1946-

This periodical reports on economic, financial, stock market information, and trends from Afghanistan to Vietnam. Some regular sections are: reports on market indicators, prices of commodities, currencies, and countries. The annual to this is *Asia Yearbook*.

502. Sameeksha Trust. *Economic and Political Weekly*. Bombay: Sameeksha Trust. ISSN 0012-9976. LCCN 67002009. Weekly. 1966-

This weekly covers economic and political events in India with current statistics on macroeconomic indicators such as: commodities, fuel, manufactured products, cost of living index, money supply, foreign trade, exports, and imports.

503. Toyo Keizai Shinposha. *Tokyo Business Today*. Tokyo: Toyo Keizai Shinposha. ISSN 0911-7008. LCCN 86-647918. Monthly. 1986-

This journal contains information on business, economics, finance, industry outlook, policy, stocks, and corporations for the Asia region from a Japanese perspective.

504. University of Michigan. *Journal of Asian Business*. Ann Arbor, MI: Southeast Asia Business Program. University of Michigan. ISSN 1068-0055. LCCN 93-641551. Quarterly. 1993-

Trends, economic development, economic policy, emerging markets, entrepreneurship, and international relations are some of the topics covered by this periodical.

Europe

505. Business International. *Business Eastern Europe*. Geneva: Business International, SA. ISSN 1351-8763. LCCN sn83-12188. Weekly. 1976-

This weekly summarizes business news, markets, legal watch, and what's new in the automotive, aviation, consumer goods industry, finance opportunities, business travel, environmental issues, company case study, and legal and tax updates for business managers of East European operations. Some country coverage include: Bulgaria, CIS/Russia, Turkmenistan, Czech Republic, Hungary, Lithuania, and Slovakia.

506. Business International. *Business Europe*. Geneva: Business International, SA. ISSN 0007-6724. LCCN sf 93-94849. Weekly. 1960-

This publication informs European, Middle Eastern, and African managers of events by surveying: business outlook, critical issues and problems, alerts and updates, environmental issues, business mood, research and development, trade policy, taxation, and financial markets.

507. Commission of the European Communities. *European Economy*. Luxembourg: Office for Official Publications of the European Communities. ISSN 0379-0991. LCCN 82-642524 Quarterly. 1978-

The journal includes the reports and communications from the European Commission to the Council and Parliament on the economic situation, borrowing and lending activities, and economic policy problems including: one market, one economy; the impact of the international market by industrial sector, the challenge for member states, and the path of reform in Central and Eastern Europe. Two supplements accompany the periodical: Series A covers economic trends and Series B covers business and consumer survey results.

508. The Economist Intelligence Unit. *European Trends*. London: The Economist Intelligence Unit. ISSN 0014-3162. Quarterly. 1964-

This updates the directives that have been incorporated by the member states into National Law. It indicates the progress of the European community's movement to a single market.

509. The Economist Intelligence Unit. *Marketing in Europe*. London: Economist Intelligence Unit. ISSN 0025-3723. Monthly. 1962-

This monthly provides information on: (1) EC member states covering area, population, GDP, consumer prices, and rates of exchange (2) trade reviews for about 30 products and product sectors and (3) market surveys analyzing the current structures and characteristics of national markets for specific consumer products, production, exports, imports, and trends. Products reviews include: food, drink, tobacco; clothing, furniture.

510. The Economist Intelligence Unit. *Retail Business: Retail Trade Reviews*. London: The Economist Intelligence Unit. LCCN sn 87044734. Quarterly. 1987-

This British periodical has statistical analyses and forecasts for individual retail trade sectors. Each sector is reviewed once a year, and there is an annual review of the United Kingdom retail business. Some areas covered are: grocery retailers, cooperative societies, specialist food shops, and company profiles.

511. The Economist Newspaper. *Economist*. London: The Economist Newspaper. ISSN 0013-0613. LCCN 08017464. Weekly. 1843-

This periodical provides business, economic, financial, social, and political news from a British perspective. Data on output, demand and jobs, prices and wages, office rents, and commodity price index, trade exchange rates and reserves for twelve OECD countries. (Also on DIALOG File 648 - full text).

512. Euromoney Publications. *Euromoney*. London: Euromoney Publications. ISSN 0014-2433. LCCN 76010311. Monthly. 1969-

This monthly looks at world events, EC regulations, currencies, the banking industry, and business news from a monetary perspective. It reports on foreign exchange rates, and global banking and their effects on countries. It has issues on: country risk rankings and world equity markets.

513. European Scientific Association of Applied Economics. *European Economic Review*. Amsterdam: North Holland Publishing. ISSN 0014-0991. LCCN 74010994. Quarterly. 1969-

This scholarly quarterly is written by academics from Europe, the U.S. and Canada. Recent issues cover a variety of topics such as: exporting, risk sharing on the labor market, value added taxation in the EC after 1992, government policy and the firms capital structure. It also has papers and proceedings of the European Economic Association.

514. Faulkner & Gray Inc. *Journal of European Business*. New York: Faulkner & Gray Inc. ISSN 1044-002x. LCCN 89656389. Bimonthly. 1989-

This bimonthly includes marketing topics, latest updates on EC directives, member state reports, Eastern Europe news, tax watch, and statistics on European industrial production, unemployment, inflation, and monthly European currency rates.

515. MCB. *European Journal of Marketing*. Bradford, Eng.:MCB. ISSN 0309-566. LCCN 83640837. 10/year. 1975-

This scholarly journal examines various aspects of marketing such as finance, advertising, government policy, strategy and planning, product, and consumer voice, and international marketing ethics.

516. Organisation for Economic Cooperation and Development. *OECD OBSERVER*. Paris: Organisation for Economic Cooperation and Development. ISSN 0029-7054. LCCN 66098609. Annual.

Industry, trade, international relations, the environment, energy, education and economies in transition are some subjects covered by this periodical. It has a check list of indicators including GDP, inflation rate, and unemployment rate. It also has short term economic indicators for five transition countries in Central and Eastern Europe covering industrial production, construction, employment, earnings prices, domestic and foreign finance, and trade. Also it includes the OECD economic outlook.

The Caribbean and Latin America

517. American Chamber of Commerce. *Business Mexico*. Mexico City: American Chamber of Commerce. ISSN 0007-6880. LCCN sc84005016. Quarterly. 1983-

This publication's aim is to promote trade between the U.S. and Mexico and has articles on events, agreements, environmental issues that affect business and investment. The "business Mexico indicators" page has data on capital investment, construction, machinery and equipment, production of automobiles, trucks, crude oil, foreign trade, monetary, inflation and interest rates.

518. The Bank. *The IDB: Monthly News from the Inter-American Development Bank*. Washington, DC: The Bank, 1987. LCCN 89659251. 10 issues/year. 1987-

This short news letter reports on economic and social development trends in Latin America and the Caribbean. It includes the activities of the Inter-American Development Bank, foreign investment and a listing of loans in some issues by country, amount of loan, and purpose of loan.

519. Business International. *Business Latin America*. New York: Business International Corporation. ISSN 0007-6800. LCCN sn85-20778. Weekly.

This weekly for managers examines business outlook, foreign investment, regulations, comparative corporate tax rates, management alerts, trends, and a green watch.

520. Freedom Communications Inc. *U.S./Latin Trade: the Magazine of Trade and Investment in the Americas*. Miami: Freedom Communications. ISSN 1086-198X. Monthly. 1993-

This periodical includes news of the region, industry, trade calendar, commodities, trade and investment coverage in the Americas, emerging markets, and graphs on inflation, reserves and dollar value of imports and exports.

521. Latin Research Group. *The Latin American Index*. Washington, DC: Latin Research Group. ISSN 0090-9416. LCCN 73-642942. Biweekly 1973-

This brief (usually about 4 pages) Latin American newsletter covers political and economic events of Latin America and the Caribbean countries. Information includes: marketing, trade, investment, human rights, reform, World Bank and tourism issues.

522. Government Development Bank for Puerto Rico. *Puerto Rico Business Review.* New York: Government Development Bank for Puerto Rico. ISSN 0491-50860. LCCN 80643717. Monthly. 1976-

Puerto Rican business and economic trends are covered in this review with statistics on hotel registration, hotel accommodations, occupancy rate, average rate in tourist hotels and economic indicators such as construction, external trade, transportation and cargo, commercial banking and government revenues.

NORTH AMERICA

Canada

523. The Canadian Chamber of Commerce. *Canadian Business.* Montreal: The Canadian Chamber of Commerce. ISSN 0008-3100. LCCN 40038115. Monthly. 2933-

This Canadian monthly looks at business topics such as: manufacturing, management, economy, public policy, technology, international events that affect business, CEO surveys, book reviews, politics, and Canada's 500 largest companies (special issue).

524. Conference Board in Canada. *Canadian Business Review.* Ottawa: Conference Board in Canada. ISSN 0317-4026. LCCN 74645468. Quarterly. 1974-

This review covers information on business, economic conditions, companies, industry, and trends with emphasis on Canadian concerns.

United States

Business Basics

525. Advertising Publications, Inc. *Advertising Age*. Chicago, IL.: Crain Communications. Weekly. ISSN 0001-8899. LCCN 42-47059. Weekly.

This U.S. weekly is an advertising basic with information on companies, trends, rankings (who's the biggest by categories and how much is spent in advertising) and which agencies are involved.

526. Harvard University. Graduate School of Business. *Harvard Business Review*. Boston, MA: Harvard University. Graduate School of Business. ISSN 0017-8012. LCCN 25010769. Bimonthly. 1922-

This review covers articles in the area of business and management with findings on: organizations, effective management techniques, and changes and trends in management and business.

527. McGraw-Hill. *Business Week*. New York: McGraw-Hill. ISSN 0007-7135. LCCN 31006225. Weekly. 1929-

This is business from a U.S. perspective with information on corporations, economic analysis, marketing, finance, and information processing. It features the business index that has data on production indicators, foreign exchange, price, leading indicators and money market rates. Special issues such as the "The Top 1000, Corporate Scoreboard, and Rankings" rate firms according to various criteria.

528. Forbes, Inc. *Forbes*. New York: Forbes, Inc. ISSN 0015-6914. LCCN sc76000149. Weekly. 1917-

The standard coverage looks at: companies, industries, executive compensation, international business, law and legal issues, marketing, computers, money and investing. The Forbes index measures the health of the economy by the cost of service, consumer price index, manufacturer's inventories, industrial production, new housing starts, personal income, new unemployment claims, retail sales, and consumer installment credit.

529. Time. *Fortune*. New York: Time, Inc. ISSN 0015-8259. LCCN 31007716. Monthly. 1930-

This weekly classic covers U.S. management issues, competition, politics and policy, autos, innovation, money and markets, news and trends, corporate performance, executive life, book review, personal investment, and entrepreneurs. There are many special issues with rankings of companies and people, called "Fortune 500" etc.

Economic and Business Indicators

530. United States. Board of Governors of the Federal Reserve System. *Federal Reserve Bulletin.* Washington, DC: Board of Governors of the Federal Reserve System. ISSN 0014-9209. LCCN 15026318. Monthly.

For those who are looking for banking and finance industry information, this monthly has legal developments, financial and business statistics, policy concerns, interest rates, trends, weekly reports of U.S. branches and agencies of foreign banks, and industrial production.

531. United States. Board of Governors of the Federal Reserve System. *Industrial Production and Capacity Utilization.* Washington, DC: Board of Governors of the Federal Reserve System. LCCN sn 91026141. Monthly. 1990-

This monthly is packed with data on industrial production, capacity utilization, and graphs on industrial producing indexes including total industry, manufacturing, materials, products, and durable manufacturing. There are tables on industrial production, market groups covering consumer goods, equipment, defense and space equipment, industry groups, manufacturing, and mining.

SEE United States. Bureau of Labor Statistics. *Compensation and Working Conditions: CWC.*

532. United States. Bureau of Labor Statistics. *CPI Detailed Report.* Washington, DC: U.S. Government Printing Office. ISSN 0095-926X. LCCN 75641423. SUDOCS L 2.38/3: Monthly. 1974-

U.S. Consumer price index for all urban consumers (CPI-U) and consumer price index for urban earners and clerical workers (CPI-W) by expenditure category and commodity service group such as food, housing, fuel etc. are the data included in this journal.

533. United States. Bureau of Labor Statistics. *Employment and Earnings.* Washington, DC: U.S. Government Printing Office. ISSN 0013-6840. LCCN 83645868. SUDOCS L 2.41/2. Monthly. SUDOCS L 2.41/2: 1954-

Monthly statistics on employment, earnings, and unemployment with establishment data by industry sector (mining, construction, manufacturing, durable goods), productivity data, characteristics of the employed and unemployed, employment by national, state and area for the U.S. are included in this publication. The companion volume is the *Employment and Earnings.* Annual. SUDOC L 2.41/2-2:

534. United States. Bureau of Labor Statistics. *MLR Monthly Labor Review.* Washington, DC: U.S. Government Printing Office. ISSN 00098-1818. LCCN 15026485. SUDOCS L 2.6: Monthly. 1915-

This monthly includes: labor trends, major agreements expiring next month, industry output, and statistics on employment and earnings, unemployment, population, labor compensation, collective bargaining data, consumer price index, productivity statistics, international comparisons of employment and unemployment, and annual indexes of productivity and related measures for about 12 countries.

535. U.S. Congress. Joint Economic Committee. *Economic Indicators*. Washington, DC: U.S. Government Printing Office. ISSN 0013-0125. LCCN 29011002. SUDOCS Y4.EC7:EC7/ Monthly. 1948-

This monthly covers basic economic indicators such as: total output, income, spending, gross domestic product, imports, exports, net exports, employment, unemployment, corporate profits, wage, hourly earnings, production, and business activity.

536. U.S. Dept. of Commerce, Bureau of Economic Analysis. *Survey of Current Business*. Washington, DC: U.S. Government Printing Office. ISSN 0039-6222. LCCN 21026819. SUDOCS C 59.11: Monthly.

This monthly is a compilation that includes: national income and product account, corporate profits by industry, personal savings rate, international comparison of industrial production indexes, consumer price indexes, stock prices, and exchange rate, capital expenditures by majority-owned foreign affiliates of U.S. companies.

537. U.S. Dept. of Commerce, Bureau of the Census. *County Business Patterns. Washington,* DC: U.S. Government Printing Office. SUDOCS C 3.204: (also on a compact disk) 1946-

This is an annual series for each state, a U.S. summary, District of Columbia and Puerto Rico giving the number of establishments, employees, and payroll by major industry group for each county.

538. U.S. Dept. of Commerce. Bureau of the Census. *Quarterly Financial Report for Manufacturing, Mining and Trade Corporations*. Washington, DC: U.S. Government Printing Office. ISSN 0098-681X. LCCN 75644219. SUDOCS C 3.267: 1975-

Statistics on the positions of U.S. corporations based on sample surveys include: estimated statements of income and retained earnings, balance sheets, and related financial and operating ratios for all manufacturing, mining and trade corporations.

539. U.S. Dept. of Labor. *Producer Price Indexes*. LCCN 85644268. SUDOCS L 2.61: Monthly. 1985-

This monthly is the counterpart to the consumer price index and includes producer price indexes (PPI) and percent changes by stage of processing, PPI and percent changes for selected commodity groupings by stage of processing, PPI for the net output of major industry groups by durability of product and new commodity price indexes based on the movement of corresponding industry-based product price indexes.

540. U.S. Dept. of Commerce. International Trade Commission. *International Economic Review*. Washington, DC: Office of Economics. U.S. Trade Commission. SUDOCS ITC 1.29: Monthly. 1987-

The purpose of the U.S. International Trade Commission is to provide technical information and advice on international trade matters to Congressional policy makers and the executive branch. This document includes international economic comparisons with tables on annual productivity, output changes, and related measures in business, non-farm business, and manufacturing. It includes international trade developments and some forecasts.

541. U.S. Dept. of Treasury. *Treasury Bulletin*. ISSN 0041-2155. LCCN sn85021533. Quarterly. 1983- Available on web site.

This quarterly provides data on the U.S. Treasury's cash and debt operation of the federal government. The financial operation includes the profile of the economy, federal fiscal operations, federal obligations and federal debt. The capital movements section looks at total liabilities by type of holder, total liabilities by type payable in dollars, total liabilities by country and total liabilities by type and country. Also on the U.S. Dept. of Commerce. *Economic Bulletin Board*.

IMPORT/EXPORT AND TRADE PERIODICALS

542. International Trade Center. *International Trade Forum*. Geneva, Switzerland: International Trade Center UNCTAG/GATT. ISSN 0020-8957. LCCN sf 82006007. Quarterly. 1964-

This is a quarterly that focuses on export, marketing, trade promotions and techniques, import methods, market outlook and trends for specific products. It includes a listing of its publications, news on exporting topics such as: export round up, foreign capital watch, matchmakers (listing of distributors for specific products with names and addresses, production, finance, transportation, customs, and export information on specific geographical area, trade events, and taxes.)

543. North American Publishing. *Global Trade and Transportation*. Philadelphia, PA: North America Publishing. ISSN 1069-2843 LCCN sn 93650350. Monthly. 1993-

This views business and world events as they affect shippers with information on customs clearance, transport, finance, NAFTA, shipping information, regulations alert and shippers profile. Some topics in previous issues include a guide to refrigerated cargo carriers. This has a monthly update to the *U.S. Customs House Guide & Official Export* which has regulations for importers/exporters.

544. Trade Communications Inc. *Export Today*. Washington, DC: Trade Communications Inc. ISSN 0882-4711. Monthly.

This exporting periodical is similar to *Business America*. (This has its own entry.) It includes information on: trade, funding for corporations, country marketing information, transport, matchmaker information and banking.

545. Trade Data Reports. *The Exporter*. New York: Trade Data Reports. ISSN 0736-9239. Monthly. 1980-

This periodical has information for exporters covering marketing, operations, distribution, logistics, finance, legal and regulatory issues.

546. U.S. Dept. of Commerce. International Trade Administration. *Business America: The Magazine of International Trade* Washington, DC: U.S. GPO. ISSN 0190-6275. LCCN 79640406. SUDOCS C 61.18: Biweekly. 1978- Also available on *NTDB*.

The aim is to help American exporters penetrate overseas markets by providing them with current and timely information on trade opportunities, market news, methods and cultural information. It includes: calendars for world trader, international trade exhibits, and new books and reports. (This is also included in *National Trade Data Bank.)*

547. World Trade. *World Trade*. Irvine, CA: World Trade. ISSN 1054-8637. LCCN 91-660008. Monthly. 1988-

This trade journal has articles on: trends in the industry, marketing tips, country profiles, "doing business in ...(country)," movers and shakers of world trade, manufacturing, and trade barriers. Special January issue has year's best foreign markets.

INTERNATIONAL

548. Business International. *Business International.* New York: Business International. ISSN 0007-6872. LCCN 64001908. Weekly. 1954-

This is a weekly for international managers with news on marketing, corporate culture, environmental practices and problems, and prospects for profits. It covers different countries with political climate, economic prospects, investment outlook and currency forecasts.

549. Economist Intelligence Unit. *Business International Money Report.* New York: Business, Economist Intelligence Unit. ISSN 0161-0384. LCCN 78642271. Weekly. 1975-

This is a weekly intended for international executives with news on monthly foreign exchange tables, country currency forecasts, country interest rate forecast, country economic outlook (GDP), inflation, current accounts, trade balance, financial hotline on currencies and interest rates, and monthly rate table of major currencies.

550. Economist Intelligence United. *Crossborder Monitor*. New York: Economist Intelligence Unit. ISSN 1070-5961. LCCN sn 93043189. Weekly. 1993-

This weekly keeps international executives informed about business, economics, and trade issues covering the world in brief, the Americas, Western Europe, Eastern Europe, Asia and the Pacific, Africa and the Middle East. It gives specific forecasts such as: Hungary Forecast 1994-1998 with GDP growth, CPI, current accounts, GNP, and population.

551. Economist Intelligence Unit. *Multinational Business*. London: Economist Intelligence Unit. ISSN 0300-3922. LCCN 72622279. Quarterly. 1971-

This periodical looks at events that affect multinational corporations such as acquisitions and mergers, currency updates, management perspectives, legal aspects, workforce, and political and economic changes.

552. Federal Reserve Bank of St. Louis. *International Economic Trends*. St. Louis, MO: Federal Reserve Bank of St. Louis. Quarterly. 1995-

This publication includes foreign economic data, U.S. trade, money aggregates, real gross domestic product, consumer prices, and monetary growth rates for the G-7 countries which include: the U.S., Canada, Japan, France, Germany, Italy and the United Kingdom.

553. Graduate School of Business. Columbia University. *Columbia Journal of World Business*. New York: Graduate School of Business, Columbia University. ISSN 0022-5428.

This journal publishes studies and opinions on international business in the following areas: economics, finance, political science and management.

554. International Business. *Journal of Global Marketing*. New York: Haworth Press. ISSN 0891-1762. LCCN 87655798. Quarterly. 1987-

This scholarly journal treats marketing issues from a global perspective with theoretical, conceptual, and empirical articles covering topics as: global strategic marketing planning, comparative market systems, cross national/cultural decision making and consumer purchasing and selection behavior across cultural nations.

555. International Monetary Fund. *IMF Survey*. Washington, DC: International Monetary Fund. ISSN 0047-083x. LCCN 72626146. Semimonthly. 1972-

The purpose of the International Monetary Fund is to promote international monetary cooperation; to facilitate the expansion and balanced growth of trade, to promote exchange rate stability, and assist in the establishment of a multilateral system of payments. This is its newsletter with information on its progress.

556. John Wiley & Sons. *International Executive*. New York: John Wiley & Sons. ISSN 0020-6652. LCCN 63052025. 3 times/year. 1963-

This scholarly journal covers topics of interest to global managers on government, cultural differences for marketers, the role of the various international organizations, trade agreements, and analysis of events that affect business.

557. MCB University Press. *International Marketing Review*. West Yorkshire, England: MCB University Press. ISSN 0265-1335. LCCN sn8412269. Quarterly. 1983-

This scholarly journal examines aspects of international marketing. Some past titles are: consumer profiles and perceptions, market concentration versus market diversification and internationalization, impact of host country market characteristics on the choice of foreign entry mode, exporting as an innovative behavior, and sales training practice: a cross national comparison.

558. United Nations. Centre on Transnational Corporations. *Transnational Corporations*. New York: United Nations. Centre on Transnational Corporations. ISSN 1014-9562. LC 92645953. Triennial.

Transnational corporations are changing the world and this refereed journal discusses the effects of these corporations in the area of business, economics, finance, politics, government policy and law.

NEWSPAPERS

559. Barron's. *Barron's National Business and Finance Weekly*. Chicopee, MA: Dow Jones & Co. ISSN 0005-6073. LCCN 23018506. Weekly. 1942-

This weekly covers financial, investment, and business topics. It includes: round table discussions with expert economists, investment news and views, recommendations to buy or sell certain stocks, global stock market reports with percent change, 52 week range in local currencies and U.S. dollars, and reviews of the Dow industrials and Dow world index.

560. Dow Jones & Company. *Asian Wall Street Journal*. New York: Dow Jones & Company, Inc. ISSN 0377-9920 LCCN sn78006295. Weekly. 1976-

This Asian equivalent of the *Wall Street Journal* covers

Asian/Pacific and London stock transactions as well as the New York Stock Exchange, American Stock Exchange, and over the counter.

561. Dow Jones & Co., Inc. *Wall Street Journal.* Chicago: Dow Jones & Co., Inc. ISSN 0163-089X LCCN sn79004570. Daily. 1951-

This is an authoritative daily with comprehensive coverage on business, the economy, commodities, money rates, daily stock market prices on the NY stock exchange, American stock exchange, over the counter, and foreign exchange rate. The first page has a world wide business and finance summary.

562. Financial Post. *Financial Post.* Toronto: Financial Post. ISSN 0838-8431. LCCN cn88-31057. Daily. 1923-

This Canadian daily includes information on Canadian business, finance, investment, stock market wrap-up, mortgage rates, market highlights, current quotes, corporate information, weekly banking statistics for the Bank of Canada, housing starts, CPI, industrial product price index, and Canadian Stock Exchange.

563. F. T. Times. *Financial Times.* New York: F. T. Times. ISSN 0884-6782. LCCN sn 85006603. Daily. 1985- Also available on *DIALOG.*

This is the British equivalent of the *Wall Street Journal*. It has worldwide coverage of business events, company information, and the stock exchange. There are several editions to this journal.

564. Investor's Business. *Investor's Business Daily.* Los Angeles, CA: Investor's Business. ISSN 1061-2890 LCCN sn 91-17844. Daily. 1991-

This newspaper covers world events from an investor's view. There is stock coverage, industry prices, charts, and graphs on general market indicators which include: S & P 500 Index, Dow Jones

Industrial, Consumer Index, Dow Jones Transportation, and High Technology Index. (similar to *Wall Street Journal*).

565. Journal of Commerce Inc. *Journal of Commerce and Commercial.* New York: ISSN 0361-5561. LCCN sn 78004930. Daily. 1978- (Also available on *DIALOG*).

This newspaper publishes export opportunities, agricultural trade leads, trade list exhibits, shipping schedules, futures trading/open interest and sales, spot chemicals (prices of chemicals) trends, and government regulations affecting the industry.

566. New York Times Co. *New York Times*. New York: New York Times Co. ISSN 0362-4331 LCCN sn78004456. Daily. 1857- Also available on *DIALOG.*

This is an American daily with the most complete international coverage of economic, political, and social events.

567. Nihon Keizai Shimbum, Inc. *Nikkei Weekly*. Tokyo: Nihon Keizai Shimbum, Inc. Weekly. LCCN 91-26020. 1991-

This is a financial weekly with news on the Tokyo Stock Exchange, weekly closings, news on Asia & Pacific in brief, summaries on politics and society, market outlook, and the economy.

CHAPTER VII

STATISTICS

This chapter covers social, economic, financial, and demographic data for regions. It begins with guides for understanding the statistics. Then it categorizes statistical sources by region, investment, and trade. Under region, the data cover areas such as: Asia, Europe, Latin America, and international. There are some statistical sources that cover the world or use the term "international," therefore, the use of "international" for this area. An example is: *International Financial Statistics*.

Under investment, there is statistical information for foreign investments. Under trade, there are data for trade trends and trade issues.

For country specific statistics, consult Chapter IV and the *National Trade Data Bank*.

GUIDES

568. Bailey, Victor B. and Sara R. Bowden. *Understanding United States Foreign Trade Data*. Washington, DC: U.S. International Trade Administration. 1985. 189 p. SUDOCS C 61.2:F 76/5

This source provides background information on foreign trade including: definition, changes of U.S. foreign trade data systems, the role of international organizations in standardizing and improving the comparisons of foreign trade data, and the evolution of the U.S. Trade Data Classification System to meet the needs of international data comparison. Tariff Schedules of the United States or TSUSA for imports and Schedule B for exports and SITC are covered. This source doesn't cover the Harmonized Commodity and Coding Classification System which the U.S. has used since January 1, 1989. SEE ALSO *Guide to Foreign Trade Statistics*.

569. Barbuto, Domenica M. *The International Statistics Locator: A Research and Information Guide.* New York: Garland, 1995. 338 p. ISBN 0815314833. LCCN 9401999.

This locator provides access to statistical resources with a description of the twenty-two sources. It is arranged alphabetically by country.

570. Economist Books. *The Economist Guide to Global Economic Indicators: The Economist Books, Ltd.* New York: John Wiley & Sons, 1994. 216 p. ISBN 0471305537. LCCN 93-013996.

This guide explains over 100 important global economic indicators such as: definition, coverage, significance, source, publisher, reliability, revisions and interpretations. Tables include: world output and trade, the period for comparison, and comparative inflation rate, 1960-90. It ranks government statistical agencies for 10 industrialized countries by statisticians. Also it has a listing of useful national statistical publications.

571. Johnson, David B. *Finding and Using Economic Information: A Guide to Sources and Interpretation.* Mountain View, CA: Mayfield Pub. Co, 1993. 512 p. ISBN 1559341009. LCCN 91036786.

This is a guide to understanding economic statistics with an explanation about the data series, the construction, overview, and analysis of data, and sources for the data. Chapter 17 covers international trade and finance. The appendix has the release date of some important data series.

572. Organisation for Economic Co-operation and Development. Statistics Directorate. *Sources and Methods: Consumer Price Indices=Sources et Methodes: Indices des Prix e la Consommation.* Paris: OECD, 1994. 86 p. LCCN 9264041133.

This special issue of *Main Economic Indicators* provides a description of member OECD country consumer price indices with basic concepts underlining the consumer price indices, selection of reference population, the determination of its consumption expenditure structure, and the choice basket of goods and services, and the organization of price observation. (Text in English and French)

573. U.S. Bureau of the Census. *Guide to Foreign Trade Statistics*. Washington, DC: U.S. Government Printing Office. 1992. LCCN 74642459. SUDOCS C 3.6/2:F 76/992

This guide explains foreign trade statistics from data filed with the U.S. Customs service; export and imports filed with the Census Bureau; and exports to Canada from Canadian import data. The most significant change in collecting foreign trade data occurred in January 1989, when the U.S. adopted the Harmonized Commodity Description and Coding System. This source includes: description of the foreign trade statistical program, U.S. merchandise trade, special reports and services, printed reports, foreign trade products on CD-ROM, conversion table, and reference and order forms.

REGIONALLY ORIENTED STATISTICS

Asia

574. Economic and Development Resource Center. Asian Development Bank. *Key Indicators of Developing Asian and Pacific Countries*. Manila, Philippines: The Bank. ISSN 0116-3000. LCCN 91-656125. Annual. 1990-

Current statistics and key indicators of developing Asian and Pacific Countries are included in this publication. Part I compares the performance of the region to industrialized countries and the world. Part II looks at member countries in the areas of: population, adult literacy rates, TV receivers, age distribution, infant mortality, per capita energy consumption, total and per capita GDP. Part III has country tables with data on labor force, national accounts, production, energy, price indexes, money, banking, external trade and exports by SITC and by principal commodity. Countries include Afghanistan to Western Samoa. New coverage includes: Viet Nam and Mongolia. (This description is for a 1992 issue.)

575. United Nations. Economic and Social Commission for Asia and the Pacific. *Economic and Social Survey of Asia and the Pacific 1993*. Bangkok: United Nations. ISSN 0252-4704. LCCN 76643956. 1974-

This source analyzes global, economic and social development in the Asia/Pacific area and compares them to the world economy. Some topics are: macroeconomic performance, summary of this developing region, developments in agriculture, industry, external trade, finance, and initial conditions of growth and structural transformation. ESCAP regions include: Afghanistan, Australia, Bangladesh, Bhutan, Brunei, Darussalam and China.

576. United Nations. Economic and Social Commission for Asia and the Pacific. *Statistical Yearbook for Asia and the Pacific. Annuaire Statistique pour l'Asie et le Pacifique*. Bangkok: Economic and Social Commission for Asia and the Pacific. ISSN 0252-3655. LCCN 76641968. 1973- Annual.

This statistical yearbook provides population, national accounts, agriculture, forestry, fishing, industry, external trade, finance and social statistics for countries such as: Afghanistan, Australia, Bangladesh, Bhutan, China, and for Micronesia. Also values of imports and exports by SITC chapter, transport and communications, and number of tourists are other data listed in this yearbook.

577. United Nations. Industrial Development Organization. Industrial Statistics and Sectoral Surveys Branch. *ASEAN Industry in Figures*. New York: United Nations Industrial Development Organization, 1993. 99p.

This publication provides indicators of the remarkable growth and structural changes of ASEAN countries which include: Brunei, Darussalam, Indonesia, Malaysia, the Philippines, Singapore and Thailand.

It has international comparisons with tables on: distribution of GDP by sector of origin; annual growth of GDP, total and by sector of activity; GDP per capita, manufacturing value added (MVA) per capita and their growth; share of industry groups in total MVA; structure of MVA; per capita trade in goods and services and its growth; Part II has country indicators for ASEAN countries with tables on distribution of GDP by sector of origin; indices of relative specialization in manufacturing ASEAN countries, etc.

Europe

Eastern Europe and Commonwealth of Independent States

578. Karasik, Theodore, W., ed. *USSR Facts & Figures Annual*. Gulf Breeze, FL: Academic Press International. ISSN 0148-7760. LCCN 77-644197. Annual. 1977-

This source analyzes social, political, economic, and statistical data including: economic profile, production of commodities, GNP of the Soviet Union and the Republic (1987 data) and industry such as the Ukrainian industry compared to other countries, Kazakstan Consumer goods export/import for 1990, economic affairs chronology for 1991 (in the 1992 edition). There is no index.

579. Organisation for Economic Cooperation and Development. *Short-Term Economic Statistics, Commonwealth of Independent States-Statistiques Economiques a Court Terme, Communaute des Etats Independents, 1980-1993*. Paris: OECD, 1993. 176 p. ISBN 926403884. LCCN 94-124813.

This has statistical tables for Armenia, Azerbaijan, Belarus, Kazakhstan, Kyrgystan, Republic of Moldova, Russian Federation, Tajikistan, Turkmenistan, and Uzbekistan. The data include industrial production: total, industrial production for mining and quarrying, manufacturing, electricity, construction and crude steel, wages, and consumer prices. The text is in English and French.

580. Pockney, B. P. *Soviet Statistics Since 1950.* New York: St. Martin's Press, 1991. 333 p. ISBN 0312040032. LCCN 91-29226.

Population and labor, mortality rates, demographics, percentage of urban population, nationalities, level of education, demographics, regional trends, women in the economy, wages and earnings, and investments, growth national accounts, employment, defense, electricity, manufacturing and food, rates of selected sectors of industry, foreign trade, and industrial accidents are some areas covered in this publication.

581. Wiener Institut fur Internationale Wirtschaftsvergleiche. *Comecon Data.* New York: Greenwood Press, 1989. ISBN 0313278385. LCCN 86-641182. Annual. 1979-

This handbook of statistical data covers production for the Council for Mutual Assistance or better known in the West as Comecon. The countries included in this group of planned economies are: Bulgaria, the former Czechoslovakia, the former German Democratic Republic, Hungary, Poland, Romania, and the USSR. The data include: production and distribution, foreign trade, debt, energy, and standard of living. These are statistics for the time before these states were restructured.

582. World Bank. *Statistical Handbook: States of the Former USSR.* Washington, DC: World Bank, 1992. ISSN 1020-0991. LCCN 93642587. Annual. 1992-

This handbook has data for fifteen countries of the former USSR. The first part has comparative statistics on population growth, projection, production, growth of consumption and investment, general government expenditure, and merchandise imports and exports by end use categories. Part two has a profile of the 15 countries with population, natural resources, main industrial activities, currency, GDP, and GDP per capita, and tables on population, employment at current prices for a range of years, total trade, ferrous metals, chemicals and products, and light industry.

OECD Countries

SEE also Organisation for Economic Cooperation and Development. *Foreign Trade by Commodities*.

583. Organisation for Economic Cooperation and Development. (OECD) *Main Economic Indicators*. Paris: Organisation for Economic Cooperation and Development. ISSN 0474-5523. LCCN 64-33608. Monthly. 1965-

Series A has data on economic development in OECD countries. They include GDP, industrial production and leading indicators on construction, passenger cars, producer prices, consumer price index, retail sales, and unemployment rates, national income and production in manufacturing-durable goods, consumer goods, raw material, domestic trade, wages, prices, and foreign trade.

584. OECD. *OECD Economic Outlook*. Paris: Organisation for Economic Cooperation and Development. ISSN 0474-5574. LCCN 91-656029. Semiannual. 1967-

This publication gives an overview of the current economic situation and prospects of the twenty-four member OECD countries with graphs on consumer confidence, private consumption, business climate and industrial production. Individual OECD countries are covered with recent development, policies and prospect.

585. Organisation for Economic Cooperation and Development. *OECD Financial Statistics, Financial Statistics Monthly, International Markets*. Paris: Organisation for Economic Cooperation and Development. LCCN 86468729. Monthly. 1983- Also available on diskette.

These statistics are in three parts. Part I, has financial statistics divided into: international and domestic financial markets on bond issues and interest rates (monthly) for 19 countries. Part 2 has financial accounts of OECD countries (monthly), and Part 3 has non-financial enterprises financial statements which includes balance statements of income and sources and uses of funds for a sample of companies. (Annual)

586. OECD. *The OECD STAN Database for Industrial Analysis=La Base de donnees STAN de l'OECD pur l'analyse de l'industrie*. Paris: Organisation for Economic Cooperation and Development. LCCN 95650546. Annual. 1972- Also available on diskette and at Website http://www.oecd.org/dsti/.

This structural analysis industrial database provides international comparisons of OECD data on industrial activity for 21 OECD countries and Korea from 1975-1994. The STAN coverage includes: food, beverage and tobacco; textiles; leather and products; footwear; wood products; chemicals; motor vehicles; and transport activity. It looks at production, value added, labour compensation, and exports and imports.

587. Organisation for Economic Cooperation and Development *Quarterly National Accounts*. Paris: Organisation for Economic Cooperation and Development. ISSN 0304-3738. Quarterly. 1983-

Part I has information on OECD member countries national account aggregates with tables on gross domestic product by type of expenditure and the second part consists of data for each country.

The Caribbean and Latin America

588. United Nations. *Economic Survey of Latin America and the Caribbean*. Santiago, Chile: United Nations. ISSN 0070-8720. LCCN 50003616. Annual. 1982-

This UN document covers basic economic indicators such as GDP, GNP, population, and per capita GNP, short term economic indicators and consumer prices, terms of trade, exports and imports of goods and services for Latin America and the Caribbean. It also gives a country by country breakdown of economic trends from Argentina to Venezuela.

589. University of California. Los Angeles. Latin America Center. *Statistical Abstract of Latin America*. Los Angeles: University of California. ISSN 0081-4687. LCCN 56063659. 1955-

These statistics are from over 200 sources with the latest for twenty countries of Latin America. These include a series to reveal future trends; selected commodities in foreign trade, exports of major commodities, food trade, forestry, manufacturing and merchandise; and production statistics for gasoline, motor vehicles, steel, and television, and wheat flour.

International

590. Dreifus, Shirley and Michael Moynihan. *The World Market Atlas*. New York: Business International Corporation, 1992. 513 p. LCCN 91-077832.

This is a comparative source with statistics on population, GDP, trade, industry, manufacturing, and country profiles in graph form. The trade section has graphs on exports and imports, world exports and imports by country shares (1990) and world exports and imports by region.

591. The Economist. *The Economist Book of Vital World Statistics*. New York: Times Books, 1990. 254 p. ISBN 018129187701. LCCN 90033986.

This fascinating book of vital world statistics reflects the culture, social, and economic conditions of individual countries. The data compares: economic strengths, richest and poorest, living standards, economic growth, components of GDP, industrial efficiency, manufacturing, commodities, vehicle ownership, post and telecommunications, inflation, composition of visible trade, health, education, and family life.

592. Euromonitor. *International Marketing Data and Statistics* London: Euromonitor. LCCN 76647987. Annual. 1975-

This is an annual with statistical data on the Americas, Asia, Africa, and Oceania for market planners including: marketing geography, demographic trends and forecast, economic indicators, finance and banking, labor force indicators, industrial resources and output, and consumer expenditure patterns, trends in number of telex lines. (Excludes Europe which is covered in *European Marketing Data and Statistics*.) SEE Entry 224.

593. Gale Research Inc. *World Market Share Reporter*. Detroit, MI: Gale Research Inc. ISBN 1078-6783. LCCN sm 04--1387/ Biennial.

This has market share profiles for regions, excluding North America and Mexico. The information is alphabetically arranged by product with market size, end product use, trends, and rankings producing countries. SEE ALSO Entry 334, *Market Share Reporter*.

594. Gale Research, Inc. *Statistical Abstract of the World.* Detroit: Gale Research, Inc. ISSN 1077-1360. LCCN 95640698. Annual. 1995-

This statistical abstract covers demographics, health expenditures, development assistance for health, religion, educational rate, military expenditure and arms transfer, GNP, imports, exports, foreign aid, import and export of commodities, top mining products, GDP and manufacturing.

595. International Monetary Fund. *Balance of Payments Statistics Yearbook.* Washington, DC: International Monetary Fund. ISSN 0252-3035. Annual. 1981-

The data in this source is based on reports sent to the Fund by the 146 member countries with coverage of: current accounts for goods and services, merchandise exports/imports, trade balance, direct investment and other long term capital, and short term capital.

596. International Monetary Fund. *International Financial Statistics.* Washington, DC: International Monetary Fund. ISSN 0020-6725. LCCN 4900225141. Monthly. 1948- Also on compact disk.

This publication has information on money, banking, production prices, charts on international reserves, trade, national accounts, and world tables on international banking, measures of money, interest rates, real effective exchange rate indexes, international trade, commodity prices, and country tables covering Afghanistan to Zimbabwe.

597. Mitchell, Brian R. *International Historical Statistics: Africa, Asia & Oceania 1750-1988.* New York: Stockton Press, 1995. 1089 p. ISBN 1561590630 LCCN gb 95060243.

This source covers historical statistics on Africa, Asia, and Oceania from 1750-1988 on: population, labor force, agriculture, industry, external trade, transport, communications, finance, prices, industrial production indices, and national accounts.

598. Organisation for Economic Co-operation and Development. (OECD) *External Debt Statistics*. Paris: Organisation for Economic Co-operation and Development. ISSN 1015-4159. LCCN 87-658141. Annual. 1984-

Statistics on the external debt of over 150 developing countries and territories, Central and Eastern Europe with numbers on long term debt : export credits, bank claims and other claims and short term debt: bank and export credits.

599. OECD. *Geographical Distribution of Financial Flows to Developing Countries= Repartition geographique des resources financieres mises a la disposition des pays en developpement*. Paris: Organisation for Economic Co-operation and Development. LCCN sc 82008028. Annual. 1969-

The external financial resources to developing countries are listed with tables on: receipts of each developing country and tables for individual recipients by origin of resources.

SEE ALSO *Indicators of Industrial Activity*.

600. OECD. *National Accounts Statistics* Paris: Organisation for Economic Co-operation and Development. LCCN 83-141020. Annual. 1952-

The *National Accounts* is published in two volumes. Volume 1 has main aggregates for each country. Volume 1, Part I has graphs for each country with growth in terms of GDP and expenditures. Part 2 contains aggregates by zone (OECD total, OECD - Europe, and EC) expenditures on gross domestic product, and Part 3 gives main aggregates in national currencies for each country. Volume 2 has detailed national accounts for each country.

601. United Nations. *Monthly Bulletin of Statistics*. New York: United Nations Statistical Office. ISSN 0041-7432. LCCN 50003951. Monthly. 1947-

This periodical provides data on: population, manpower, industrial production, mining, manufacturing, external trade with total exports and imports by region and country, imports and exports by value and index numbers of quantum and unit value, and exchange rates, and consumer price index. (Cumulated in *Statistical Yearbook*)

602. United Nations. *Statistical Yearbook: Annuaire statistique*. New York: United Nations. ISSN 0082-8459. LCCN 50002746 1948- Annual.

This yearbook compiles basic social, economic, business, and industrial statistics for countries of the world from the *Monthly Bulletin of Statistics*. It informs with numbers on population, education and literacy, health and child bearing, nutrition, national accounts, government finance, labor force, wages and prices, manufacturing, and international trade.

603. United Nations. Educational, Scientific and Cultural Organisation. *Statistical Yearbook*. Paris: United Nations Educational, Scientific and Cultural Organisation. ISSN 0082-7541. LCCN 65003517. Annual. 1963-

Information on: population, education, science and technology, expenditures on research, culture and communication, libraries, book production, broadcasting and international trade in printed matter for the countries of the world are included for comparison.

604. World Bank. *Social Indicators of Development*. Washington, DC: World Bank, Socio-Economic Data Division. ISSN 1012-8026. LCCN 88647378. Annual. 1987- Also available on diskette.

This has information on size, growth, structure of population, fertility, mortality, labor force, educational attainment, natural resources, access to safe water, GNP per capita, total household income, expenditure on food and cereal imports. The data indicate trends and differences for more than 170 countries. There is a statistical appendix of environmental tables on water availability, air quality, agricultural production, and energy resources.

605. World Bank. *World Debt Tables*. Washington, DC: World Bank. ISSN 0253-2859. LCCN 82-642205. Annual.

This annual reports on the debt figures for countries of the world including: total debt stocks, debt repayments, interest payments, GNP, and exports and imports.

606. World Bank. *World Tables*. Baltimore: Published for the World Bank by the Johns Hopkins University Press. ISSN 1043-5573. LCCN 89-647121. Annual. Also available on a diskette.

This source contains data for 146 countries for analysis of economic and social trends in developing countries with tables on: gross national product per capita (U.S. dollars) that cover a range of years, gross national income per capita, gross domestic product by average annual growth, industry contributions to growth of gross domestic product, social indicators such as fertility rate, infant mortality rate, agricultural labor force, female labor force, manufacturing activity, employment, and a glossary of terms that include definitions such as quasi-money.

INVESTMENT

SEE ALSO *Directory of Foreign Manufacturers in the U.S.*

607. Garman, Nancy, ed. *Directory of Foreign Investment in the U.S.: Real Estate and Business.* Detroit: Gale Research, Inc. ISSN 1050-8694. LCCN 91656076. 1991 -

This source has foreign owned firms in the U.S. arranged by SIC code number with the name of the company, address, description of line of business, and country of origin. It also includes: investment and real estate owned by foreign investors, value, purchase date, price, joint venture, and contact information, trends in foreign investment with investment outlays by industry, foreign direct investment in the U.S. by country, and a directory of foreign owned U.S. real estate firms broken down by state, listing the name of the company and country.

608. Organisation for Economic Co-operation and Development. *International Direct Investment Statistics Yearbook=Annuaire des Statistiques d'investissement Direct Internationale.* Paris: Organisation for Economic Co-operation and Development. ISBN 9264038876. LCCN 93-647875. Annual. 1993-

This annual presents a series of foreign direct investment statistics for OECD countries for analyses and trends that includes summary tables on: direct investment flows in OECD countries, direct investment flows abroad from OECD countries, international direct investment position of selected OECD countries, and direct investment positions abroad of OECD countries. The 1993 edition reports that "OECD foreign direct investment flows increased at an unprecedented pace in the 1980's before declining in the early 1990's. OECD countries accounted for more than 95% of world-wide outflows of foreign direct investment and approximately 80% of inflows."

609. United Nations. Centre on Transnational Corporations. *World Investment Directory. Foreign Direct Investment, Legal Framework and Corporate Data*. Vol. 1. Asia and the Pacific. New York: United Nations. 1992. LCCN 92656265.

Analysis of foreign direct investment trends and their impact on a region or country is covered by this source. It includes an overview of foreign direct investments in Asia and the Pacific during the 1980's with coverage of inward and outward foreign direct investment, regulatory framework, inward and outward foreign direct investment trends, and country/territory tables from Bangladesh to Taiwan.

610. U.S. Dept. of Commerce. Bureau of Economic Analysis. *Foreign Direct Investment in the United States: 1992 Benchmark Survey Final Results*. Washington, DC: U.S. Government Printing Office, 1995. 270 p. SUDOCS C 59.2:F 76/4/992/Final.

This is a benchmark survey that gives data on the operations of U.S. affiliates of foreign companies including: balance sheets, income statements, sale of goods and services, external financial position, U.S. merchandise trade, research and development expenditures, and U.S. land owned or leased. It includes 166 tables. The number of U.S. affiliates was 18,223. Of that number 12,672 reported in the survey and 5,551 were exempt from reporting.

611. U.S.. Dept. of Commerce. Bureau of Economic Analysis. *Foreign Direct Investment in the United States: Operations of U.S. Affiliates of Foreign Companies*. Washington, DC: U.S. Government Printing Office, 1993. LCCN 87644253. SUDOCS C 59.20.

This source has foreign direct investment in the U.S. by selected financial and operating data of affiliates, by industry of affiliate; selected financial and operating data of affiliates, by country and industry of ultimate beneficial owner (UBO); number of affiliates with property, plant, and equipment or employment, state by country of UBO.

612. U.S. Dept. of Commerce. Bureau of Economic Analysis. *U.S. Direct Investment Abroad*. Washington, DC: U.S. GPO. ISSN 0730-9847. LCCN 81602504. SUDOCS C 59.20/2: Annual. 1977-

This source has estimates that are eventually revised for operations of U.S. parent companies and their foreign affiliates. These estimates supplement those in U.S. multinational companies: operations *Survey of Current Business*. (The data are about two years behind).

613. U.S. Dept. of Commerce. Economics and Statistics Administration. *Foreign Direct Investment in the United States: Establishment Data for Manufacturing, 1994*. Washington, DC: U.S. GPO, 1994. LCCN 93-649189. SUDOCS C 59.2:F 76/8 1988-

This document gives an overview of foreign direct investment in the U.S. for manufacturing establishments by industry, country and state with data on (1) employment, value added by manufacture, value of shipments of foreign-owned and all U.S. establishments by detailed industry; (2) employment and employee compensation of foreign owned establishment by industry; state by industry and state by country and tables with number of foreign owned establishments.

614. U.S. Dept. of Commerce. Economics and Statistics Administration. *Foreign Direct Investment in the United States. Review and Analysis of Current Developments. A Report in Response to a Request by U.S. Congress*. Washington, DC: U.S. GPO, 1991. 103 p. SUDOCS C 59.2: F76/6.

The role and significance of foreign direct investment in the United States from 1977 to 1988 with updates to 1990 with coverage of factors driving foreign direct investment in the U.S., macroeconomic setting for foreign direct investment, patterns and trends in foreign direct investment are areas covered by this study. This is the first report of three.

615. U.S. Dept. of Commerce. Economics and Statistics Administration. *Foreign Direct Investment in the United States: An Update. Review and Analysis of Current Developments*. Washington, DC: U.S. Government Printing Office, 1995. 130 p. SUDOCS C 59.2:F 76/6/Update/995.

This third report examines foreign direct investment in the U.S.(FDIUS) by the changes in FDIUS and its impact on the U.S. economy. It looks at the characteristics of U.S. affiliates by detailed industry groups and occupational structure of foreign owned manufacturing establishments. Some highlights are: FDIUS grew at a slower pace over the 1990-92 period than in the 1980; Japan surpassed the U.K. in 1992 as the largest foreign direct investor in the U.S. and remained so in 1993; foreign-owned U.S. firms tend to invest in larger and more capital intensive establishments than U.S. owned establishments and they pay higher wages; labor productivity tends to be higher, and foreigners tend to invest in research intensive U.S. industries. Second report has the same title. (SUDOC C 59.2:F 76/6/update)

616. U.S.. Dept. of Commerce. International Trade Administration. *Foreign Direct Investment in the United States... Transactions*. Washington, DC: U.S. Government Printing Office. ISSN 0732-0418. LCCN 82641818. SUDOCS C 61.25/2: Annual. 1979-

This report analyzes foreign direct investment transactions in the U.S. for trends. It gives: an overview of foreign direct investment in the U.S.; investment by source country, megadeals, investment by industry, mode of investment transactions and location of investment by states.

617. Yoshitomi, Masaru and Edward M Graham, ed. *Foreign Direct Investment in Japan*. Aldershot. Hants. UK: Brookfield, VT: E. Elgar. 1995.

TRADE

618. International Monetary Fund. *Direction of Trade Statistics: Yearbook*. Washington, DC: International Monetary Fund. ISSN 0252-3019. LCCN 82-646788. Annual. 1981-

This yearbook includes import and export data for 161 countries with value of merchandise, and exports and imports by trade partners. The classification includes: industrial countries, developing countries, and others not included elsewhere. There are quarterly issues that precede the yearbook.(also available on a compact disk) A guide to this periodical is: *A Guide to Direction of Trade Statistics*.

619. Organisation for Economic Co-operation and Development. *Foreign Trade by Commodities=Commerce exterieur par produits. Ser. C.* Paris: OECD. Dept. of Economic and Statistics. LCCN 85650241. Annual. 1983-

This publication has total trade statistics for member OECD countries including: imports, exports, food and live animals, meat and meat preparations, dairy products and birds, eggs, fish, crustaceans, mollusks, cereals, vegetables and fruits, sugar preparation, coffee, tea, beverages and tobacco, textile fibers and their waste, organic chemicals, and plastics in primary form. The statistics cover foreign trade by commodities from country of origin to world, OECD total, non OECD, Africa, America, Middle East, Far East and Oceania. Coverage includes the following countries: Austria, Belgium, Luxembourg, Finland, France, and the Netherlands, Germany, Iceland, Italy, Norway, Sweden, Switzerland, United Kingdom, U.S., Japan, New Zealand, Spain and Turkey, Canada, Australia, Denmark, Greece, and Portugal. There are four or five volumes per year.

620. Organisation for Economic Co-operation and Development. *Monthly Statistics of Foreign Trade*. Paris, France: Organisation for Economic Co-operation and Development. ISSN 0474-5388. LCCN 83647272. Monthly.

This monthly provides statistics on foreign trade for member OECD countries with total trade, imports, exports, food and live animals, meat and meat preparations, dairy products, fish, crustaceans, mollusks, cereals, vegetables, textile fibers and organic chemicals. Part I analyzes trade flows. Part II shows volume and average value indicator, and Part III show trade by SITC chapters. Part IV has foreign trade of OECD members with partner countries. In November 1994, Mexico was added. The data for this publication are cumulated in *Foreign Trade by Commodities*.

621. United Nations. *International Trade Statistics Yearbook. Annuaire statistique du commerce international*. New York: United Nations. Department of International Economic and Social Affairs, Statistical Office. LCCN 86648144. Annual. 1983-

There is information on external trade for each country with trends in current value, volume, price and trading partners and significance of imported and exported commodities. Volume 1 has trade by country:

total imports and exports by region and country and value as a percentage of world total. Volume 2 has trade by commodity: world exports by commodity classes and growth of world exports by commodity classes. 152 countries are covered. Text is in English and French.

622. U.S.. Central Intelligence Agency. *OECD Trade with Asia: A Reference Aid.* Washington, DC: U.S. Central Intelligence Agency, The Directorate. Distributed by National Technical Information Service. 1992. 149 p. LCCN sn 95-33626. Order number PB92-928000.

This source has commodity statistics of OECD countries with Asia, and trade of the five largest OECD countries with the region and key Asian countries.

623. U.S.. Central Intelligence Agency. *OECD Trade with Mexico and Central America: A Reference Aid.* Washington, DC: U.S. Central Intelligence Agency. Distributed by National Technical Information Service. 1992. LCCN sn90-661153. 116 p. order number IR92-10006, RTT92-10020.

Commodity trade statistics of OECD countries with Mexico, Central America including five of the largest OECD countries with the region and individual Mexican and Central American countries are included in this source.

624. US. Central Intelligence Agency. (CIA) *OECD Trade with South America: A Reference Aid.* Washington, DC: U.S. Central Intelligence Agency, The Directorate. Distributed by National Technical Information Service. (NTIS) 1992. 128 p. LCCN 90661152. PB92-928015.

This statistical source includes data on: OECD exports and imports to and from South America (SA), data on five of the largest OECD countries' imports and exports to S.A. and to individual S.A. countries. The five largest OECD members are: France, Germany, Japan, United Kingdom, and the U.S. Some data include: France's exports to SA, and France's imports from SA, and other member OECD country's imports and exports to South America, then individual countries in S.A. The data covers over a ten-year time period.

625. U. S. CIA. *OECD Trade with Sub-Saharan Africa: A Reference Aid*. Washington, DC: U.S. Central Intelligence Agency. The Directorate. Distributed by NTIS, 1992. 189 p. LCCN 93643225. Order number PB92-928000.

This source includes trade statistics for commodities of the OECD countries with Sub-Saharan Africa with data on trade with the five largest OECD countries with the region and with individual countries.

626. U.S. CIA. *OECD Trade with the USSR and Eastern Europe: A Reference Aid.* Washington, DC: U.S. Central Intelligence Agency. The Directorate. Distributed by NTIS, 1992. PB92-928000.

This has commodity statistics of OECD Trade with the USSR and Eastern Europe including trade with the five largest OECD countries with the region and US trade with individual countries of the region.

SEE ALSO Entries 342 to 341 for U.S. import, export, and trade data.

CHAPTER VIII

ELECTRONIC SOURCES

This chapter includes: computerized sources and internet and worldwide web sites. Computerized sources allow rapid and timely access, although there are online charges for convenience and timeliness with services such as *DIALOG* and *LEXIS/NEXIS*. The cost varies with the file as well as print and telecommunications charges. Check with your librarian for the charges on these databases.

The electronic indexes such as *ABI/Inform* are indicated in Chapter VI and are not listed in this chapter.

Internet, web sites, ftp (file transfer protocol), and telnet sites are listed in this chapter as this new technology can't be ignored. However, the sites are volatile and subject to change. The sites listed here were active on April 1, 1996.

There are also search tools for locating information on the internet and world wide web in this chapter.

COMPUTERIZED SOURCES

627. Congressional Information Service. *Statistical Masterfile. [compact disk]* Bethesda, MD: Congressional Information Service. ISSN 1064-4695. LCCN 92-644453.

This compact disk allows searching statistics on population, business, finance, and trade (similar in coverage to the *County and City Data Book*) including data from *American Statistics Index, Statistical References Index,* and *Index to International Statistics.*

628. Dialog Information Services. *DIALOG* (Dialog Information Services,) Inc. Palo Alto, CA.

This online source is a subsidiary of Knight-Ridder, Inc. It offers more than 350 databases and approximately two-thirds have business applications. The online charges vary from file to file.

Some business files on DIALOG include:
Business International (File 627)
Canadian Newspapers File (File 727)
Cancorp (File 491)
Disclosure Database (File 100)
Dun & Bradstreet Asia Pacific Dun's Market Identifiers (File 522)
Dun & Bradstreet Canadian Dun's Market Identifiers (File 520)
DUN & Bradstreet European Dun's Market Identifies (File 521)
Dun & Bradstreet European Financial Records (File 523)
Dun & Bradstreet International Market Identifiers (File 518)
EIU: The Economist Intelligence Unit (File 8)
Financial Times (File 196)
Kompass Asia/Pacific (File 592)
Kompass Canada (File 594)
PTS International Forecasts (File 83)
PTS PROMPT (File 16 and 216)
Teikoku Databank: Japanese Companies (File 502)
Trade & Industry ASAP (File 648)
TRADSTAT Plus

SEE ALSO *Fulltext Sources Online*.

629. Journal of Commerce. *PIERS (Port Import/Export Reporting Service)*. New York: Journal of Commerce. Monthly. Also available on *DIALOG* File 637.

This is an online database that provides statistics on inbound and outbound cargoes including product weight and country of origin or destination and shipper/consignee name. Tabulations can be customized. Service is by paid subscription. (212) 837-7054.

630. *LEXIS/NEXIS*. Dayton, OH: LEXIS/NEXIS, a division of Reed Elsevier, Inc. (U.S. 1-300-346-9759) New York: Reed Elsevier, Inc.

This is a comprehensive full text online service with charges for the information. It includes information on business, company, financc, legal aspects, tax, industry, country, and news. Each database is called a library with files of related information including full text of the *Times* (of London), Economist Intelligence Unit country forecasts, and industry analysis from the *National Trade Data Bank*. Its file includes: a World Library, and other libraries by region such as the Asia and Pacific Rim Library.

631. U.S. Bureau of the Census. Data User Services Division. *CENDATA*. Washington DC: U.S. Bureau of the Census. Data User Services Division. Also available on *DIALOG* File 580.

This is an online database available through private vendors such as DIALOG (DIALOG File 580) and CompuServ. The data and information originate from the U.S. Census Bureau and the information covered includes census data, U.S. merchandise exports and imports, press releases, data products, and is updated daily.

632. U.S. Dept. of Commerce. *Economic Bulletin Board (EBB)* United States. Dept. of Commerce. Washington, DC: U.S. Dept. of Commerce. SEE ALSO Website at University of Michigan Documents Center. It has the *EBB* available free, STAT-USA, and gopher site at the University of Michigan gopher -- una.hh.lib.umich.edu/11/ebb

This bulletin board allows users with personal computers to access business, economic, industrial, and trade data including consumer price index, employment and unemployment, industrial statistics, foreign trade data, and personal income. It originates from the Dept. of Commerce, Office of Business Analysis. There are over 700 files updated daily. Some agencies that distribute information on this bulletin board are: Federal Reserve Board, U.S. Dept. of Agriculture, Office of U.S. Trade Representative, International Trade Administration, and Bureau of Labor Statistics. The information is volatile and changes quickly. (For subscription information, call the Bureau of the Census (202) 482-1986.)

633. U.S. Dept. of Commerce. Economics and Statistics Administration. *National Trade Databank* [compact disk] (NTDB) Washington, DC: U.S. Dept. of Commerce. Economics and Statistics Administration. LCCN 920644644. ISSN 1064-9913. SUDOCS C 1.88: Available on web site such as: STAT-USA.

This is one of the most comprehensive exporting source on two disks. Disk 1 offers information on trade, marketing research reports, export promotion, overview, country profile, population, basic marketing and exporting guides, statistics, financial information, trade exhibit and fairs, and names of specialists who can assist exporters. Disk 2 has a *Commercial Service International Contacts* (formerly *The Foreign Trade Index)*, and *Export Yellow Pages*, and previous trade opportunities, and country studies.

634. U.S. Dept. of Commerce. Bureau of the Census. *U.S. Exports of Merchandise* [compact disk] U.S. Dept. of Commerce, Bureau of the Census, Data User Services Division. Washington, DC: U.S. Dept. of Commerce. SUDOCS C 3.278/3: Monthly.

This monthly disc has exports of merchandise by the Harmonized Code. It has domestic and foreign exports listed by quantity-F.A.S.(free along side ship), export value; shipment by vessel, F.A.S. export value, shipping weight, shipments by air, F.A.S. export value and shipping weight. It has monthly and cumulative data.

635. U.S. Dept. of Commerce, Bureau of the Census, Data User Services Division. *U.S. Imports of Merchandise* [compact disk] U.S. Dept. of Commerce, Bureau of the Census, Data User Services Division. Washington, DC: U.S. Dept. of Commerce. LCCN 92655127. ISSN 1057-8765. SUDOCS C 3.278: Monthly.

This disk has imports for consumption by Harmonized Commodity Code. The data cover dutiable value, calculated duty on general imports and imports for consumption. Customs value, import charges, import C.I.F. charges are some of the figures given.

INTERNET AND WORLDWIDE WEB SITES

The worldwide web search tools provide site and subject access and links to web sites as many organizations, countries, newspapers, companies, and government agencies have their own home page. Hypertext markup language (HTML) allow web site operators to link their home page to other remote sites anywhere in the world.

These sites are subject to rapid changes and are known to dissolve into cyberspace but these are listed to inform people about the types of information available on the web and at Internet sites.

636. Some worldwide web search tools are:

Alta Vista	http://altavista.digital.com/
C-NET	http://www.search.com/
CUSI	http://www.ucnet.hinet.net/cusi/cusi.html
EINet Galaxy	http://galaxy.einet.net/
Galaxy	http://www.einet.net/www.html
InfoSeek Search Page	http://www.infoseek.com/
Lycos Search Page	http://www.lycos.com/
The McKinley Internet Directory	http://www.mckinley.com/
W3 Search Engines	http://cuiwww.unige.ch/meta-index.html
Web Crawler Page	http://webcrawler.com/
The Whole Internet Catalog	http://nearnet.gnn.com/sic/index.html
Yahoo Search Page	http://www.yahoo.com/

637. Asia Business Connection
http://asiabiz.com/int/index.html

This sites covers Asia business contacts, directories, business services, and sources.

638. BISNIS Online. Business Information Service for the Newly Independent States
http://www.itaiep.doc.gov/bisnis/bisnis.html

BISNIS On-Line is the home page for the U.S. Dept. of Commerce Business Information Service for the Newly Independent States

(BISNIS), the U.S. government's site for the Newly Independent States and Russia including: BISNIS country reports, NIS market information, sources of finance for trade and investment in the NIS, business leads and promotional events, and economic and trade overview.

639. Bloomberg
http://www.bloomberg.com/

The coverage is world markets and financial services and includes the world equity indexes (for DJIA, TSE, Europe/Africa and Asia), new, products and services.)

640. Business & Economics Numeric Data (Larry Schankman)
http://www.clark.net/pub/lschank/web/ecostats.html

This is a good site for economic information, government statistics, census, international, employment, economic and trade data by country (1983-1993) and links to other sites.

641. Business & Economics Reference (Larry Schankman)
http://www.clar.net/pub/lschank/web/mu-biz.html

This site includes links to: an 800 number directory, Business Yellow Pages, Canadian Statistics, company information, Country Reports-Economic Policy and Trade Practices, and GATT and NAFTA.

642. Business Sources on the Net (BSN)
gopher Niord.SHSU.edu
gopher refmac.kent.edu (Kent State University)

FTP ksuvxa.kent.edu (files are in library directory)

BSN is organized by subject with a listing of people that put the site together so if there are questions, the people can be contacted. This has a listing of many good sources.

643. Bureau of Labor Statistics
http://stats.bls.gov

This web site has information on the U.S. economy, industry, labor market, employment and unemployment from the U.S. Dept. of Labor, Bureau of Labor Statistics.

644. Census
http://www.census.gov

This has information from the U.S. Department of Commerce, Bureau of the Census on U.S. population and housing, economy and geography.

645. Center for Global Trade Development
http://www.cgtd.com/global/

The Center for Global Trade Development is an independent, research organization monitoring socio-economic events and trends for over 220 countries focusing on issues relating to local, national, and global economic development, industrial, and trade growth with emphasis on the emerging market economies.

646. Currency Exchange Web Site
http://www.olsen.ch/cgi-bin/exmenu

This includes exchange rates and forecasts, currency converter, products and services available from Olsen and Associates.

Economic Bulletin Board (U.S. Dept. of Commerce) SEE STAT-USA or University of Michigan Documents Center,

647. EDGAR
http://www.sec.gov/edgarhp.html

This has information from the U.S. Securities and Exchange Commission (SEC) and it has company information such as: name, SIC, state of incorporation, address, and other financial information filed with the SEC.

648. EUROPA
http://www.cec.lu

This EUROPA web site provides information about the European Union and its institutions, history, the Commission, and Union's policies, and next step to integration. It is run by the European Commission, and it includes the Maastricht Treaty and other official documents from the Union.

649. European Union Internet Resources (University of California)
http://www.lib.berkeley.edu/GSSI/eu.html/

This is a rich site of web sources on the European Union with links to EU documents, servers, research and development, and the European parliament online.

650. Government Information Locator Service (GILS)
http://www.access.gpo.gov/su_docs/gils/gils.html

This is a government program to help the public access federal information systems.

651. GPO Access (these are available at many depository libraries)
telnet://swais.access.gpo.gov (login as guest)
http://www.access.gpo.gov/su_docs/aces/aaces001.html

Some better web sites for searching GPO Access are:

Purdue
http://thorplus.lib.purdue/gpo/

Univ. of California, San Diego
http://ssdc.ucsd.edu/gpo/

This has the *Congressional Register, Federal Register, Congressional Bills, Economic Indicators, Congressional Directory,* public laws, and more full text.

652. Japan & APEC Member Economies
http://apec.tokio.co.jp/member/index.html

This site has APEC member country information from a Japanese perspective including population, history, economy, trading partners, and treaties. It has Japan's aid: Loans to the particular country, and Japanese direct investment in the country. It also includes facts and figures about APEC members. It is run by the Ministry of Foreign Affairs, Japan.

653. OECD
http://www.oecd.org/

This is the Organisation for Economic Cooperation and Development. It has a listing of member countries, activities, economics, and news events and statistics, and links to other sites.

654. Rice University Information by Subject Area
http://riceinfo.rice.edu.RiceInfo/Subject.html
gopher riceinfo.rice.edu:70/11/Subject

Rice University has one of the best information by subject area on its web site. Its gopher menu includes Business Sources on the Net, CIA World Factbook, Economic Bulletin Board, and International Business Practices Guide.

655. Standard Industrial Classification Codes (SIC)
http://weber.u.washington.edu/~dev/sic.html

This is the complete listing of the Standard Industrial (SIC) codes. It describes industries and not occupations. SEE ALSO *Standard Industrial Classification Manual.* Also this is at the University of Michigan Documents Center web site and others.

656. STAT-USA
http://www.stat-usa.gov

This has business, economic, and marketing information from over 50 federal agencies including many programs from the *National Trade Data Bank* and Dept. of Commerce *Economic Bulletin Board.* SEE *National Trade Data Bank* and *Economic Bulletin Board.* This is available

National Trade Data Bank and *Economic Bulletin Board.* This is available at some federal depository libraries free and is available for subscription.

657. Trends in Developing Economies
http://www.ciesin.org/IC/wbank/tde-home.html

This site provides brief reports on the World Bank's borrowing countries with economic trends. SEE ALSO book with this title.

658. U.S. Business Advisor
http://www.business.gov/

The U.S. Business Advisor is a business site from the executive office of the U.S. Vice President. It includes information on exports, postal service, running a small business, international trade, laws, and regulations, women in business, and business statistics, and many links to other good sites.

659. U.S. Dept. of Commerce. International Trade Administration homepage
http://www.ita.doc.gov/

The International Trade Administration's (ITA) purpose is to help U.S. companies sell their products and services abroad. This site has information by geographic region including: Africa and the Near East, Asia and the Pacific, Europe and the western hemisphere. It has links to country information, trade, export issues, and other government agencies.

660. University of Michigan Documents Center
http://www.lib.umich.edu./libhome/Documents.center

This has comprehensive sites for the Dept. of Commerce *Economic Bulletin Board,* the Bureau of Census economic data, economic indicators, and EconData (from the University of Maryland), and highlights of foreign trade.

661. Virtual Africa: International Trade with South Africa
http://www.africa.coml/docs/satrade.html

This has a directory of South African companies on the South African stock exchange with name of the company, company secretary, line of business, SIC code, bankers, auditors, assets, and liabilities.

662. World Bank
http://www.worldbank.org/html/

The World Bank site includes information on: the World Bank, current events, country project information, and publications, and research studies.

663. The World Trade Organization (WTO)
http://www.unicc.org/wto/

This has information about the WTO including: press releases, trade policy issues, the Uruguay Round, international trade, its publications, and WTO membership.

Chapter IX

DIRECTORIES

The directories are divided into: (1) corporate directories by region, (2) export (3) import/trade and (4) government/organization. Some are basic for finding company information such as address, telephone and fax number, sales, employees, and the officers. Others such as *Principal International Business* and *Ward's Business Directory of U.S. Private and Public Companies* group companies in the same industry by standard industrial classification code (SIC number) as well as alphabetically. Others such as *Moody's International Manual* include comprehensive financial company information with capital structure, assets, liabilities, history, joint venture, and research activities.

The directories for government agencies such as the *U.S. Government Manual* are a good source for agency information, purpose, history and phone number for principal officials. Some useful agencies for trade are: International Trade Administration and Dept. of Commerce for contacting industry specialists. Another handy government directory for advice on local trade regulations and customs in a foreign country is the *Key Officers of Foreign Service Posts*. It has contact personnel and numbers.

CORPORATE DIRECTORIES BY REGION

Asia and Oceania

664. Carr, Jennifer L., ed. *Major Companies of the Far East and Australasia 1994/95*. London: Graham & Trotman. Distributed by Gale Research, Inc. in the U.S. and Canada, 1995. 3 v. ISBN 1859660984. LCCN sn90022932.

This directory is arranged alphabetically by country, then by the name of the company with address, telephone number, and principal activities. Some company information also includes: chairman, directors, parent company, sales turnover, profit before tax, share capital, total assets, and number of employees. There are about 6,500 major companies of the Far East and Australasia listed.

665. Dun and Bradstreet Information Services. *Dun's Asia/Pacific Key Business Enterprises 1995/96*. Sydney, Australia: Dun & Bradstreet Information Services, 1995. 2v. ISSN 1050-5172. LCCN 93-640854. Also available on CD-ROM.

Volume 1 has businesses listed geographically with profile of countries, principal cities, foreign commerce, trade balances, inflation rates, best export prospects, principal trading partners and currencies. Volume 2 has companies listed alphabetically and then by product classification and also the top 2,000 companies.

666. ELC International. *Asia's 7,500 Largest Companies,* 5th ed. London: ELC International, 1995. LCCN sn 85-021462. ISBN 0948058444. 583 p. Also available on disk for any IBM or compatible personal computer.

Besides basic company information of name, address, phone and fax number, this directory includes: (1) capital markets of Asia giving brief background of the stock exchanges of Asia, (2) national profiles of key performance indicators (3) largest quoted companies ranked by pretax profits, profit margin, etc. (4) money losers, (5) country by country business activity. Also there is coverage of privately owned companies.

667. Euromonitor. *Asia: A Directory and Sourcebook*. London: Euromonitor. Distributed by Gale Research, Inc., 1992. 534 p. ISBN 086334226. LCCN gb93-15052.

This source has business information sources, company profiles, and economic trends for China, Hong Kong, Indonesia, Malaysia, Pakistan, Philippines, Singapore, South Korea, Sri Lanka, Taiwan and Thailand.

668. Euromonitor. *Directory of Major Companies in South East Asia*. London: Euromonitor. Distributed by Gale Research, Inc. in U.S. and Canada. 1994. 3 v. ISBN 0863385559.

There is coverage for over 1,500 emerging companies in South East Asia with information on: the role of multinational corporations, foreign investment, company structures as well as basic company information. The countries include: Brunei, Hong Kong, Indonesia, Malaysia, Philippines, Singapore, South Korea, Taiwan, and Thailand.

669. Mead Ventures. *Asian Finance Directory*. Phoenix, AZ: Mead Ventures. ISSN 1044-4718. LCCN 90657463. Annual. 1990-

This is a listing of foreign financial companies operating in the U.S. with company name, address, phone, fax, telex, type of business, country of affiliation, and key contact and general information. Index A arranges company alphabetically by name; Index B arranges by country of owner/affiliate, and Index C lists the companies by state.

670. Rickson, Richard, ed. *Asian and Australian Companies: A Guide to Sources of Information*. Kent, England: CBD Research. Distributed by Reference Press. 1994. 334 p. ISBN 0900246618. ISSN 1352-3198.

This is a listing of information sources for Asian and Australian companies including print, online, directories, and periodicals.

Australia and New Zealand

671. Dun & Bradstreet International. *Jobson's Year Book of Public Companies of Australia and New Zealand*. Sydney, Australia: Dun & Bradstreet International. ISSN 0075-3785. LCCN 86-641405. Annual.

This publication surveys Australian and New Zealand public companies with name, address, subsidiaries, directories, secretary, auditors, authorized capital, paid up capital, major capital moves, and year ends. Includes a directory of directors and index of subsidiaries.

China

672. Chinese Business Press. *Chinese Trade Directory=Chung-kuo wai mao kung shang ming lu*. Eugene, OR: Chinese Business Press. 1993. LCCN 94-645626.

This directory lists 1,100 of the most important government agencies, corporations and trade organizations. Volume I is an alphabetical arrangement by name of company, address, phone, fax, and telex when available. Volume II has industry listing. Volume III has province listing from Anhui to Zhuhai.

673. N.C.N. Limited. *China Directory of Industry and Commerce, 3rd edition*. Hong Kong: N.C.N. Limited. ISSN 0734-1725. LCCN 82644768. 1982-

This is a directory with a listing over 10,000 industrial and commercial companies. Volume 1 includes agriculture, chemical industry, commercial material, communication, construction, and postal service. Volume 2 includes machinery industry, medical industry, metallurgical, and textile and volume 3 has government organs, corporations, and an investment guide to China's 30 provinces with a listing of contacts, statistics on foreign trade, and economics, laws and regulations.

Hong Kong

674. Croner Publications. *Business Directory of Hong Kong*. Queens Village, NY: Croner Publications, Inc., 1990. LCCN 78643122.

This source arranges Hong Kong firms by subject such as: accountants, advertising agents, air cargo forwarders, banks, computer services, department stores, hotels, importers, exporters, and manufacturers. Information includes name of company, address, telephone, fax, products, and contact person.

675. Hong Kong Productivity Council. *Directory of Hong Kong Industries*. Hong Kong: Hong Kong Productivity Council, 1991. 1253 p. LCCN 78-643122

The Census & Statistics Dept. compiles data for Hong Kong manufacturing companies arranging the directory by product (beginning with food manufacturing) and then alphabetically by the name of the company with name, address, telephone, factory address, directors, products, annual turnover, and brand name.

India

676. Informatics (India) Ltd. *Kompass India*. New Delhi, India: Informatics (India) Ltd. 1995. 3 vols. ISBN 81855410501.

This source includes: Indian economic statistics, products and services, and companies. The company information includes: name, address, telephone and fax number, and number of employees.

SEE KOMPASS. *Standard Trade & Industry Directory of Indonesia*.

Japan

677. Diamond Lead Company. *Diamond's Japan Business Directory 1993*. Tokyo: Diamond Lead Co. 1993. 1563 p. ISBN 4924360015. LCCN 75-647718.

This directory has (1) brief industry surveys on fishery & foodstuffs, construction, textile, pulp and paper, chemicals, pharmaceutical, petroleum and mining, iron and steel, nonferrous, metal, machinery, and electrical machinery, (2) financial company information on balance sheet, fixed assets, liabilities, capital, profit and loss statement and (3) Diamond's analysis of the company.

678. International Culture Institute. *The Complete Directory of Japan*. Hong Kong: International Culture Institute and Asia Press. LCCN 87-658574. 1985- Annual.

This is a directory of Japanese sources on: national and local government information, commerce, industry, foreign diplomatic corps, foreign organizations, enterprises, colleges and universities, trade and non-profit organization and Japanese business abroad. The government chapter has names of the members of the House of Representatives, Defense Agency, and Environmental Agency.

679. Japan External Trade Organization. *Directory: Japanese-Affiliated Companies in USA & Canada: Beikoku Kanada Nikkei kigyeo kairekutori*. Tokyo: Japan External Trade Organization. 1995. 821 p. LCCN 89650850.

This is a directory of Japanese companies listing restaurants with affiliations in the U.S. and Canada. Grouping is by state, then alphabetically by company name, with address, telephone number, chief executive, year established and parent company. Appendix A lists companies by product classification. Appendix B is an alphabetical index of U.S. companies. Appendix C is Canadian companies by product. Appendix D is an alphabetical arrangement of Canadian companies.

680. Japan Press, Ltd. *Japan Directory*. Tokyo: The Japan Press, Ltd. LCCN 85-642336. Annual. 1984-

This Japanese directory is arranged in two volumes. Hotels, restaurants, clubs, hospitals, classified telephone directory, embassies, and foreign residents are in volume one while business firms, business associations, clubs, Japanese government organizations, and phone numbers are in volume two. The information provides name, address, telephone and fax number, product or service, and name of contact person. The classified include job placement firms, theaters, translators and interpreters.

681. Nihon Beoeki Shinkeokei. *Japan Trade Directory 1995-96.* Tokyo: Japan External Trade Organization. Distr. by Gale Research, Inc. 1995. 1 v. ISBN 482240698. LCCN 83-646013. Irregular.

This is a dircctory for products and services for Japanese importers and exporters arranged first by products, then by prefectures. It lists about 24,000 products and 3,000 companies with name, address, telephone, telex, and fax number, and other useful financial information.

682. Nihon Shoko Kaigisho. *Standard Trade Index of Japan.* Tokyo: Japan Chamber of Commerce and Industry . Distributed by Taylor & Francis. 1 v. ISSN 0585-0444. LCCN sn87-22789. Annual 1957-

This is listing of a commodity and service firms indicating if the company is a Japanese manufacturer, importer, or exporter. It also includes: brand name index; company with address, telephone and fax number, telex and product; and government agencies, trade and industrial organizations with address, telephone and fax number.

683. Teoyeo Keizai Shinpeosha. *Japan Company Handbook.* Tokyo: Toyo Keizai, Inc. ISSN 0288-9307. LCCN 79-647242. Quarterly. 1985-

This gives investment information for Asian companies listed on the Japanese Stock Exchange. Companies are alphabetically arranged by name, and firms are listed by industry with data on outlook, income, graph of stock price movement, stocks, shares out, financial data, principal office, sales breakdown, prices (highs and lows) finance, facility investment, highest in current profit, R & D expenditure, chairman and overseas office.

Malaysia

684. Kompass Publishers. *Kompass Malaysia 1991 Trade Information Book*. Kuala Lumpur, Malaysia: Kompass Publishers. ISSN 0127-7847. LCCN 88-942661. Annual.

This source is arranged alphabetically by: (1) Malaysian companies (2) products, and (3) main product groups with four digit classification code (not SIC code).

Europe

685. Adams, Robert W., ed. *Directory of European Industrial & Trade Association*. Beckenham, Kent: CBD Research Ltd. distributed by Gale Research, Inc. 1991. ISSN 0952-3626. LCCN sn86035059. Irregular.

This directory compiles over 2000 European industrial and trade associations with address, telephone number, date of incorporation, abbreviation, activities, language used, and publication. (This does not include Great Britain and Ireland). It has a subject index in English, French, and German.

686. Cambridge Market Intelligence. *Directory of European Business*. London: New York: Bowker-Saur. 1992. ISBN 0862916178. LCCN 92030040.

This directory covers eastern and western Europe, the Soviet Union, and the Commonwealth of Independent States. The coverage includes: 4,500 service companies, government agencies, international organizations, and manufacturing companies. It looks at the political, economic, legal, and social system.

687. Didik, Frank X. *Eastern Europe Business Database*. [computer file] Springfield, VA: U.S. Dept. of Commerce. National Technical Information Service. 1993. LCCN sn 94-42526. Order No. PB93-506210/CAU.

This database contains information on Eastern European with references on the largest state and private companies which account for 92 percent of the total economic output. Database includes company name, location, product, factory, economic, and trade information.

688. Didik, Frank X. *Eastern European Business Directory*. Detroit, MI: Gale Research Inc., 1992. LCCN sn 92-22147. Annual.

This directory covers over 8,000 of the largest corporations in the former East Germany, the former Soviet Union, Poland, the former Czechoslovakia, Hungary, Bulgaria, and Romania with the name, address, telephone, fax and telex numbers, types of products and services, agents and contact name. Listing is divided into: (1) products & services (2) geographic listing (3) alphabetic listing (4) products & services and alphabetical listings to the former East Germany.

689. Disclosure Incorporated. *Compact Disclosure. Europe*. [computer file]. Bethesda, MD: Disclosure Incorporated, 1991. Quarterly with each disk being cumulative.

Full text financial information for European companies are included on this compact disk with name, address, telephone, and financial information such as: assets, liabilities, and subsidiaries.

690. Dun & Bradstreet. *D & B Europa 1995*. Bucks, U.K.: Dun & Bradstreet Ltd. ISSN 0957-5812. LCCN 93-640860. Annual.

This four volume source contains information for 60,000 leading European and Israeli corporations with company name, address, telephone, telex, year started, executives, principal business activity, export sales, importer/exporter, nominal capital issued, issued capital, and annual sales. Vol. 4 has a statistical profile for country by sales and SIC presenting top 5,000 companies ranked by sales in ECU, top 500 banks ranked by total assets, 5000 companies ranked by employees, top companies in each main business activity.

691. Euromonitor. *Eastern Europe: A Directory and Sourcebook*. London: Euromonitor. Distributed by Gale Research, Inc., 1992. 436 p. ISBN 0863384102.

Business information sources, company profiles, economics, market and consumer trends are covered in this sourcebook.

692. Euromonitor. *The European Directory of Consumer Brands and Their Owner*. London: Euromonitor Publications Limited, 1992. 1 v. LCCN 92850051.

This European directory lists consumer goods, brand name products, and their companies with name, address, telephone, and telex.

693. Euromonitor. *The European Directory of Consumer Goods Manufacturers*. London: Euromonitor Publications Limited, 1992. 1 v. ISSN 0952-9586. LCCN 90-648674.

This directory profiles over 6,000 European companies involved in the manufacturing of "fast moving" consumer goods, household durables, electrical appliances, consumer electronics, cosmetics and toiletries. Companies are arranged alphabetically from Austria to West Germany and exclude importers and distributors except in the foodstuff sector with name, address, telephone, telex, parent company, major subsidiaries, products and financial year end and turnover.

694. Gale Research, Inc. *European Wholesalers and Distribution Directory*. Detroit: Gale Research Inc., 1992. ISSN 1063-8288. LCCN 92-650272.

695. Graham & Trotman. *Major Companies of Europe 1994/95*. London: Graham & Trotman Ltd. Distributed by Gale Research, Inc. 1994. ISBN 1859660991. LCCN 92-045001. Annual.

This four volume directory has a geographical breakdown of European companies from Austria to the United Kingdom with name, address, telephone, telex, board of directors, products, parent companies, subsidiaries, sales, turnover, principal bankers, and number of employees.

696. Koek, Karin E., ed. *European Consultants Directory*. Detroit: Gale Research, Inc. 1992. 1038 p. ISSN 1060-1880. LCCN 92-040571.

Consultants are arranged geographically by country, then subdivided by different categories similar to the arrangement in the companion U.S. publication, *Consultants and Consulting Organizations Directory*.

697. Times Books. *The Times 1000.* London: Times Books. 1 vol. LCCN 72617301. Annual. 1967-

An annual with rankings of leading industrial and financial companies including leading companies in Europe, United Kingdom, United States, Japan, Canada, Australia, and South Africa.

698. Whiteside, R.M., ed. *Major Chemical and Petrochemical Companies of Europe 1995.* London: Graham & Trotman. Distributed by Gale in the U.S. and Canada. ISBN 1859661114. LCCN 90-649995. Annual.

Major European companies in the petrochemical industries with name of company, telephone, cable, telex, telefax, supervisory board, principal activities, subsidiary companies, principal bankers, financial information, sales turnover, profit after tax, principal stockholders and number of employees are included in this source.

Commonwealth of Independent States

SEE ALSO *Directory of European Business*

699. Loiry, William S., ed. *The U.S.-Soviet Trade Sourcebook.* Chicago: London: St. James Press, 1991. 203 p. LCCN 93-132104

This source includes consultants and trading companies, U.S. law firms and legal organizations that specialize in Soviet law, U.S. government resources, Soviet government and other resources, advertising firms, and insurance agencies, and freight forwarders are others included in this directory.

700. National Market Research Institute. (Soviet Union) *The Business Directory of the New Independent States.* (the former USSR). Moscow: VNIKI MVES, National Market Research Institute. Distributed by Market Knowledge, 1992. 1v.

This is a directory of the new independent states arranged alphabetically by name of company, SIC codes, then geographically, and imports, and exports arranged by SIC.

701. U.S. Russian Business Development Committee. *Russian Defense Business Directory*. U.S. Dept. of Commerce. Bureau of Export Administration. 1993. 1 v. SUDOCS C 57.121:R 92-

This directory profiles 62 Russian defense enterprises with name, address, telephone, fax, general overview, primary business, former ministry subordination, employees, principal officers, ownership, year established, product lines, civil product line, key technologies, equipment, and conversion projects.

France

702. Kompass. *Kompass France 1994 Produits & Services*. Paris: Kompass France. Croner Publications, Inc. 1994. ISSN 0759-5689. LCCN 83643069. Annual. Also available on DIALOG.

This is a directory with a listing of 115,000 French companies (1994 ed.) Products and services are listed alphabetically, citing name, address, telephone number, and a product listing of economic sectors 1-36. (product suppliers by main industry groups). Volume 2 has economic sectors 37-89. Volume 3 has a geographical directory of companies, and volume 4 has a numerical index of NAF codes (French activities nomenclature).

Germany

703. Frankfurter Allgemeine Zeitung Gmbh. *Germany's Top 300, a Handbook of Germany's Largest Corporations,* 2nd ed. Frankfurter, GE: Information Services, 1992. 401 p. ISBN 392487591X. LCCN sn92-24122. Annual.

This source ranks Germany's leading corporations for 1991 by sales turnover with a packed one page profile with name, address, year established, telephone and fax number, line of business, product and activities, SIC codes, management, employees, major subsidiaries, turnover, pre-tax profits, capital, shareholders, dividend, high and low share price for 1991. Includes a chart of a statement of income that a German company must disclose in its annual profit and loss account.

704. Frankfurter Allgemeine Zeitung GmbH. *Germany's Top 500.* Frankfurt, Germany: Frankfurter Allgemeine Zeitung GmbH. Distributed by The Reference Press, 1995. LCCN sn95-26615. Annual. 1992-

This directory profiles Germany's top 500 companies with name, address, phone and fax number, number of employees, sales, profits, assets, line of business, and subsidiaries.

Ireland

705. *Thom's Commercial Directory* Dublin: Thom's Directories Limited. ISSN 0002-4224.

This directory covers Ireland in the following areas: government departments, professional associations, trade association, banks, finance houses, manufactures, companies, and Who's Who in Ireland.

United Kingdom

706. Dun & Bradstreet. *Key British Enterprises, 1995: Britain's Top 50,000 Companies.* High Wycombe, U.K.: Dun & Bradstreet International. 1995. 6 v. ISBN 0901491977

Volume 1-4 lists British companies alphabetically with full name, headquarters, address, telephone, fax and telex numbers, line of business, UK SIC codes, U.S. SIC codes, trade names, warrants help, parent co., trade awards. Volume 5 ranks the 5,000 largest employers, by sales and employees within county and line of business, and volume 6 provides cross referencing.

707. *Kelly's Business Directory,* 105th. East Grinstead, U.K.: Kelly's Directories, Ltd. 1993. ISSN 0269-9265. LCCN 86-651566. Annual.

This is a one volume manufacturing directory with a product chapter arranged by manufactures' names, wholesalers, and firms giving address, telephone and fax number. Its chapters include: oil and gas industry, company information, exporters and services.

The Caribbean and Latin America

708. Dun & Bradstreet Information Services. *Dun & Bradstreet's Key Business Directory of Latin America*. Bethlehem, PA: Dun & Bradstreet. ISSN 1069-3041. LCCN 93-642357. Annual.

Volume 1 has the firms geographically arranged, then alphabetically by the name of the company. The information includes the name of the company, address, telephone and fax number, line of business by industry classification and a ranking by number of employees.

709. Dun and Bradstreet. *Dun's Latin America Top 25,000*. Parsippany, NY: Dun's Marketing Service. ISSN 0742-9849. LCCN 84-846677. Annual. 1984-

Section (Sec.) 1 has Latin American companies arranged by country then alphabetically with name, address, sales figures expressed in local currency, year started, SIC, product, and number of employees. Sec. 2 has businesses by product classification, and Sec. 3 has firms alphabetically arranged.

North America

Canada

710. Canadian Manufacturers' Association. *Canadian Trade Index*. Toronto: Canadian Manufacturers' Association. ISSN 0068-9904. LCCN 1421699. Annual.

Vol. 1 gives an alphabetical listing of products and trademarks manufactured in Canada, French glossary of product headings. Vol. 2 is the export chapter which includes alphabetical listing of exporting companies providing name, address, telephone number, fax number, distribution chapter, and geographical offices of manufacturers.

711. Canadian Newspaper Services International. *Blue Book of Canadian Business*. Toronto: Canadian Newspaper Services International. ISSN 0381-7245. LCCN 76-382127. Annual.

This source profiles prominent Canadian companies by citing history, management, philosophy, directors and officers. It gives brief executive biographies, ranks the Canadian 500 companies, and alphabetically lists companies with address, phone number, employee number, other locations and nature of business.

712. Disclosure Incorporated. *Compact Disclosure. Canada* [computer file]. Bethesda, MD.: Disclosure information Group. 1990 -

This has full text for the Toronto Stock Exchange companies. SEE ALSO *Compact Disclosure* (U.S.)

713. Dun & Bradstreet. *Canadian Key Business Directory*. Toronto: Dun & Bradstreet Canada, 1995. ISSN 0315-0879. Annual.

This directory profiles more than 20,000 Canadian companies which include hotels with the following characteristics: $10,000 sales, or 75 employees, or $3,000,000 net worth, and 250 employees at branch location. It arranges the firms alphabetically with name, address, telephone number, sales, employees, SIC codes, and company officers. Also there is a classification by SIC code and a geographical arrangement of companies.

714. Dun & Bradstreet Canada. *Guide to Canadian Manufacturers*. Toronto: Dun & Bradstreet Canada. ISSN 0227-2059. LCCN 9364861. Annual. 1978-

This Canadian manufacturing directory is arranged (1) alphabetically with the name of the company, address, telephone, SIC number, line of business, employees, and principal selling territory (2) geographically and (3) organizationally by line of business. Graphs and charts on: major industry group distribution, manufacturers' distribution, company size distribution, percentage of new business starts, and company size distribution.

715. Financial Post DataGroup. *Financial Post Survey of Industrials*. Toronto: Financial Post DataGroup. ISSN 0071-5050. Annual.

This directory covers more than 2,000 Canadian listed and unlisted industrial corporations with names, addresses, telephone numbers, stock symbols, and transfer agents. The firms are in manufacturing, real estate, forestry, investment holding, communications and transportation. The data include: price range, operating revenue, long term debt, financial statistics, total assets, current liabilities, subsidiaries and earning per common share and return on equity.

716. Financial Post Co. *Survey of Mines and Energy Resources*. Toronto: Financial Post. ISSN 0833-9600. LCCN 95-648074. Annual.

This source lists Canadian mining and energy companies including publicly traded corporations involved in exploration, development and production of base metals, overview of investment opportunities, company information with name, head office with address, telephone and fax number, key personnel and financial statistics, unlisted stock prices, and statistical overview with price range of selected metals for current years.

717. Globe and Mail. *The Globe and Mail Report on Business: Canada Company Handbook*. Toronto: Globe and Mail Publishing, 1993. ISBN 092192545X. ISSN 0847-2831. LCCN cn90030368.

Financial information for public Canadian companies includes: line of business, current news, ratios, P/E ratios, dividend share, book value per share, balance sheet, price and performance, charts, stock symbol, and summary of the year.

718. Scott's Directories. *Scott's Directories: Atlantic Manufacturers*. Oakville, Ontario: Scott's Directories. ISSN 0831-1854. LCCN cn 86-30476. Biennial.

This is similar to *Scott's Directories: Western Manufacturers* except it covers Newfoundland, Prince Edward Island, Nova Scotia, and

New Brunswick. SEE ALSO *Scott's Directories: Western Manufacturers* for type of information contained.

719. Scott's Directories. *Scott's Directories: Greater Toronto Business Directories*. Don Mills, Ont.: Scott's Directories. ISSN 1199-7494. LCCN cn 89-34121. Annual.

Directory listing for companies in the Greater Toronto area.

720. Scott's Directories. *Scott's Directories: Metropolitan Toronto and Toronto Vicinity Trade*. Oakville, Ont.: Scott's Directories. ISSN 0828-914X. LCCN cn89-34121. Annual.

This directory is similar to *Scott's Directories: Western Manufacturers*.

721. Scott's Directories. *Scott's Directories: Western Manufacturers*. Oakville, Ontario: Scott's Directories. ISSN 829-2248. LCCN cn85-39051.

The directory covers Manitoba, Saskatchewan, Alberta, and British Columbia and its arrangement is: (1) alphabetical list of Canadian firms, (2) company profile, (3) product classification, (4) industrial contacts, and government and municipal development information. Some are small companies with as few as 5 employees.

722. Scott's Directories. *Scott's Repertoires, Fabricants du Quebec = Scott's Directories: Quebec Manufacturers*. Quebec: Scott's Directories. ISSN 0829-2221. LCCN cf85-35196. Biennial.

This directory is similar to *Scott's Directories: Western Manufacturers*. SEE ABOVE entry.

United States

723. *Directory of American Firms Operating in Foreign Countries,* 1996. 3 vol. New York: Simon & Schuster. ISSN 0070-5071. LCCN 55039067. 1955-

The directory covers over 2,500 U.S. corporations and their 18,340 subsidiaries spanning 138 countries. Volume 1 has an alphabetical index including accounting, brokerage, investment, manufactures, transportation and advertising companies arranged alphabetically with address, telephone and fax number, number of employees, personnel (president, foreign officer, or personnel director,) subsidiary, and product. Volume 2 and 3 have listings by country from Algeria to Zimbabwe of American foreign firm operations.

724. Disclosure Incorporated. *Compact D/SEC* [computer file]. Bethesda, MD: Disclosure Inc. ISSN 1062-8525. LCCN 92-64415. Monthly.

This has the full text corporate information on publicly held U.S. companies filing with the Securities and Exchange Commission with name, address, telephone, description of business, current outstanding shares, number of employees, five year summary of sales, net income, annual liabilities, and key annual financial ratios and other information.

725. Dun & Bradstreet Corp. *America's Corporate Families.* Parsippany, NJ: Dun & Bradstreet Corp., 1995. ISSN 0733-1592. LCCN sn86025463. Annual.

This directory covers U.S. ultimate parent companies with two or more business locations, 250 or more employees at a location, $25 million sales volume or net worth greater than $500,000. Volume 2 has ultimate parent, subsidiaries, division, and major branches, and volume 3 has ultimate parent companies and selected international subsidiaries.

726. Dun & Bradstreet Corp. *Million Dollar Directory*. Parsippany, NJ: Dun & Bradstreet Corp., 1995. ISBN 1562033875. Annual. Also on a CD-ROM referred to as Dun's Million Dollar Disc.

A brief profile for 160,000 U.S. firms is given which includes: name, address, phone number, officers, directors, products, sales, number of employees, SIC code, and stock exchange as well as the founding date and state where incorporated. Companies must have assets greater than $500,000 or sales greater than $25 million.

727. Gale Research, Inc. *Brands and Their Companies*. Detroit: Gale Research, Inc. ISSN 1047-6407. LCCN 900802. Annual.

This two volume directory has access to more than 268,000 consumer brands and about 46,000 manufacturers and importers. The arrangement is: consumer brands are alphabetically listed in volume 1; volume 2 is a company directory with name, address, telephone and fax number. SEE ALSO *International Brands and Their Companies* or *International Companies and Their Brands*.

728. Gale Research, Inc. *Gale Business Resources*. [computer file]. Detroit: Gale Research, Inc., 1995. ISBN 1081-6712. LCCN sn95-004394.

This is a directory of about 210,000 companies with basic directory information, histories, market share reports, and statistics.

729. Gale Research, Inc. *Ward's Business Directory of U.S. Private and Public Companies*. Detroit: Gale Research, Inc., 1996. ISSN 1048-8707. Annual.

The first three volumes list U.S. companies alphabetically with name, address, SIC, and officers. Volume 4 has a geographic listing and volume 5 has companies ranked by sales within a 4 digit SIC code.

730. Moody's Investors Service. *Moody's Industrial Manuals*. New York: Moody's Investors Service. ISSN 0545-0217. LCCN 56014721. Annual. 1954-

There is comprehensive company coverage which includes: capital structure, history, joint venture, business segments, research activities, properties, subsidiaries, letters to the shareholders, income accounts, balance sheets, and independent auditor's reports. (Also in this series is *Moody's Bank and Finance Manual, Moody's Public Utilities Manual, and Moody's Transportation Manual.*)

731. National Register Pub. Co. *Directory of Corporate Affiliations*. Skokie, IL: National Register Pub. Co. ISSN 1066-9779. Annual. 1973-

Volume 1 lists U.S. companies alphabetically including name, telephone and fax number, year founded, ticker symbol, assets, earnings, liabilities, net worth, approximate sales, number of employees, fiscal year end, standard industrial classification code (SIC), officers and subsidiaries, computer systems/hardware, joint venture, non-U.S. holdings, non-U.S. plants, and exports. Vol. 2 has a geographic index, SIC index, corporate personnel index for U.S. public companies. Vol. 3 has an alphabetical index, company listing, SIC index, corporate personnel index for private companies. Vol. 4 has international and private companies, alphabetically arranged, company information, geographic index, SIC index, corporate personnel. Vol. 5 has a master index.

732. Spain, Patrick J. and James R. Talbot. *Hoover's Handbook of American Companies*. Austin, TX: The Reference Press, 1996. 1059 p. ISBN 1878753878. (Hoover's has a web site)

This handbook profiles 500 American companies giving an overview, history, financial information on sales, net income, income as percent of sales, earnings per share, stock price, P/E debt ratio, return on equity, cash, current ration, long term debt. Also ratings such as 100 largest companies in 1990, most profitable companies in 1992, 100 largest employers, leading brands in U.S. by category.

733. Standard & Poor's Corporation. *Standard & Poor's Register of Corporations, Directors and Executives*. New York: Standard & Poor's Corporation. ISSN 0361-3623. Annual.

This is a three volume directory for U.S. companies with name of company, address, telephone number, chief executive officer, president, secretary and treasurer, primary bank, products and SIC code number. Vol. 2 has an alphabetical listing of directors and executives with brief biographical information. Vol. 3 has a listing by SIC code, geographical index, and a new company additions listing.

734. Thomas Publishing Co. *Thomas Register of American Manufacturers and Thomas Register Catalog File*. New York: Thomas Publishing Co. 26 vols. ISSN 0362-7721. LCCN 06043937. 1905-

For a specific product or service of a U.S. manufacturing firm, this is the most comprehensive annual source. There is a listing of product and services alphabetically, a directory for the names of the companies alphabetically arranged with address, ZIP codes, telephone number, asset rating, company officials, and trademarks and the catalog file alphabetically by company name and cross references to other volumes.

International

735. American Marketing Association. *Green Book*. New York: New York Chapter, American Marketing Association. ISSN 8756-534X. LCCN 08645228. Annual. 1978-

This directory has an alphabetical listing of companies with name, address, telephone, fax, branch office, and description of its services; company services index; a market/industry specialties index, and a computer program index. In the geographical section, U.S. companies are listed by state and international companies by country. City name and telephone number accompany each listing.

736. Arpan, Jeffrey S., David A. Ricks, and Edith Flower Kilgo. *Directory of Foreign Manufactures in the United States*. Atlanta, GA: Georgia State University Business Press, 1993. 419 p. ISBN 0884062554. LCCN 79-4146. 1975-

This source includes a summary of the current status of foreign direct investment in the U.S., parent companies ranked by the number of foreign owned U.S. manufacturers, states ranked by the number of foreign owned U.S. manufacturers, and industrial classification ranked by the number of foreign owned U.S. manufacturers, and an alphabetic listing of foreign manufacturers in the U.S. with name, address, telephone, SIC, parent company and its address, and an index of products by SIC.

SEE ALSO *Directory of Foreign Investment in the U.S.: Real Estate and Business*.

737. Dun & Bradstreet. *Directory of the World's Largest Service Companies*. New York: Dun & Bradstreet. ISSN 1014-8507. LCCN 91-649766. 1990- Irregular.

The service industries are categorized alphabetically by subject including: accounting, advertising, air transport, construction, hotels, legal services, market research, and publishing with name, legal status, home country, headquarters, phone, fiscal year, ownership, board of directors. There is company information on background, structure, products, consolidated data worldwide including billings, gross income, operating income, net income, subsidiaries and affiliates.

738. Dun & Bradstreet. *Principal International Businesses*. New York: Dun & Bradstreet. ISSN 0097-6288. LCCN 75-642277. Annual. 1974-

This directory arranges corporations geographically by country, then alphabetically by company name, citing address, telephone number, year incorporated, SIC code, number of employees, product with sales figures expressed in local currency, a product index, and company index.

739. Euromonitor. *The World's Major Companies Directory*. London: Euromonitor. Distributed by Gale Research, Inc., 1995. 756 p. ISBN 086338559.

Multinational companies are profiled with financial information on companies for three years with subsidiaries, turnover at home and abroad, and rankings.

740. Gale Research, Inc. *Companies International.* [computer file] Detroit, MI: Gale Research, Inc., 1994. ISBN 08103-64859.

This compact disk directory has information on companies involved with international trade with: name, address, phone, fax, financial information, 4-digit SIC code, number of employees, and import/export information. It also has names of personnel and contact person.

741. Moody's Investor Service. *Moody's International Manual.* New York: The Service. ISSN 0278-3509. LCCN sc820030291. Annual. 1981-

This listing of corporations includes Algeria to Zimbabwe, profiling people, geography, government, economy, outstanding loans, transportation, electric power, and foreign trade by principal countries. The corporate chapter has information on history, line of service or product, directors, balance sheet, principal subsidiaries, long term debt, and capital stock. It also lists lending institutions such as the African Development Bank, the Asian Development Bank, and European Investment Bank with history, functions, membership, callable capital, operations and ratings of these organizations. It is updated with *Moody's International News Reports*.

742. National Register Publishing Co. *Standard Directory of International Advertisers & Agencies*. Wilmette, IL: National Register Publishing Co., 1993. 1430 p. ISBN 0872171442. LCCN 84-62414.

This directory presents an overview of more than 4,200 advertising companies, agencies, subsidiaries, division and affiliates with name, address, telephone , telex, approximate revenue, year founded, SIC, product, names of officers, media type, and advertising appropriations for advertiser. Indexes to advertisers and advertising agencies; brand name index; a geographical index; and a product index by classification code are included. This is the counterpart to the *Standard Directory of Advertising Agencies* and the *Standard Directory of Advertisers* for the U.S.

743. Shih, Catherine, ed. *International Corporate Yellow Book: Who's Who at the Leading Non-U.S. Companies*. New York: Monitor Pub. Co. ISSN 1058-2894. LCCN 92640558. Semiannual. 1992-

This semi-annual has corporations with name, address, facsimile number, officers, management, major subsidiaries, division, and affiliates of non-U.S. companies.

744. Spain, Patrick J. and James R. Talbot, eds. *Hoover's Handbook of World Business*. Austin, TX: The Reference Press, 1995. 608 p. ISBN 1878753436.

This handbook presents country profiles by region, then individual country with: an overview of the area, history of the country, statistics on population, GDP, exports, imports, consumer inflation, purchasing power, and prominent leaders such as prime minister, ambassador with address, phone and fax number. Company information is also included with history, statistics on sales, net income, income as percentage of sales, return on equity, assets, current ratio, long term debt and president, CEO, personnel manager, number of employees, key competitors and product lines.

745. Stetler, Susan L. and Allison K. McNeill, eds. *International Brands and Their Companies 1993-94: Over 97,000 International Consumer Products and Their Manufacturers, Importers and Distributors*. . . 3rd ed. Detroit: Gale Research, Inc., 1992. 1163 p. ISBN 0810369478. ISSN 1050-8376.

This directory provides information for consumer products manufactured or imported worldwide (except for the U.S. SEE *Brands and Their Companies)* with a product and company breakdown. The product information includes: trade name, brief description, company that manufactures or distributes it, and original source. It includes companies with name, address, phone and tax numbers.

746. Stetler, Susan L. and Allison K. McNeill, eds. *International Companies and Their Brands 1993-94: International Manufacturers, Importers, and Distributors*. Detroit, MI: Gale Research, Inc., 1993. 848 p. ISSN 1050-8384.

This is like the above source except the international companies are arranged before the brands.

747. Stopford, John, M.. and R.H.A. Purkis, eds. *Directory of Multinationals*. New York: Stockton Press, 1992. 2 vols. ISBN 1561590533. LCCN gb92-51183.

Volume 1 profiles corporations with information on: directors, structure, products, background, and current situation, major shareholders, financial information on product sales, total net sales, operating profit, identifiable assets, long term debt, capital expenditure, earnings per share, total employees and principal subsidiaries and affiliates. There is a table with the name of firm, country, foreign sales, and total sales.

748. Times Books. *The Times 1000*. London: Times Books. LCCN 72617301. Annual.

This annual ranks the leading industrial and financial world companies, the top European companies, top American, Japanese, Canadian, British, Australian and South African companies,

749. Uniworld Business Publications. *Directory of Foreign Firms Operating in the United States,* 7th ed. New York: Uniworld Business Publications, 1992. 687 p. ISBN 0836000374. LCCN 26794521.

This is a listing of foreign firms operating in the U.S.

750. Wright Investor's Service. *Worldscope Industrial Company Profiles*. Bridgeport, CT: Wright Investor's Service. 5 vol. ISSN 0504-32060. LCCN 89-156536. 1987- Also available on a compact disk. ISSN 1069-0867.

This five volume set covers companies in Asia, Africa, Australia, Europe, and North America. The information includes: company name, address, telephone, country, ticker symbol, exchange that it trades on, SIC codes, major industry groups, description of business, revenues, number of employees, market value, auditor, ownership, product segment data with sales, assets, capital expenditures, building materials, graphic segment data, officer, key financial items, market capital, common equity and growth rates.

EXPORT DIRECTORIES

751. Journal of Commerce, Inc. *Directory of United States Exporters*. New York: Journal of Commerce Inc., 1996. 1661 p. ISSN 1057-6878. LCCN 92-643845. Annual. Also available on diskette.

This is a directory of U.S. exporters with an alphabetical company listing, product index, numerical product index by Harmonized number, and company listing by state.

752. Swiss Office for the Development of Trade. *Swiss Export Directory: Products and Services of Switzerland*. Zurich, Switzerland: Swiss Office for the Development of Trade. 1 vol. Biennial.

Population, geography, largest towns, economy, embassies, company listing with address, telephone number, director and subsidiaries are some subjects covered with an index of products and services.

753. Thomas International Pub. *American Export Register*. New York: Thomas International Pub. Co. 1 vol. ISSN 0272-1163. LCCN 80648882. Annual. 1980-

This source lists American products and services by subject and company profiles alphabetically with name of contact person, key executives, export sales and fax number, and transportation services such as international air cargo carriers and couriers and freight forwarders.

754. Venture Publishing. *Export Yellow Pages*. Washington, DC: Venture Publishing, N.A. 1 vol. Annual. 1991- Also available on the *National Trade Data Bank*.

This export directory divides U.S. companies into: service providers, trading companies, and producers. The information given is: name of company, address, telephone and fax number, contact person and title. There is also an alphabetical and geographical index and a listing of International Trade offices by state.

IMPORT/TRADE DIRECTORIES

755. Blytmann. *International Directory of Importers Asia/Pacific* Healdsburg, CA: Blytmann International, 1996. 2 vol. ISSN 1050-5539. LCCN 90643777. Eighteen month frequency.

International commodity index, listing of importers from Australia to Thailand with name of the company, address, manager, year established, employees, telephone, telex, cable and products are included in this directory.

756. Blytmann International. *International Directory of Importers South/Central America*. Healdsburg, CA: Blytmann International. 1996. ISSN 1050-5547. LCCN 90643779. Eighteen month frequency.

The arrangement is the same as the directory above except this directory covers the countries of Argentina to the West Indies.

757. Croner Publication Inc. *Trade Directories of the World*. Queens Village, NY: Croner Publication Inc. ISSN 0564-0482. LCCN sc793363.

This loose-leaf volume with updates divides information sources by continents, then country including manufacturing directories, guides, largest companies associations, and a list of regional trade directories such as the Akron (Ohio) International Trade Directory.

758. Gale Research, Inc. *World Trade Resources Guide*. Detroit, MI: Gale Research, Inc., 1992. ISSN 1058-1618. LCCN 92-659025. Semiannual.

This directory has a listing of over 11,000 trade contacts, information on foreign trade sources including country information, organizations, agencies, banks, financial institutions, government agencies, research centers, publications, statistical sources, freight forwarders and shipping lines, and agents.

759. Hilary House Pub. *International Trade Directory of Contacts/Sources/Services*. Boca Raton, FL: Hilary House Pub., 1992. 556 p. ISBN 0934464200. LCCN 92-229742.

This directory has a subject index to: advertising agencies, air cargo carriers, airlines, banks, customs house brokers, embassies in DC, employment opportunities, foreign owned firms in U.S. and importers. The advertising agencies with international clients are divided alphabetically by state, then city, with contact person, name of company, address and telephone number.

760. Interdata. *International Directory of Importers: North America*. Healdsburg, CA: Interdata. 1992. LCCN 9064-3781. ISSN 1050-5466. Eighteen month frequency.

Canadian and U.S. importers are the subject of this directory with the following arrangement: (1) commodity index, (2) Canadian companies alphabetically arranged by name with address, telephone, year established, telephone and fax number and product (3) Canadian product index and (4) U.S. importer index alphabetically arranged by name of company, and then by product.

761. Loiry, William *U.S. - East European Trade Directory*. Chicago: Probus Pub. Co., 1991. 269 p. ISBN 1557381917. LCCN 91015859.

This is a reference source for doing business in Poland, Hungary, the former Czechoslovakia, the former Yugoslavia, Bulgaria, Romania, and Albania.

762. Meara, Meghan A.O. and Kimberly A. Peterson, eds. *World Business Directory*. Detroit, MI: Gale Research, Inc., 1994. 4 v. ISSN 0162-1172. LCCN sn920004526. Annual.

There are four volumes of company listings for 140,000 international trade corporations with name, address, telephone and telex number. Volume 1-3 has company listings alphabetically arranged within geographic sections, and volume 4 has a product index, industry, and alphabetic index. Small and medium sized companies are listed. Names and locations of possible business partners are listed.

763. Johnson Pub. Co. *Worldwide Chamber of Commerce Directory*. Loveland, CO: Johnson Pub. Co. ISSN 0524-78660. Annual. 1987-

This directory of the Chambers of Commerce in the U.S. is alphabetically arranged by states, then cities with contact person, address, and phone number.

GOVERNMENT/ORGANIZATION

764. Congressional Quarterly, Inc. *Washington Information Directory*. Washington, DC: Congressional Quarterly, Inc. ISSN 0887-8064. LCCN 75646321. Annual. 1975-

This directory has information on the federal government including: agencies with name, address, telephone number, and contact person; Congress, and nongovernment organizations; a listing of foreign embassies and state department desk officers.

765. Gale Research, Inc. *Consultants and Consulting Organizations*. Detroit, MI: Gale Research, Inc., 1996. ISSN 0196-1292. LCCN sn79-009748. Annual. 1979-

The 1996 directory lists 23,000 consulting organizations and consultants alphabetically arranged with name, address, phone, fax, email, date founded, staff, and consulting activities.

766. Gale Research, Inc. *Encyclopedia of Associations*. Detroit, MI: Gale Research, Inc. LCCN 76-046129. Annual. Also available on compact disk ISSN 0071-0202.

This is a directory of associations with name, address, telephone, fax, contact person, publication, and meeting dates. This has U.S. organizations.

767. Gale Research, Inc. *Encyclopedia of Associations. International Organizations*. Detroit, MI: Gale Research, Inc. ISSN 1041-0023. LCCN 89-645065. Annual.

This is a directory with the name of association, address, telephone and fax number, date established, and publication and meeting or conference dates for international organizations.

768. Hernandez, Ricardo and Edith Sanchez, eds. *Cross-border Links: A Directory of Organizations in Canada, Mexico, and the United States*. Albuquerque, NM: The Inter-Hemispheric Education Resource Center, 1992. 269 p. ISBN 09112133874. LCCN 92071799.

This book is arranged into the following sections: networks for fair trade, environment, advocacy organizations, academic institutions, government agencies, business groups, and electronic networks. The directory on organizations for Canada, Mexico, and the U.S. has name, address, phone, contact person, and publications.

769. Martens, Hans. *EC Direct: A Comprehensive Directory of EC Contacts*. Oxford, UK. Cambridge, MA: Blackwell, 1992. 230 p. ISBN 0631187960. LCCN 92024062.

This source is for managers and others who need information about Europe and the proper person to solve a business problem. It includes the role of the EC Commission in the decision making process, an organization chart of the Commission, the various departments and people with phone and fax numbers. It has a table for the implementation of Single Market Rules for members as of April 1992.

770. Union of International Associations. *Yearbook of International Organizations*. New York, London: Union of International Associations, 1993. ISSN 0084-3814. LCCN 49-22132. Annual.

This yearbook enumerates international organizations with name, address, telephone and fax number with contact person, year founded, structure, language, staff, finance, events, publications, and members.

771. U.S. Dept. of Commerce. *Export Program: A Business Directory of U.S. Government Services*. Washington, DC: U.S. Government Printing Office, 1994. 1 vol. SUDOCS C 1.2:EX 7/5.

The purpose of this pamphlet is to give an overview of government export assistance available. It lists the program with description, phone numbers, and addresses. It includes export counseling, country and regional business centers, international trade contacts, financing and insurance, and investment feasibility studies program.

772. U.S. Dept. of Commerce. International Trade Administration. *International Financing Programs and U.S. International Economic Competitiveness*. Washington, DC: U.S. Government Printing Office, 1990. 72 p. SUDOCS C 61.2:F 49/2.

This source describes the use of foreign assistance and other government international financing programs to advance national, industrial and commercial interests on the part of the United States, France, Germany, Japan, and the United Kingdom. Also it examines ways to enhance United States international economic competitiveness through financing programs.

773. U.S. Dept. of State. *Diplomatic List*. Washington, DC: U.S. Government Printing Office. ISSN 0012-3099. LCCN 10016292. SUDOCS S 1.8: Quarterly. 1976-

This source lists the names of members of the diplomatic staff with their address, telephone and fax number, and national holidays for each country.

774. U.S. Dept. of State. *Foreign Consular Officers in the United States*. Washington, DC: U.S. Government Printing Office. ISSN 0071-7320. LCCN 32026478. SUDOCS S 1.69/2: Semiannual. 1932-

This guide profiles consular officers in the United States. It includes national holidays from January to December and the chancery offices in the United States.

775. U.S. Dept. of State. *Key Officers of Foreign Service Posts: Guide for Business Representatives*. Washington, DC: U.S. Government Printing Office. ISSN 0023-0790. LCCN 64061222. SUDOCS S 1.40/5: (Also on the National Trade Data Bank)

The key officers of foreign service posts help companies arrange appointments with government officials and provide information on local trade regulations, laws and customs. Economic officers report on trends and policies that affect the U.S. and its programs. This source lists U.S. embassies, consulates, Department of Commerce District Offices, information and special notices from Albania to Zimbabwe, ambassadors, deputy chief of mission, commercial officers, economic officers, and agricultural officers, and desk officers.

776. U.S. Office of the Federal Register. *United States Government Manual*. Washington, DC: U.S. Government Printing Office. ISSN 0092-1904. LCCN 73646537. Annual. 1973- Also available on web sites.

It is a good source for agency information, listing the purpose, history, address, phone number, principal official, and organization chart of each agency.

CHAPTER X

DICTIONARIES

Dictionaries are useful for defining and understanding many business, trade, and other terms. No one dictionary covers every term and different dictionaries offer slightly different definitions. Consulting several dictionaries for a term makes for a more complete definition. In some dictionaries, the definition for a term such as GATT resembles a brief article with definition, description, goals and members of international organizations.

777. Ammer, Christine and Dean. *Dictionary of Business and Economics*. New York: The Free Press, 1984. 507 p. ISBN 0029007909. LCCN 83-48175.

This dictionary has good definitions and explanations on how information is derived, economic theory of past and present, and biographies of the most important economists.

778. Baker, Michael J. *Dictionary of Marketing & Advertising*. New York: Nichols Publishing, 1990. 271 p. ISBN 0893973718. LCCN 90-7454.

This defines marketing and advertising terms in a concise and informative way. Organizations and brief biographies are also included. Good definition of GATT with definition, goals, historical background.

779. Drost, Harry. *What's What and Who's Who in Europe*. New York: Simon & Schuster, 1994. 646 p. ISBN 0304341177. LCCN 95-148041.

This is a dictionary of people, ethnic groups, places, organizations, terms and events.

780. Fry, Gerald. *The International Development Dictionary*. Santa Barbara, CA.: ABC-CLIO, 1991. 445 p. ISBN 0874365457. LCCN 91-018796.

This is a dictionary of international development that includes: theorists, leaders, and analytical concepts. It includes terms and explains their significance. Some examples are: commodity agreements, comparative advantage, counter trade, export processing zone.

781. Gipson, Carolyn R. *The McGraw-Hill Dictionary of International Trade and Finance*. New York: McGraw-Hill, 1994. 419 p. ISBN 0070236003. LCCN 93021390.

This is a dictionary of international trade and financial terms including acronyms, abbreviations, organizations, and associations such as GATT (General Agreements on Tariff and Trade), ESCAP (Economic and Social Commission for Asia and the Pacific) and FAS (free alongside ship). There are cross references, a brief history of organizations, and some foreign phrases used in trade.

782. Hart, Norman and John Stapleton, eds. *The Marketing Dictionary,* 4th ed. Oxford, England: Butterworth Heinemann, 1991. 252 p. ISBN 0750602082. LCCN gb91-90942.

Entries for over 3000 marketing terms including research, management, packaging, advertising, and selling can be found in this dictionary.

783. Hindle, Tim. *Field Guide to Marketing: A Glossary of Essential Tools and Concepts for Today's Manager.* Boston, MA: Harvard Business School Press, 1994. 195 p. ISBN 0875844359. LCCN 93023865.

This is a marketing dictionary that looks at marketing issues and defines marketing terms including: mini essays on terms such as: global brand, brief biographies, acronyms, and agency giants such as Dentsu with sprinkling of humorous quotations.

784. International Chamber of Commerce. *INCOTERMS: International Rules for the Interpretation of Trade Terms.* Paris: ICC Pub., 1990, 215 p. ISBN 9284200873.

The purpose of this source is to define the most commonly used trade terms to prevent misunderstandings in different countries. The main reason for the revision of ICOTERMS was to adapt terms for electronic data interchange. It includes terms such as: FAS (free alongside ship), CFR (cost and freight), and DDP (delivery duty paid). See also *Guide to Incoterms 1990.*

785. Links, Albert N. *Links International Dictionary of Business Economics.* Chicago, IL: PROBUS Publishing Co., 1993. 293 p. ISBN 155738505x. LCCN 93-193426.

This dictionary defines over 2,500 terms, including many international trade terms and phrases.

786. Miller, William J. *Encyclopedia of International Commerce.* Centreville, MD: Cornell Maritime Press, 1985. 391 p. ISBN 0412280108. LCCN 90-123510.

This source contains the terminology of international trade with definition, description, goals and members of international organizations.

SEE Also *National Trade Data Bank* for trade terms.

787. Presner, Lewis A. *International Business Dictionary and Reference*. Lewis A. Presner. New York: J. Wiley, 1991. 486 p. ISBN 0417545945. LCCN 91-9328.

Definitions give brief legislative history, goals (such as the Caribbean Basin Initiative), and some detailed explanation on how terms are derived or calculated. There are many trade terms included.

788. Ramberg, Jan. *Guide to Incoterms*. Paris: ICC Publishing, SA, 1991. 152 p. ISBN 9284210887.

This is a guide for Incoterms in 1990 with an introduction, the importance of trade terms, the trends toward delivered terms, the use of electronic data interchange, and changes in transportation techniques. This guide gives an overview of the buyers and sellers obligation and analysis of the 13 Incoterms section.

789. Rosenberg, Jerry. *Dictionary of International Trade*. New York: J. Wiley, 1994. 314 p. ISBN 0471597325. LCCN 93-5188.

More than 4,000 entries are included in this dictionary with definitions, symbols, acronyms, and abbreviations. For terms such as General Agreements on Tariff and Trade (GATT) there is a brief article with date treaty was signed, and the effects of treaty on consumers.

790. Rosenberg, Jerry M. *Encyclopedia of the North American Free Trade Agreement, New American Community, and Latin-American Trade*. Westport, CT: Greenwood Press, 1995. 562 p. ISBN 0313290695. LCCN 94016984.

This encyclopedia covers specific issues, rationales, ideologies, controversies, and actions needed to increase understanding in the pursuit of cooperation and productivity if the New American Communities are to be incorporated into future treaties.

791. Rosenberg, Jerry M. *The New Europe: An A to Z Compendium on the European Community*. Washington, DC: Bureau of National Affairs, 1991. 206 p. ISBN 0871796694. LCCN 90-48878.

There are 2,500 definitions of the European Community with a brief background on the institutions of the European Community such as: European Commission, Council of Ministers, European Parliament, Court of Justice, and legislative process of this body. Explanation of policies, identification of people, places and events, and structure and chronology of the European community are contained in this dictionary.

792. U.S. Dept. of Commerce. *Reference Terms of International Trade: The Uruguay Roundtable*. Washington, DC: U.S. Government Printing Office, 1987. 8 p. SUDOCS C 61.2:T 27.

This pamphlet has a selective list of trade acronyms and terms used by GATT.

Chapter XI

REGULATIONS, LAWS, AND TRADE AGREEMENTS

Laws, regulations, and agreements that affect business and trade such as the North American Free Trade Agreement and the U.S. Generalized System of Preferences are included in this chapter and also studies of the effects of these agreements. This chapter provides an overview of some regulations and legal requirements. These regulations and laws are not to be interpreted as all-encompassing or construed as legal advice.

The chapter is divided into: regulations and laws, export/import and trade agreements.

Some examples of publications on regulations are: *Export/Import Procedures and Documentation,* a procedure and documentation manual; *U.S. Export Administration Regulations*, a source covering export licensing requirements and a commodity control list for national security purposes.

The National Trade Data Bank has regulations on import duty for some foreign countries on certain products.

The trade agreements include: GATT and Uruguay, Maastricht, and the North American Free Trade Agreement.

REGULATIONS AND LAWS

793. Baudot, Barbara Sandberg. *International Advertising Handbook: A User's Guide to Rules and Regulations*. Lexington, MA: D.C. Heath and Co., 1989. 359 p. ISBN 0669170704. LCCN 87-45968.

The advertising rules and regulations of a country are a reflection the origins of regulations in the different countries. It covers: an introduction to regulatory environments around the world, issues, laws, and regulations, and the role of international organizations as they attempt to protect Third World countries. This handbook is not intended as a comprehensive summary for advertising regulations.

794. Gottschalk, Jack A. *The Global Trade and Investment Handbook: a Country-by-Country Reference to Business Practices, Regulations and Laws*. Chicago, IL: Probus Publishing Co. 1993. 675 p. ISBN 1557384762.

There are over 155 nations covered in this source with information on political environment, foreign investment policy summary, types of permitted business organizations, rights and obligations of foreign investors, labor, accounting requirements, currency controls, taxation, legal system, protection of intellectual property, immigration and residence, and a foreign assistance directory.

795. Graham, John, ed. *The International Handbook of Corporate and Personal Taxes,* Second Edition, 1994. London: Chapman & Hall. 679 p. ISBN 041247910. LCCN gb94-60717.

This handbook arranges countries alphabetically for tax purposes from Argentina to the USA including: corporate taxes, resident companies, non-resident companies, tax year and filing requirements, taxes imposed, rate of tax, income subject to tax, capital gains, losses, dividends, and deduction, value added tax and sales tax.

SEE ALSO *Lexis/Nexis*

796. Manser, W.A.P. *Control from Brussels*. London: Economist Intelligence Unit, 1994. 175 p. ISBN 0206124212. LCCN93248101.

This is a survey of European Community Laws that affect corporations. It is a readable and comprehensive without jargon or undue legal details including: the freedom of movement of persons, job notification and standardized training, European standards, movements of goods, problems of VAT (value added tax) excise duties, public procurement and European Company Law. It covers the regulation of company organization and management, the rules for creating branches and subsidiaries, mergers, and takeovers, finance, accounting and taxation. This survey is adapted from the Economist Intelligence Unit report *Control from Brussels...* completely revised and updated.

SEE ALSO *National Trade Data Bank.*

This database has unique information on tariff, taxes and other regulations. For example, there is a compilation of world motor vehicle import requirements, value-added taxes, the North American Free Trade Agreement, *Country Reports on Economic Policy and Trade Practices*, General Agreement on Tariffs and Trade, and tariffs and taxes on various industries. Some are specific, such as taxes on a particular industry. The listing changes monthly.

SEE ALSO Price Waterhouse. *Price Waterhouse Information Guide Series.*

797. Tax Management Inc. *Tax Management Portfolios: Foreign Income.* Washington, DC: Tax Management Inc, 1996. ISSN 0494-8270. LCCN 90643888.

This is a series that is divided into: foreign income and U.S. income and estates, gifts and trust. The foreign income section has a distinctive title, i.e. *Business Operations in ...* (name of the country). The portfolio provides country information and efficient ways of doing business in a particular country. The information is heavy on taxes but includes: the country, its people and economy, operating a business in the country, forms of doing business, principal taxes, taxation of resident corporations, taxation of foreign corporations, taxation of branch, and taxation of partnerships. Worksheets include forms such as: corporate income returns, inheritance and gift tax rates.

798. United Nations. Commission on International Trade Law. *Yearbook - United Nations Commission on International Trade Law*. New York: United Nations. ISSN 0251-4265. LCCN 72625945. Annual. 1972-

Part I has the Commission's report and action of the United Nations Conference on Trade and Development and by the General Assembly. Part II has a reproduction of the list of documents considered at the 25th session (description for 1992 edition). Also there are selected working papers on studies and reports on specific subjects such as: international payments and international countertrade. Part III contains the model law on international credit transfer, the Convention on Limitation Period in the International Sale of Goods as amended by the Protocol.

799. Verzariu, Pompiliu. *International Countertrade: Individual Country Practices*. Washington, DC: US. Government Printing Office, 1992. SUDOCS C 61.2:C 82/2. 33 p.

This document defines countertrade. Some forms of countertrade are: offsets, barter, buyback and counterpurchase. Countertrade practices are covered by region, then individual country. The regions covered are: Eastern Europe and the CIS, Latin America, Africa, and Asia.

EXPORT/IMPORT

800. Johnson,Thomas E. *Export/Import Procedures and Documentation*. New York: AMACOM, 1994. 439 p. ISBN 0814402372. LCCN 94-0063.

Part I explains organizing for exporting. It includes procedure and documentation manuals for the export/import department, export organization charts, export order processing, and a chart for workflow pictures. Part II has exporting procedures and documentation examples. Some subjects covered are: compliance with foreign law, export controls licenses, countries of restricted destination and commodity control lists.

Some subjects covered are: compliance with foreign law, export controls licenses, countries of restricted destination and commodity control lists.

801. Stowell, Alan M. ed. *U.S. International Trade Laws*. Washington, DC: Bureau of National Affairs, 1989. 730 p. ISBN 0871796147. LCCN 89009749.

This is a compilation of import and export laws such as: The trade Act of 1974, Trade Agreements Act of 1979, Trade and Tariff Act of 1984, Export Administration Amendments Act of 1985, Omnibus Trade & Competitiveness Act of 1988 and U.S. Canada & Free Trade Implementation Act. The source cites the titles and paragraphs in the United States Code.

802. U.S. Dept. of Commerce. Bureau of Export Administration. Office of Technology and Policy Analysis. *Annual Foreign Policy Report to Congress*. LCCN sn92-40957. Washington, DC: U. S. Government Printing Office. SUDOCS C 61.11/2: Annual. 1988-

There are extensions and revisions to the U.S. Exports Control programs maintained for security purposes. This annual includes description, licensing policy, purpose for controls regarding crime control equipment, supercomputers, and other instruments that might be used for military equipment, embargoed countries, and biological agents.

803. U.S. Dept. of Commerce. International Trade Administration. *Foreign Regulations Affecting U.S. Textile/Apparel Exports*. Washington, DC: U.S. Government Printing Office, 1994. 341 p. LCCN sn92-23659. SUDOCS C 61.2:F 76/

Restrictions and requirements of 60 countries are listed from Argentina to the former Yugoslavia that affect the U.S. textile and apparel export sales. The 60 countries represent top markets and the report includes: tariffs, import bans, license or permit requirements, special taxes, fees, or surcharges and quota requirements. Also tables are included on exports to particular countries.

804. U.S. Dept. of Commerce. International Trade Administration. *U.S. Export Administration Regulations*. Washington, DC: U.S. Government Printing Office. LCCN 90-649431. SUDOCS C 61.23: Irregular.

This regulation guide answers questions on export licensing requirements for products that are subject to export controls. The U.S. participates with 16 other countries in the Coordinating Committee for Multilateral Export Controls (COCOM). The Bureau of Export Administration (BXA) publishes a commodity control list for security purposes. This commodity control list includes arms, ammunition, implements of war as well as computers, software, electronics, and technical data.

805. U.S. Dept. of Treasury. Customs Service. *Customs Valuation Encyclopedia*. Washington, DC: U.S. Government Printing Office, 1995. ISBN 0160480248. SUDOCS T 17.2:EN 1/.

This encyclopedia includes: valuation statutory provisions, portions of the Customs Valuation Code, judicial precedent, and rulings of U.S. Customs Headquarters: The table of contents includes: assists, counter trade, currency conversion, duties and taxes and invoice requirements.

806. U.S. Dept. of Treasury. Customs Service. *NAFTA, the North American Free Trade Agreement: a Guide to Customs Procedures*. Washington, DC: U.S. Government Printing Office, 1994. 51 p. ISBN 0160430410. SUDOCS T 17.26:571/994.

This is a manual on customs procedures regarding NAFTA. It explains chapters 4 and 5 of the North American Free Trade Agreement that describe the rules of origin and procedural obligations relating to customs administration and gives an overview of the benefits and requirements for importers, exporters, and manufacturers.

807. U.S. Dept. of Treasury. *Customs Regulations of the United States*. Washington, DC: U.S. Government Printing Office, 1994. 51 p.ISBN 0160430410. SUDOCS T 17.9:

This publication covers U.S. import and export regulations that must bc strictly observed. It includes: vessels in foreign and domestic trades, packing, stamping and marking, special classes of merchandise, cargo container and road vehicle certification pursuant to international customs convention, and customs relations with Canada and Mexico.

SEE ALSO U.S. Dept. of the Treasury. U.S. Customs Service. *Importing into the United States*.

808. U.S. International Trade Commission. *The Year in Trade: Operations of the Trade Agreement Program.* Washington, DC: U.S. Government Printing Office. SUDOCS ITC 1.24: Annual. 1993-

This is an annual report of the International Trade Commission to Congress including its trade policies and activities for the year. The 1994 issue includes: information on its trade policy and its administration including: GATT, Uruguay Round, creation of WTO, NAFTA, and multilateral activities. It gives a summary of 1994 trade agreement activities.

809. U.S. Office of the Federal Register. National Archives and Records Administration. *Code of Federal Regulations. 15 Commerce and Foreign Trade*. Title 15. Washington, DC: U.S. Government Printing Office SUDOCS AE 2.106/3:15/pt. 0-299/.

These U.S. regulations relate to commerce and foreign trade such as: general requirements for exporters and exporting carriers.

810. United States. Office of the Federal Register. National Archives and Records Administration. *Code of Federal Regulations. Title 19, Customs Duties*. Washington, DC: U.S. Government Printing Office. SUDOCS AE 2.106/3:19/.

These are U.S. regulations relating to customs duties.

811. U.S. Office of the President. *U.S. Generalized System of Preferences (GSP)* Washington, DC: U.S. Government Printing, 1991. 129 p. SUDOCS PREX 9.2:G 28

This publication describes briefly the requirements for importing articles duty free under this program and lists articles eligible for duty free treatment. Presents changes in the designations of eligible articles or countries under the GSP.

TRADE AGREEMENTS

GATT

812. Hudec, Robert E. *Enforcing International Trade Law: the Evolution of the Modern GATT Legal System.* Salem, NH: Butterworth Legal Publishers, 1993. 630 p. ISBN 0880633558. LCCN 9310758.

This book includes the legislative history of the General Agreement on Tariffs and Trade, the evolution of this organization and its legal structure, the dispute settlement mechanism, and a profile of GATT dispute settlement cases. The appendix lists a chronological table of complaints from 1948 to November 1989. The purpose of GATT is the reduction of tariffs among the signatories and nondiscrimination or Most Favored Nation (MFN) -- meaning every trade advantage given to any GATT member is given unconditionally to its other members.

In the 1990s, there is an effort to restructure GATT at the Uruguay Round in the areas of: service, intellectual property rights, and trade related investment measures.

813. GATT Publications. *Trade Policy Review*. Geneva, Switzerland: GATT Publications Service, 1992. 2 v.

The objective of the Trade Policy Review is to achieve compliance of contracting parties to GATT (General Agreements on Tariff and Trade) rules, disciplines and commitments. It is not the basis for enforcement of GATT obligations. Each issue reviews a specific country including trade policy features and trends, trade policy and foreign trading partners, recent economic performance, and structure of trade policy objectives, and trade disputes. Some of the countries reviewed are: Finland, Korea, and the United States. Volume 2 has concluding remarks by the chairman of the council and a report of the government of the country being reviewed.

814. U.S. Congress. House. Committee on Foreign Affairs. Subcommittee on Economic Policy, Trade and Environment. *GATT, the Expert's View: Hearing Before the Subcommittee on Economic Policy, Trade, and Environment of the Committee on Foreign Affairs, House of Representatives, One Hundred Third Congress, second session*. Washington, DC: U.S. Government Printing Office, 1994. 46 p. ISBN 0160448956. SUDOCS Y 4.F 76/1:T 67/17.

GATT will take effect in the twenty-first century, and it will provide substantial benefits to the American economy in the areas of agriculture, services, and intellectual property. It will liberalize trade which will reduce tariffs, eliminate all "voluntary" export restraint agreements, and will result in gains that are estimated to be about $70 billion by the Institute for International Economics.

815. U.S. Office of the President. *Final Act Embodying the Results of the Uruguay Round of Multilateral Trade Negotiations*. Washington, DC: U.S. Government Printing Office, 1993. 1 vol. ISBN 0160430372. SUDOCS PREX 1.2: EM 1.

This is the final act of the December 1993 version of the Uruguay

Round of Multilateral Trade Negotiations with the actual text of the agreement that includes: the scope, functions, and structure of the Multilateral Trade Organization, its relations with other organizations, and its decision making consensus under the GATT 1947 agreement.

816. U.S. Office of the President. *The GATT Uruguay Round Agreements: Report on Environmental Issues*. Washington, DC: U.S. Government Printing Office, 1994. 35 p. ISBN 0160451558. SUDOCS PREX 9.2:UR 8/14.

The purpose of The General Agreements on Tariffs and Trade (GATT) is to provide a secure and reliable trading environment. However, the dispute mechanism is not effective, so members meet in Uruguay to launch the Uruguay Round of Multilateral Trade Negotiations. This report addresses environmental concerns which will strengthen economic growth but may increase environmental problems. It includes: an overview of the Uruguay Round Agreements, trade and environment issues under the current GATT agreement, provisions of the Uruguay with potential effects on U.S. environmental laws, and agreement on technical barriers to trade.

817. U.S. Office of the President. *Report of the Services Policy Advisory Committee (SPAC), on the Results of the GATT Uruguay Round Negotiation*. Washington, DC: U.S. Government Printing Office, 1994. 27 p. SUDOCS PREX 9.2:UR 8/6.

The service sector is important in the world economy but it has never been addressed by GATT. As a result of this agreement, there is a reduction of trade barriers in the service industry so U.S. firms can compete effectively. However, the trading partners are unwilling to make commitments in audio visual,financial, and telecommunications services (a disappointment to the SPAC Committee). The creation of rules and disciplines for services trade and investment is accomplished although they are non-binding.

818. United States. Office of the President. *The Uruguay Round of Multilateral Trade Negotiations*. Washington, DC: U.S. Government Printing Office, 1994. 77 p. SUDOCS PREX 9.2: UR 8/4.

The Uruguay Round Table seeks to expand the GATT system to include services, intellectual property, and investment, and to improve its function. The report is divided into two categories: (1) market access and trade rules (2) other codes and expansion of the GATT system.

819. U.S. Office of the President. *Report of the United States Trade Representative's Intergovernmental Policy Advisory Committee (IGPAC) to the agreements reached in the Uruguay Round of Multilateral Trade Negotiations: Submitted to the Congress, January 14, 1994.* Washington, DC: U.S. Government Printing Office, 1994. 33 p. SUDOCS PREX 9.2:UR 8/9.

Although the Intergovernmental Policy Advisory Committee (IGPAC) endorsed the Uruguay Round of Multilateral Trade Negotiations, the Committee does not approve all aspects of the agreement. On the whole, the panel feels "...the Uruguay Agreements provide a foundation for the construction of a freer and fairer world trading system that should benefit American economic growth and competitiveness."

820. United States. Office of the President. *The Uruguay Round of Multilateral Trade Negotiations: Report of the Industry Sector and Functional Advisory Committees (ISAC/IFAC)*. Washington, DC: U.S. Government Printing Office, 1994. 1 vol. SUDOCS PREX 9.2:UR 8/2.

This report has policy, technical advice, information and recommendations to the Secretary and USTR on the following industries: Aerospace Equipment, Capital Goods, Chemicals and Allied Products, Consumer Goods, electronics and instrumentation, ferrous ores and metals, standards and intellectual property rights. It includes trade related investment measures that the Uruguay Round needs to address such as:

investment barriers, dispute settlement, and the establishment of the World Trade Organization to facilitate implementation of trade agreements in the diverse area of trade in goods and services.

821. U.S. Office of the President. *The Uruguay Round of Multilateral Trade Negotiations: Report of the Investment Policy Advisory Committee*. Washington, DC: U.S. Government Printing Office, 1994. 21 p. SUDOCS PREX 9.2:UR 8/8.

The Investment Policy Advisory Committee represents the private sector and provides advice to the President, the Congress and the U.S. Trade Representative on investment policy issues relating to international economic activity. This report begins with a review of transnational investments on U.S. and global economic growth, and it concludes that fostering transnational investment promotes the economic interest of the U.S. It recommends approval of the Uruguay Round although the committee was disappointed that trade related investment measures were not a success.

822. U.S. Office of the President. *The Uruguay Round of Multilateral Trade Negotiations Report of the Labor Advisory Committee (LAC)*. Washington, DC: U.S. Government Printing Office, 1994. SUDOCS PREX 9.2:UR 8/7.

LAC for Trade Negotiations and Trade Policy feels that the proposed Uruguay Round of Multilateral Trade Agreements offers little to the U.S. workers and in some cases is detrimental to their interest. Nevertheless, the Committee will continue to work with the Administration and Congress to craft a better agreement.

823. World Trade Organization. Information and Media Relations Division. *WTO Focus*. Geneva, Switzerland: World Trade Organization. Information and Media Relations Division. ISSN 0256-0119. LCCN sn 9520147. 10/year.

This newsletter informs with outlook, issues, and events that affect trade policy and includes excerpts from the Trade Policy Review Body. Past issues include: WTO establishment, function, structure, and members.

Maastricht

SEE ALSO Europa web site for full text of this treaty.

824. Corbett, Richard. *The Treaty of Maastricht: from Conception to Ratification: A Comprehensive Reference Guide*. Harlow, Essex, U.K.: Longman Group, 1993. 512 p. ISSN 0582209064. LCCN 93-161402.

This is a legislative history of the Treaty on European Union. It includes the text of the Treaty; various Community and member states' documents that led to its signature and ratification; and a chronological table of contents, and a glossary.

North American Free Trade Agreement

825. Globerman, Steven and Michael Walker, eds. *Assessing NAFTA: a Trinational Analysis*. Vancouver: Fraser Institute, 1993. 314 p. ISBN 0889751560. LCCN 93200727.

This collection of papers analyzes the North American Free Trade Agreement (NAFTA) from an American, Canadian and Mexican perspective. It gives an overview of NAFTA, the impact of the agreement on the different industrial sectors such as: automotive, agriculture, textiles and apparel, and financial services as well as the countries involved. Other areas discussed are dispute settlement, investment provisions, and environmental considerations. The conclusion is that NAFTA is worthwhile and will contribute to liberalizing trade arrangements in North America, and the gains will be more immediately available to Mexico.

826. Hastings, Paul et al. *North American Free Trade Agreement: Summary and Analysis*. New York, NY: M. Bender, 1993. 112 p.

This summary and analysis are not intended to be exhaustive but to present highlights to help users focus on understanding the basic objectives of the NAFTA agreement and help clients spot areas in which the implementation of this treaty may affect their interests. (This analysis was prepared in 1992).

827. Hufbauer, Gary Clyde and Jeffrey Schott. *North American Free Trade: Issues and Recommendations*. Washington, DC: Institute for International Economics, 1992. 369 p. ISBN 0881321206. LCCN 92008206.

This study examines the North American Free Trade Agreement providing: an overview, national objectives, issues, recommendations, and the economic implications for U.S., Mexico, Canada, and non-member countries. It also gives a sectoral analyses covering: energy, automobiles, steel, textiles, and agriculture.

SEE ALSO Moran, Robert T. and Jeffrey D. Abbott. *NAFTA: Managing the Cultural Differences*.

828. Reams, Bernard D. and Jon S. Schultz. *The North American Free Trade Agreement (NAFTA): Documents and Materials including a Legislative History of the North American Free Trade Agreement Implementation Act: Public Law 103-182*. Buffalo, NY: William S. Hein & Co., 1994. 29 v. ISBN 0899418996. LCCN 94077540.

829. Rugman, Alan M. *Foreign Investment and NAFTA*. Columbia, SC: University of South Carolina Press, 1994. 340 p. ISBN 0872499936. LCCN 93048267.

NAFTA will accelerate economic changes in North America. It is an economic regionalization based on the European Community, Japan and North America markets. This regionalization is driven by multinational enterprises. Mexico will have the greatest gain from NAFTA although there will also be costs.This source includes the economics and politics of NAFTA and NAFTA's treatment of foreign investment.

830. U.S.. Dept. of Agriculture. National Library of Medicine. *North American Free Trade Agreement (NAFTA) Mexico United States-Canada Trade Accord*. Washington, DC: U.S. Government Printing Office, 1993. 1 v. SUDOCS A 17.18/6:93-01.

Mostly this is a listing of periodical articles which give information on NAFTA from 1987 to 1992 and goals such as: tariff elimination, increased trade in agriculture, reduced textile and apparel barriers, expanded trade in financial services, and protection of intellectual property rights.

SEE ALSO U.S. Congress. House Committee on Government Operations. *The North American Free Trade Agreement (NAFTA) and Its Impact on the Textile/Apparel/Fiber and Auto and Auto Parts Industries*.

831. U.S. Executive Office of the President. *1993 North American Free Trade Agreement between the Government of the United States of America, the Government of Canada and the Government of the United Mexican States*. Washington, DC: U.S. Government Printing Office, 1993. 5 vols. (ISBN 0160419603-vols. 1-2; ISBN 016041962x-vol. 3; ISBN 0160419654-vol.4; ISBN 01640419611-vol. 5.) SUDOCS PREX 1.2:T 67/993-2/vols. *(NAFTA)*

This five volume document has the objectives of the NAFTA

agreement, definitions, treatment and market access for goods, rules of origin, customs procedures, investment services and related matter. It establishes a free trade zone for the three countries. Volume 2 discusses specific rules of origin covering live animals, animal products, beverages, spirits and vinegar, mineral products, plastics and articles. Volume 3-5 covers the tariff schedule of Canada, Mexico (in Spanish) and the United States with base rate and staging category (different time periods for the elimination of tariff barriers).

832. U.S. Office of the Federal Register. *U.S. Statutues at Large* 107 (1993): *North American Free Trade Agreement Implementation Act.103-182*. Washington, DC: U.S. Government Printing Office, 1993. 1 v. SUDOCS AE 2.111:103-182.

This is the law to implement the North American Free Trade Agreement.

SEE ALSO : Web site Business and Economic Reference for links to sites on NAFTA.

CHAPTER XII

CLASSIFICATION CODES

There are various classification codes used in business and trade. This chapter is divided into: industrial and commodity classification.

Three most commonly used classification codes from a U.S. perspective will be identified and defined, and a brief background will be given. The following manuals can be used to identify the classification codes:

Standard Industrial Classification Code (SIC)
Standard International Trade Classification Code
Harmonized Commodity Description and Coding System

The **Standard Industrial Classification Code (SIC)** is an industry classification. Its purpose is the collection, tabulation, and analysis of data related to establishments in the U.S. by the type of company activity. Other countries have their counterparts to this industry classification and they are listed.

The SIC Code is not interchangeable with the commodity or product classification. The SIC number reflects an establishment classification and identifies the individual commodity or commodity group. It is a four digit number. There are commercial publications that modify this SIC number such as the Dun & Bradstreet (expands the SIC code to 8 digits) and Predicasts. The commercial publishers extend the SIC number to reflect more quickly the changes in the industry.

Some sources used to identify the SIC numbers and modified SIC are:

Standard Industrial Classification Manual
Standard Industrial Classification Manual 2 + 2

Some publications that use the SIC code are: *Annual Survey of Manufacturers*, *Census of Manufacturers* and *County Business Patterns*, and *Predicasts Basebook.*

Some corporate directories include the SIC number for a company. *Ward's Business Directory...* also ranks corporations by the SIC number, such as companies with the largest sales, number of employees, and assets. *Predicasts Basebook* uses a modified 7 digit SIC code to specify a segment of the industry. Some counterparts to the U.S. SIC are:

The European counterpart is NACE.

The United Nations counterpart is International Standard Industrial Classification (ISIC).

The Canadian equivalent is the Standard Industrial Classification, 1980.

In the U.S., there are concerns and criticisms about the SIC system, for example, that it is not effective for collecting, tabulating, and analyzing data. A committee, the Economic Classification Policy Committee, was established in 1992 by the Office of Management and Budget to examine this economic classification system.

The Committee is working on a new system which will include Canada and Mexico. This new system will be called the North American Industrial Classifications System (NAICS). It will be implemented some time in 1997.

The Standard International Trade Classification. Where the SIC number refers to the establishment or line of business, the standard international trade classification code classifies a commodity or product. It is an international system. Its history began with attempts at standardizing commodities for trade purposes in the 1930's when the League of Nations published a report called the *Minimum List of Commodities International Trade Statistics (Minimum List)* based on a 1937 revision of the League's Draft Custom Nomenclature.

The *Minimum List* was soon outdated by the rapid changes in international trade and the needs of countries for comparing trade data.

The United Nations recommended revising the *Minimum List*. The United Nations Secretariat with the assistance of government and experts drafted the 1950 edition of the United Nations Standard International Trade Classification (SITC) referred to as the original SITC and the Economic and Social Council accepted the resolution.

The classification system served as a basis for systematic analysis of world trade and a standard for reporting trade statistics to international trade agencies, thus alleviating the burden on governments. The Council urged all governments to accept this system of classification and to modify it as necessary to meet national requirements without disturbing the framework of the classification.

At the same time the SITC was being developed, many European and non-European countries were using a different system called the Customs Tariff Nomenclature. It was based on the 1955 Tariff Nomenclature (BTN) of the Customs Cooperation Council which was headquartered in Brussels. This nomenclature grouped products according to the nature of the materials.

Data based on BTN data had to be regrouped and this regrouping of the BTN data into the form of the original SITC involved numerous subdivisions of the BTN items.

Experts from countries and intergovernmental agencies using both the original SITC and the BTN prepared the SITC revision. The source used to identify the SITC number is the *Standard International Trade Classification, Revision 3.*

Some United Nations publications list products or commodities by the SITC number such as: *Foreign Trade by Commodities*, *International Trade Statistics Yearbook* and the *Monthly Statistics of Foreign Trade.*

The Harmonized Commodity and Coding System was adopted by the U.S. and its major trading partners on January 1989. The Harmonized System (HS) is an international standardized product nomenclature. It describes, classifies, and codes goods for customs, tariff, and statistical purposes. It is a means to standardize import and export information and enhance data collection internationally. It obligates contracting countries to use the six digit nomenclature as the basis for their customs, tariff, and statistical nomenclature for imports and exports. The HS is a written description with a corresponding numerical code for a product. The HS encodes information in a digital system as compared with the manual system of the Customs Cooperation Council.

Using this numerical code for product, government and industry can examine import and export statistics from countries around the world. From these import/export statistics, growth and production patterns can be identified. Companies can determine the absence or presence of competition for its product or service in the target countries.

The *National Trade Data Bank* uses the HS number for the export figures of a commodity or product that the United States exports to the world (total) and then broken down by specific country. This HS number is one key to the information in the *National Trade Data Bank* and *U.S. Import* and *U.S. Exports*. (Computerized Programs)

In addition to the HS number, *The Harmonized Tariff Schedule of the United States* also gives the importers rates of duty classified into general, special, or free and lists beneficiary developing countries for the Generalized System of Preference.

INDUSTRIAL CLASSIFICATION CODE

Europe

833. Office for Publications of the European Community. *NACE: General Industrial Classification of Economic Activities Within the European Communities,* Luxembourg, Belgium: Office for Publications of the European Community, 1985. 100 p. ISBN 928255628X.

Canada

834. Statistics Canada. Standards Division. *Canadian Standard Industrial Classification for Companies and Enterprises. 1980.* Ottawa, Canada: Statistics Canada, Standards Division, 1986. 381 p. ISBN 0660119455. LCCN 87-120163.

835. Statistics Canada Standards Division. *Standard Industrial Classification, 1980.* Ottawa, Canada: Statistics Canada, Standards Division, 1980. 528 p. ISBN 0660106728. LCCN 81-198750.

United States

836. Dun & Bradstreet. *Standard Industrial Classification Manual: SIC 2 + 2*. Murray Hill, NJ: Dun & Bradstreet Information Resources, 1989. 1 v.

This manual modifies the SIC (Standard Industrial Classification) to detect and analyze changes in business activity and industrial structures.

837. U.S. Dept. of Commerce. *Concordance Between the Standard Industrial Classification of the United States and Canada*. Washington, DC: U.S. Government Printing Office, 1993. SUDOCS C 3.2:C 74 (microfiche).

This concordance was developed to compare and analyze the industrial data of Canada and the United States. Although both classification systems have many similarities, differences arise due to economic structure of the two countries in the organization of production and the size of their markets. This document compares the standard industrial classifications of the United States and Canada, their economic structure, classification criteria and includes concordance tables and explanatory notes.

838. U.S. Dept. of Commerce. National Technical Information Service (NTIS). *The Computerized SIC Index*. Springfield, VA: National Technical Information Service, 1991. Order Number PB91-507947/CAU. (diskettes)

839. U.S. Dept. of Commerce. NTIS. *Computerized SIC-Industry and Product Classification Codes*. Springfield, VA: National Technical Information Service, 1992. Order Number PB92-50171/CAU.

840. U.S. Dept. of Commerce. NTIS. *Computerized U.S. Canada SIC Concordance*. Springfield, VA: NTIS, 1992. Order number PB92-501725/CAU.

SEE ALSO *Concordance Between the Standard Industrial Classification Code of the United States and Canada.*

841. U.S. Dept. of Commerce. Economics and Statistics Administration. *1992 Industry and Product Classification Manual.* Washington, DC: U.S. Government Printing Office, 1992. 459 p. SUDOCS C 3.6/2:In 2/2/992.

842. U.S. Office of the President. Office of Management and Budget. *Standard Industrial Classification Manual, 1987.* Washington, DC: U.S. Government Printing Office, 1987. ISBN 0160043298.

The standard industrial classification code (SIC) is a United States industry classification. Its purpose is to aid in the collection, tabulation and analysis of data related to U.S. establishments by the type of activity the company is engaged in. It is not interchangeable with the commodity or product classification. This manual identifies this 4 digit SIC number. There are other commercial publications such as the Dun & Bradstreet Standard Industrial Classification Manual 2+2 and Predicasts' Basebook that use a modified SIC number. (Also available on diskettes from National Technical Information Services)

United Nations

843. United Nations. Statistical Office. *The International Standard Industrial Classification of All Economic Activities Revision 3.* New York: United Nations, 1990. 189 p. ISBN 9211613190. LCCN 75013258.

This document provides a framework for the international comparison of statistics. Its intention is to classify productive economic activities. The purpose of the International Standard Industrial Classification (ISIC) is to provide a set of activity categories. Part I has the background of the ISIC, its principles, and definitions, and its relationship to other international classifications. Part II shows broad and detailed structure of the ISIC categories.

844. U.S. Bureau of the Census. *International Concordance Between the Industrial Classification of the United Nations (ISIC REV 3) and Canada (1980 SIC), the European Union (NACE REV.1) the United States (1987 SIC)*. Washington, DC: U.S. Bureau of the Census, 1994. 261 p. ISBN 0660137461. LCCN 91-73264.

This trilateral concordance of industry classification involving the U.S., Canada, and the European communities presents detailed descriptions of industries and the underlying concepts used in classifying economic units by activity. The classification structure is similar, but the United Nations has 17 tabulation categories, Canada has 18 divisions and the U.S. has 11. Differences of the systems are discussed. A concordance table and appendices with a list of methodologies used to create the concordances and the differences in the assignment of activities to industries and industry groups are included.

COMMODITY CLASSIFICATION

Australia

845. Australian Bureau of Statistics. *Australian Standard Commodity Classification (Revised): Transportable Goods*. Canberra, Australia: Australian Bureau of Statistics, 1989. 1 v.

Europe

846. United Nations. Statistical Office. External Trade: *Nomenclature of Goods=Commerce exterieur. Nomenclature des marchandises*. Luxembourg: Office for Official Publications of the European Communities, 1988. 7 vols. ISBN 928258030X (vol.1) 9282580628 (vol. 1-7).

Canada

847. Statistics Canada, Standards Division. *Standard Classification of Goods 1992: Based on the Harmonized Commodity Description and Coding System.* Ottawa: Minister of Supply Services, 1992. 1 vol. (loose-leaf)

United States

SEE ALSO *Official Export Guide.* This has a schedule B guide with Harmonized Code for various export products.

SEE ALSO U.S. Dept. of Commerce. *1992 Industry Product Classification Manual.* Washington, DC: U.S. Government Printing Office, 1992. 459 p. SUDOCS C 3.6/2:In 2/2/992.

848. U.S. Dept. of Commerce. Bureau of the Census. *Schedule B Statistical Classification of Domestic and Foreign Commodities Exported from the United States.* Washington, DC: U.S. Government Printing Office, 1990. SUDOCS C 3.150:B/990/vols.

Schedule B is a commodity classification that is used by exporters. Schedule B is an official schedule that is based on the Harmonized System. It classifies commodities by breaking them down into 97 chapters and 22 sections. It has an index that is handy to look up a Harmonized number.

849. U.S. Dept. of Treasury. *Harmonized Commodity Description and Coding System.* Washington, DC: U.S. Government Printing Office, 1992. SUDOCS T 17.2:H 22/3/vols.

The Harmonized Commodity and Coding System (HS) was adopted by the U.S. and its major trading partners on January 1989. It is an international product nomenclature that describes, classifies, and codes goods for customs, tariff, and statistical purposes. It obligates contracting countries to use the six digit nomenclature. The HS is a written description with a corresponding numerical code for a product. This manual is used to find the HS number. The HS number can then be used on the NTDB to see the breakdown of the export and import figures of a specific product from the U.S. to various countries.

850. U.S. International Trade Commission. *Harmonized Tariff Schedule of the United States*. Washington, DC: U.S. Government Printing Office, 1994. SUDOCS ITC 1.10:

This has the import classification system based on the Harmonized System. It is used by merchandise importers for rates of duty and statistical purposes. It has a listing of countries that are designated beneficiary developing countries for the purposes of the Generalized System of Preference. It has products arranged by Harmonized numbers, article description, units or quantity, rates of duty classified into general, special, or free. Also it has an index.

United Nations

851. United Nations. Statistical Office. *Standard International Trade Classification. Revision 3.* New York: United Nations, 1986. 106 p. ISBN 9211612659. LCCN 86226177.

The standard international trade classification code (SITC) classifies a commodity or product. It is an international system used by the United Nations. SITC serves as a basis for the analysis of world trade and a standard for reporting trade statistics. There is a cross reference to the Harmonized Code in this publication.

852. United Nations. Statistical Office of the European Communities. *Classification of Products by Activity* (CPA). Luxembourg: United Nations Statistical Office, 1988. 165 p.

853. United Nations. Statistical Office. *Classification by Broad Economic Categories Defined in Terms of SITC, rev. 3*, New York: United Nations Statistical Office, 1989. 86 p. ISBN 9211612764. LCCN 87401426.

854. United Nations. Statistical Office of the European Communities. *Provisional Central Product Classification (Statistical Papers, Series M. no. 77)*. New York: United Nations, 1991. 296 p.

CHAPTER XIII

HANDBOOKS AND YEARBOOKS

This section has miscellaneous information such as international company histories, book of lists, and description of the economy in figures.

CORPORATE INFORMATION

855. Bavishi, Vinod B., ed. *CIFAR's Global Company Handbook. 1992*. Princeton, NJ: Center for International Financial Analysis, 1992. 2 v. ISSN 1060-8710. ISBN 18775870444. LCCN 92-644028. Annual. 1992-

This is an analysis of annual reports of 15,000 companies with a global comparison of 2,500 companies in 35 emerging capital markets including Eastern Europe with data on international accounting and auditing trends in 48 countries.

856. Brooklyn Public Library Business Library Staff. *Business Book of Lists*. Detroit: Visible Ink Press, 1991. 535 p. ISBN 0810394103.

This book ranks the biggest, the smallest, best and worst with the quoted source. Examples are: largest companies in Singapore and Taiwan, largest private companies in India and Britain, Canada's largest law firms, and leading Hispanic business, and five largest international textile groups.

857. Cooney, John, ed. *Louis Rukeyser's Business Almanac*. New York, NY: Simon and Schuster, 1991. 587 p. ISBN 0671907280. LCCN 91030290.

This almanac looks at industries in America such as: advertising, automobiles, beverages, and electronics. For each industry it gives a few basics facts about the industry, companies that are key players in the industry, the number of people employed in the industry, trends and forecasts of the industry. It also covers trends in federal debt, GNP, and profits by industry, and work and earnings of America.

858. Ibbotson, Roger G., *The Global Marketplace*. New York: Macmillan Publishing Co., 1995. 339 p. LCCN gb93-50822.

This source has information on the most influential companies outside of the U.S. Two thirds are based in Japan, Britain, France, W. Germany and Italy. It includes a description of companies against geographical, historical backdrops. It is a book about the people behind the companies with information on sales, profits, U.S. sales, rank, year founded, employees and headquarters.

859. Kepos, Paula et al. *International Directory of Company Histories*. Chicago: St James Press, 1995. 14 v. LCCN 89-190943.

This directory lists corporations first by industry (Mining & Metal, Paper & Forestry, Petroleum, Publishing & Printing, and Real Estate), then alphabetically by name including address, phone and fax, and sales. This directory covers the world's largest companies. It gives basic information as well as acquisitions, mergers, and subsidiaries.

860. Mattera, Philip, ed. *Inside U.S. Business: A Concise Encyclopedia of Leading Industries*. New York: Irwin Professional Publishing, 1994. 568 p. ISBN 1556233779. LCCN 90015020.

Each chapter starts with industry information, a few basic facts and observations, ranking of the top companies, profiles of leading firms, labor relations of the industries, a list of sources, and online databases. The industries covered are: book publishing, broadcasting and cable, film and video, telecommunications, beverages, mainframes, minicomputers and work stations, oil and natural gas. This is a good source to use in conjunction with the *Value Line Investment Survey* or the *Standard and Poor's Industry Surveys* as this gives history and background and the others provide recent industry overview.

STOCK MARKET AND INVESTMENTS

861. Editors of the Dow Jones & Company in Association with Morningstar, *The Dow Jones Guide to the World Stock Market.* Englewood Cliffs, NJ: Prentice Hall, 1995. 705 p. LCCN 94043722.

This source has a statistical overview of the Dow Jones World Stock Index performance with a listing of 2,500 of the biggest stocks which constitute over 80% of the market value of all stocks in the world, a directory of companies alphabetically arranged by region, then country with name, address, telephone and fax number, exchange, ticker symbol, president, sales, net income, book value, P/E ration, yield, 52 week high and low.

862. International Finance Corporations, *Emerging Stock Markets Factbook.* Washington, DC: International Finance Corporations. ISSN 1012-8115. LCCN 90649979. Annual. 1988-

This factbook presents information on stock markets in developing countries with an overview of emerging markets, trends in these emerging markets, market commentaries on various countries, a list of domestic companies, principal industries in the International Finance Corporation for Latin America and Asia. More recent issues in this factbook discuss the role of the stock markets in the economic development of the larger market.

863. Price, Margaret M., *Emerging Stock Markets: A Complete Investment Guide to New Markets Around the World.* New York: McGraw-Hill, 1994. 414 p. ISBN 0070510490. LCCN 93025979.

This investment guide looks at risks, attractions, characteristics of emerging markets and gives advice about when to invest. It has country information from an investor's view. It covers Argentina to Papua New Guinea.

864. United Nations. *World Investment Directory.* New York: United Nations, 1996. 6 vol. LCCN 96256265.

This series consists of five volumes. Volume 1 -- Asia and the Pacific; Volume 2 -- Developed Countries; Volume 3 -- Latin America and the Caribbean; Volume 4 -- Africa and West Africa and Volume 5 -- Central and Eastern Europe. Volume 6 -- Global Trends. The first volume, Asia and the Pacific, analyzes foreign direct investment trends and their impact. Coverage includes: foreign direct investment in Asia and the Pacific during the 1980's, inward foreign direct investment, outward foreign direct investment trends, sources of data, industrial and geographical breakdowns, definitions, discrepancies in data and information. There is country information from Bangladesh to Taiwan and tables on foreign direct investment: the legislative environment in the Pacific Region.

ECONOMICS AND MISCELLANEOUS

865. Besher, Alexander. *Pacific Rim Almanac.* New York: HarperCollins Publisher, 1991. 824 p. ISBN 076846960. LCCN 90055996.

This is a compendium on market trends, trade, money and finance in the Pacific Rim area. This readable almanac covers the creativity revolution, the subtle art of marketing to wealthy Asians and Japan's future. The appendix lists Asian advertising, marketing and public relations firms, and Pacific Rim Publications.

866. International Bank for Reconstruction and Development. *Trends in Developing Economies*. Washington, DC: International Bank for Reconstruction and Development. ISSN 1014-7004. LCCN 90640763. Annual. 1989- Also availablc on diskcttc.

The trends in developing countries from Albania to Zimbabwe are included covering topics such as: recent economic-social developments, public finance, balance of payments, external debt and medium term prospects, and tables on key ratios, GDP: production, GDP: expenditures broken down by private consumption, general consumption, gross domestic investment and consumer prices, and implicit GDP deflator. There is a main volume and three other volumes by regions which are extracts of the main volume. Vol. 1 is Eastern Europe and Central Asia; Vol. 2 is Emerging Capital Markets and Vol. 3 is Sub-Saharan Africa (Description is based on 1994 edition).

867. Orr, Bill. *The Global Economy in the 90's: A User's Guide*. New York: New York University Press, 1993 .

This is a facts and figures description of the global economy including macro trends, trade, fiscal and monetary balances of G-7 governments, labor, manufactures, primary products and trade geography. Irregular series.

868. United Nations. Department of International Economic and Social Affairs. *Overall Socio-economic Perspective of the World Economy to the Year 2000*. New York: United Nations, 1990. ISBN 0211091179. LCCN 90-181067. Irregular series.

The long term trends in world economic development, the widening disparities in production performance, the structural adjustment and industrial redeployment, the projections of the evolution of the world economy and the structural changes in the world production and trade are some of the concerns of this publication.

869. United Nations. Department of International Economic and Social Affairs. *World Economic and Social Survey*. New York: United Nations. ISSN 0884-1714. LCCN sn94017998. Annual. 1955-

This volume describes, synthesizes, and interprets trends, issues, and policies in the world economy citing international trade statistics, savings investment, the transfer of resources and recent trends in energy covering the international oil market.

870. United Nations. Transnational Corporations and Management Division. *Transnational Corporations as Engines of Growth*. New York: United Nations, 1992. 356 p. ISBN 9211043964.

Transnational corporations and foreign direct investment play a significant role in the world economy. This report analyzes the circumstances under which transnational corporations can contribute to the economic growth of developing countries. It looks at trends in foreign direct investment and the relative importance of activities of transnational corporations in the world economy and recent policy developments on such issues as trade related aspects of intellectual property rights.

871. U.S. National Advisory Council on International Monetary and Financial Policies. *Annual Report of the Chairman of the National Advisory Council on International Monetary and Financial Policies to the President and to the Congress for the Fiscal Year*. Washington, DC: U.S. Government Printing Office. LCCN sn91023542. SUDOCS Y 3.N 21/16:1/ . Annual. 1989-

The relationship between the United States and the International Monetary Fund is described. Included also are the following: world economic trends, international monetary relations, loans by the Multilateral Development Banks and the purchases from the International Monetary Fund, and tables on U.S. Government Foreign Grants, credits, and other assistance, Asian Development Bank, African Development Bank, and the Export-Import Bank. (The data are a bit slow).

872. World Bank. *Global Economic Prospects and the Developing Countries*. Washington, DC: World Bank. ISSN 1014-8906. LCCN 91-644001. Annual. 1991-

This source focuses on the globalization of the world economy and the effects of the international economic environment on developing countries with an analysis of economic prospects for development. The 1991 issue focused on international trade in primary commodities; the 1992 issue looked at international trade in manufactures; the 1993 issue examined international finance and 1994 reports on the international trade in commodities. It also does forecasting of the global economic prospects of the developing countries.

AUTHOR/TITLE INDEX

The arrangement of this index is alphabetical with numbers filed before letters. The various congressional committees, agencies, and departments will be under U.S. Congress. House. Committee on ... or U.S. Dept. of Commerce. The ampersand (&) is filed as the word "and". Hyphens (-) and apostrophes (') are ignored. Therefore Asia's is filed as Asias and STAT-USA is filed as the word STATUSA. Acronyms are filed as words. Corporate authors with names such as H.W. Wilson are filed under the last name. The numbers refer to page numbers.

SUBJECT/KEYWORD INDEX

Numbers refer to page numbers.